Pragmatic - Existential Psychotherapy

with
Personality Disorders

Herbert M. Potash

D0208394

Gordon Handwerk Publishers
Madison, New Jersey

Production: PS Graphics, Stephanie Barry
Cover Design and Book Jacket: Kathleen Craig
Typeface: Goudy Handtooled and CG Goudy Old Style
Printer: Quebecor Printing Book Group

Library of Congress Cataloging-in-Publication Data

Potash, Herbert M.
Pragmatic-existential psychotherapy with personality disorders /
Herbert M. Potash
   p.   cm.
   Includes bibliographical references and index.
   ISBN 0-940524-05-8
   1. Personality disorders. 2. Existential psychotherapy.
   3. Pragmatism.
I. Title.
[DNLM: 1. Personality Disorders--therapy. 2. Psychotherapy-
-methods. 3. Existentialism.   WM 190 P859p 1993]
RC554.P68 1993
616.89--dc20
DNLM/DLC
for Library of Congress   93-37456
                                CIP

Printed in the United States of America

Pragmatic-Existential Psychotherapy

With

Personality Disorders

To my wife, Janice,

who makes it all wonderful.

Preface

Until now, psychology has lacked a comprehensive theory and psychotherapeutic system to treat all personality disordered individuals. Most psychotherapy patients suffer from underlying personality disorders, and therapists have been forced to improvise their own treatment strategies to offer assistance to this group of diverse patients. I have written this text in an attempt to provide practitioners with both a systematic theory and a model of treatment to guide their work with personality disordered patients.

I have utilized an existential perspective in my therapeutic work for many years as I find it the most sensible philosophy to apply to a wide range of patients. Although existentialism has not yet gained many adherents in the psychological community, I hope this presentation of pragmatic-existential therapy for treating personality disorders will help practitioners realize the advantages of an existential approach.

In order to comply with the American Psychological Association's directive to avoid the use of sexist language, I chose to use the personal pronouns "he" and "she" in alternating chapters. These pronouns designate one person rather than sexual identity.

Often the sources cited in the text are latter-day editions of much earlier works. The reader should bear this fact in mind rather than misinterpret the reference date as the original date of publication. As one example, Kierkegaard lived in the early nineteenth century yet the version of *The Concept of Dread* referred to in the text is a 1957 publication.

Many individuals have played a significant role, both directly and indirectly, in helping me bring this project to fruition. My son, David, reviewed the initial draft of the manuscript and provided an exhaustive in-depth critique which enabled me to significantly expand and refine the text. His helpful suggestions led me to write a far better book. Leonard Handler gave the manuscript a very thorough reading and made important suggestions which are incorporated into the book. My daughter, Stephanie Barry, not only assisted with copy editing but also formatted the text into its ultimate form. I am quite grateful for her assistance.

I wish to thank my teaching assistants for their aid in this project. Daphne Shalita-Kuga compiled the bibliography, and Raphael Web assembled the index. I very much appreciate the work of Kathleen Craig who designed the book jacket and cover. I am indebted to Ervin Brody who co-led our interdisciplinary course, *The Existential Movement*, thereby providing me with important insights in reading and interpreting existential literature.

My greatest debt is to my wife, Janice. During graduate school at Michigan State University, she arranged my initial exposure to existential thinking by convincing G. Marion Kinget to lead a seminar on existential therapy. Jan has been the strongest source of support throughout my adult years. As publisher of this book, she has also served as copy editor, refining my prose through painstaking efforts. I can never thank her enough for all she means to me.

Herbert M. Potash
December, 1993

Table of Contents

Part One:
The Theory of
Pragmatic-Existentialism

One:
The Existential Roots
of Psychology

E arly in my teaching career after concluding what I thought was a very lucid lecture on psychoanalytic theory and the psychosexual stages of development, an undergraduate student approached me quizzically. She said, "I do not remember wanting to have sex with my father." I reminded her that according to Freud, she could not remember this because she must have repressed the wish. The student then replied, "I do not remember repressing it." At that moment I began to wonder whether I had effectively defined my terms or if this particular student was hopelessly dense. Following the spirit of the lecture, I was soon able to arrive at a more sophisticated hypothesis, namely, this woman was defending against the activation of her still unconscious Female Oedipus Complex.

A number of years have passed since that incident and I now view our dialogue in a radically different way. I understand that this student was telling me that Freudian theory was alien to her personal experiential world. She could not make sense of the Female Oedipus Complex because this theory contradicted what she knew about herself. The central ideas of traditional psychoanalytic theory were at marked variance with her self-image. Freudian theory negated the importance of her consciousness. My lecture had told her that whatever she knew about herself was essentially a form of self-deception for her most basic personal truths were to be considered deceptive fictions.

Psychoanalytic theory avows that the most important part of the personality is in the realm of the inaccessible unconscious. In this depth psychology model the experiences of the human being are the raw data which the psychoanalyst uses to see into the unconscious. Consequently, I told my students that it would indeed be futile for them to attempt self-understanding without the guidance of the trained professional.

This particular student was intellectually unable to master the intricate sophisticated mechanics of unconscious symbols and struggles. However, I believe that she was wiser than most of us. She would not accept a theory that both dismissed her current self-awareness and advocated psychoanalysis as the only path to self-knowledge.

Questioning One's Own Professional Training

I cannot recall the specific moment in college when I decided that I wanted to become a clinical psychologist, but once I made that decision it became imperative for me to master the tools of the trade. Like my fellow students, I accepted the theories that my professors considered to be the most valid, and I acquired the skills which they endorsed. It was some time after receiving the doctorate that I began to recognize and to neutralize some of the subtle and even major forms of indoctrination that had taken place during my graduate training. My interaction with the aforementioned student was a particular manifestation of the negative effects of that graduate training. I could not fully hear what she was trying to tell me because I, too, had previously learned to assign no real validity to the nature of a person's experience.

As graduate students we were taught to avoid the direct study of personal experience which was considered either less valid data or a significant distortion of what was "really" happening within the human being. We were taught that we could become good psychologists and psychotherapists only by deemphasizing whatever we knew about ourselves and about other humans prior to our graduate training. Instead, we were to learn the theories of the professional experts and to apply these concepts to our patients. We could only become very smart and highly competent by acknowledging, at least implicitly, how very stupid we had been prior to professional training.

Once I was a self-reliant professional, no longer under the immediate influence of my professors, I began to sense that my perceptions differed from those of my teachers. In beginning my life as a new husband, new father and wage earner, I was finally functioning as an independent adult, and I also began to focus my attention upon creating a fundamentally gratifying and fulfilling personal life.

In establishing the parameters of this personal life I knew what felt good and what did not feel good. I knew what produced pain in me, and I tried to avoid such hurt. I prided myself on being an effective problem solver, and I indeed was gaining many skills to further advance my personal and professional life. What I was most fundamentally doing was living and enjoying my conscious existence. I liked my world and the people in it. Active participation in life felt deeply gratifying to me. Like most other new professionals I was concerned about making a living and being an effective parent; and like many of us in the sixties, I worried about whether we would be alive in the seventies.

However, I felt somewhat uncomfortable because the focus of my personal life was centered on my consciousness. I was fully participating in my world, conceptualizing it, and at times even attempting to change it. I was struggling to learn how to become both an effective teacher and an effective psychotherapist. I worked hard and deliberately to improve myself. What I was doing, *i.e.*, being a human who was living a consciously directed personal life, stood in marked contrast to what I had been taught as a graduate student. My academic training in depth psychology had told me that I had little awareness of what was really going on inside me; that I, just like all other humans, was a mass of self-deceptions. Many of my deliberate actions were displacements; my pleasures were all instinct derivatives and not genuine, in and of themselves.

What I most centrally knew was that my life was being consciously led and certainly consciously enjoyed. In an ongoing way I was judging and evaluating and ultimately guiding my life through the use of my will. My professional training, nonetheless, had told me that my conscious experiences were irrelevant to my psychological being. I soon found I could no longer accept this sweeping negation of personal conscious life, a negation that stands at the center of depth psychology. Although I still valued some of the conceptual and technical contributions of these theories, I needed to find a viewpoint in psychology that primarily focused upon the importance of conscious, lived experience.

In those first few years out of graduate school I wanted to become successful, which prompted me to try to eliminate my feelings of professional deficiency. Yet I could not clearly specify then, even to myself, exactly what would increase my expertise. Retrospectively, I recognize that while graduate school effectively prepared me both to diagnose and to treat particular forms of psychopathology, it did not train me to deal with many of the questions and concerns my patients were now raising about the quality of their lives and the value decisions they had to make.

I knew what was clinically pathological and I was able to define "normal" as the absence of psychopathology, but my training had not prepared me to address the crucial life issues and choices which every human must face. When engaged in therapeutic dialogue, I could help patients reduce their neurotic anxieties; but when they were deciding whether to stay married or which life paths to follow, my professional training did not offer sound guidance. My patients were making decisions which could only be based upon personal values, and therapists do not necessarily have any better personal values than do their patients. The professional values of therapists, protecting confidentiality and working in the best interests of the patient, do not extend to directing the life choices of their patients.

Ethically I could not refuse to participate in such dialogues with my patients. Our ongoing therapeutic dialogue certainly enabled me to know these people much better than anyone else did. However, I began to realize that it was "me," the person, who was participating in these particular discussions rather than "me," the trained psychologist. Later in my readings, I discovered that, in particular, Jaspers (1955) had struggled mightily with this same problem and had decided that he could legitimately address questions of values only by functioning as a philosopher. He abandoned psychiatry for philosophy so he could address major life questions in what he considered to be their most appropriate forum.

I, too, wanted to find a different route, one that would not only legitimize my professional participation in the wide range of therapeutic dialogue but one which also would increase my therapeutic effectiveness. I continued to question and to study myself as an experiencing person, and I began to explore the writings of individuals who viewed the human as an experiencing process. I had acquired only a very minimal understanding of the nature of human experience through my formal psychological training. Now I wanted and needed more and different information in order to enhance my therapeutic skills. As I reviewed and then expanded my readings in existential literature, philosophy and psychology, I sensed an affinity with these authors. I came to believe that some of these ideas deeply enhance effective therapeutic work. Furthermore, they become especially relevant in helping patients who suffer from what diagnosticians label as the personality disorders.

Not only did the ideas of existential writers seem very applicable to my therapeutic work, but these concepts also felt very right to me as a person. These writers were my kin folk. Since then I have found that when individuals first confront the major ideas of existentialism the effect is commonly and often dramatic. In my many years of teaching existential psychology I have repeatedly seen students even become dizzy and disoriented as they attempted to rediscover themselves as experiencing beings. The ideas of existentialism grant a legitimacy to consciousness, which is a freeing and liberating experience.

For myself, once I had completed graduate school, I began to accelerate the vital process of personal and professional growth that helps to produce the effective psychologist. The lengthy process of formal graduate training is, in many ways, a reenactment of childhood. Students must conform to multiple authority figures (professors) who may exhibit strong disagreements with each other as well as share a common underlying sets of beliefs. In order to survive, to acquire a professional identity and ultimately to receive a doctorate, students must adopt the faculties' set of beliefs as their own. Graduate students will necessarily be strongly influenced by their mentors, and it is extremely difficult for these students to recognize the profound extent to which their thinking is shaped by their graduate training.

After graduate school it is necessary to experience a kind of professional adolescence where one seriously questions the beliefs that were acquired through graduate training. Unfortunately, because of the intricate and numerous pressures that have comprised graduate training, new psychologists are typically unaware of the degree to which they have been strongly influenced. Certainly graduate students often will loudly critique certain theories and perhaps consider particular intervention strategies inappropriate, but the students may not be able to recognize that they have been routinely accepting many ideas without rigorous questioning.

For example, consider the length of an individual psychotherapy session. When I was in graduate training, psychotherapy was routinely conducted in a fifty minute hour. I was never provided with any cogent reason as to why fifty minutes was the best time limit. As students we were told that a ten minute break between patients would allow us to make necessary notes on the session. There is nothing particularly sacred about a fifty minute hour other than the hour is a commonly used time period in our culture. In the past fifteen years many therapists have changed this to a forty-five minute session. I believe many therapists later made the shift simply in order to fit an additional patient into their daily work schedule. However, therapists still do not know what is the optimal time period for a therapy session. It is also unlikely that they will conduct research to answer this question, as I find it difficult to believe that therapists would place half of their patients in forty-five minute sessions and half in fifty minute sessions, attempt to match them for level of pathology, and then evaluate differences in success rates.

Certainly it is legitimate and necessary for a psychologist to question some sacred cows such as the length of the therapeutic hour, but the answers will have to come out of one's own personal experiences. New professionals must struggle with themselves to determine the best ways for them to practice psychology. One's performance as a capable professional is diminished if the particular ideas instilled during training are accepted without any further questioning.

When new professionals begin to behave in ways that are at variance with the norms of early professional training, they are very likely to feel much anguish. Whenever one dares to be innovative, one can be labelled as having unresolved countertransference issues. However, innovation is the only way in which psychology or any other discipline can grow and develop.

Therefore, in order to become truly effective professionals, psychologists need to evaluate the nature and scope of their formal professional training. They must question the degree to which their university education allowed for open and unbiased presentations of opposing points of view. Such questioning occurs all too rarely. In his description of the problems with graduate education in German philosophy departments, Jaspers' comments (Wallraff, 1970) apply all too readily to current graduate education in clinical psychology. Jaspers stated that graduate students are invested in becoming successful professionals and therefore experience subtle pressures to accept the points of view of their major professors. Consequently, they quickly learn there are simply two camps of philosophy: the "right" one which is endorsed by their professors and the "wrong" ones which are taught elsewhere. When these philosophy students become teachers, they continue to propagate the same strong beliefs in the right *vs* the wrong approaches in their particular discipline.

In psychology graduate programs as well, students routinely endorse the approach to psychology which is promulgated in their doctoral programs. In research design courses the students are provided with the vision of the truly objective unbiased scientist. This vision is primarily a myth, for rarely do research scientists conduct open and objective psychological inquiries. When the results of a psychological experiment affirm the basic hypothesis of the experimenter, the procedure is considered to have been a valid paradigm. However, in those instances where the results do not confirm the experimenter's hypothesis, the research design is routinely criticized as faulty. As a result of this strategy, experimenters typically can maintain their beliefs or hypotheses, irrespective of the outcomes of their experimentation.

I needed to be completely removed from the role of graduate student before I was able to recognize that my experimentally-minded professors were not the fully objective scientists they claimed to be. These academicians used a scientific pose and language to intimidate the clinical students and were adept at providing an incise critique of depth psychology for its use of fuzzy, non-operational concepts. The analytic theories were labelled as deficient and unscientific by these experimentally-minded psychologists. Any theory which eluded reductionistic experimentation was labelled of little worth.

In the typical Ph.D. programs the clinical psychology students who espoused an affiliation with depth psychology were considered "second class" psychologists by the experimentally-minded faculty. These students certainly could not effectively argue against the experimentalists who were practicing the "real" psychology routinely defined by most introductory textbooks as the scientific study of behavior. I have long suspected that the rapidity with which behaviorism assumed dominance in clinical psychology was, in large part, due to the need of clinicians to become "first class" psychologists, accepted by their experimental counterparts.

Motivation to Become a Clinical Psychologist

Then, just as now, the overwhelming majority of clinical psychologists entered the discipline in order to become psychotherapists. This intention was often at variance with the model of training offered by graduate programs which attempted to prepare individuals to do much more than simply practice psychotherapy. If students wanted to obtain a degree, they had to follow the prescribed regimen of course work and experimentation. The very first accommodation clinical graduate students had to make was to accept the common textbook definition of psychology as the valid description of the discipline, and most introductory psychology textbooks define psychology as the scientific study of behavior. Consequently, if the therapy-oriented clinicians were to become legitimate psychologists, they needed to study behavior scientifically.

This common textbook definition of psychology is, however, far too restrictive as it puts primary emphasis upon behavior and therefore subsumes the entire field of psychology under the school of behaviorism. Psychology is comprised of many different and opposing schools of thought and to define the discipline only in behavioral terms is grossly misleading. The fundamentally powerless graduate student who is expending most of his energy trying to survive the rigors of training is very unlikely to think he can legitimately challenge or even question the very definition of psychology itself.

However, psychology has not always been defined as the scientific study of behavior. Non-behaviorists must necessarily reject this particular definition for it brings into question the very legitimacy of their professional actions. To define psychology as the scientific study of behavior is to focus only upon observable actions of organisms. As a result, any professional who studies human experiences or who investigates unconscious processes would be seen as ignoring the basic realm of psychological inquiry. This behavioral definition of psychology further demands that only professionals who define themselves as scientists have a legitimate right to call themselves psychologists. The applied psychologist who does not use scientifically based insights is deficient, according to such a definition of the discipline.

It is far beyond the scope of this book to attempt a fuller connection among the different definitions of psychology; nonetheless, it certainly is necessary to have a definition of the discipline which does not restrict valuable forms of psychological inquiry. Furthermore, such a definition must endorse the earliest forms of psychological study especially since some of these types of inquiries are still vital to our understanding of humans. In fact, the existential approach to psychology specifically endorses the original nineteenth century definition of psychology as opposed to the later behavioral definition.

Redefining Psychology Through Use Of Its Historical Context

Every field of study must define its boundaries and thereby specify the types of inquiries that constitute its legitimate operations. Particular difficulties arise with definitions of psychology because of certain subspecialties which are applied in nature and other branches of study which are considered pure science. Some individuals define the overall discipline as a science, and other professionals define the subspeciality of clinical psychology without any particular attention to a scientific definition.

Psychology *per se* has changed radically over the years since its inception, and the current definition offered by behaviorists is totally unacceptable to certain professionals. We can understand the evolution by first turning to *Webster's College Dictionary* (1991) which documents the American perspective on psychology. Webster's first defines the psyche as the human soul, following the Greeks, and secondly defines psyche as the mind. Most people enroll in their first psychology course expecting to learn about the mind and are very disappointed when they discover that the mind is not the focus of psychological inquiry.

To continue with basic definitions, Webster's on *psychology* states "1. the science of the mind or of mental states and processes 2. the science of human and animal behavior." It is this second definition which is primarily used in introductory psychology textbooks even though a number of psychologists prefer the first definition. When the authors of introductory psychology texts choose the second as opposed to the first definition, they displace the mind from the role of primary topic of inquiry. This second definition of psychology, however, satisfies only those psychologists who call themselves behaviorists. Defining psychology as the science of human and animal behavior is the same as implicitly considering behaviorism to be the core of psychology.

The enormous power and influence of this behavioral school of psychology can also be seen in the transformation of the meaning of *empirical*. Webster's defined empirical as "1. derived from experience or experiment 2. depending upon experience or observation alone, without scientific method or theory, esp. in medicine 3. verifiable by experience or experiment." The study of experience without the use of experiment is currently described as a negative endeavor. This point is made even more apparent by Webster's definition of the related word "empiric," which is explained as "1. a person who is guided primarily by experience" and "2. a quack or charlatan."

In the nineteenth century, the word *empirical* denoted only the study of experience, and psychology at that time was defined as an empirical discipline. Now, in the late twentieth century, *empirical* means relying on and using scientific experimentation, a state of affairs which is quite different from the actual study of experience. To carefully study and record one's own personal experiences and to use these discoveries as a basis of knowledge is to violate the tenets of the dominant behavioral psychologists.

The ways in which psychology defined empiricism also changed its epistemological stance. This consequent redefinition of the scope and method of acquiring knowledge has been disputed by some psychologists, for many of the clinicians eschew research as their basic method of discovering truth.

The examination of psychology's history readily discloses that the careful study and recording of personal experience provided our earliest psychological data. For example, the pioneering work in psychophysics by Weber, as documented by Boring (1963), was an attempt to categorize the relationship between personal experience and the nature of the external, objective world. Weber's experiments represented the first laboratory work in psychology and Weber functioned as his own subject. He attempted to answer the major question posed by nineteenth century psychologists, *i.e.*, what type of relationship exists between one's personal experiences of reality, one's sense of touch, and the objective realities of the external world. Today, studies of this nature are relegated to the subdiscipline of psychophysics.

Following Weber, both Fechner and Wundt investigated human experience using other people as the subjects for their inquiries. Wundt attempted to discover the basic units of the mind and developed the method of trained introspection as a way of teaching his subjects to report on their conscious experiences. Wundt's approach was quite reductionistic and appears to have been heavily influenced by the philosophy of the British associationists, particularly by the writings of Locke. Wundt, in agreement with Locke, believed that the human mind was composed of simple elements which operated in various combinations. Wundt's proposed task was to discover these fundamental units of consciousness and to determine how these elements combined.

Many consider Wundt the true "Father of Psychology" because he used a laboratory to acquire his data. Certainly Wundt created his own particular method of collecting information, but this data was acquired by directing the subject's experience. His subjects were not asked to simply describe their experiences but were told to direct their minds in a particular direction and then report on their subsequent experiences. In fact, today's scientific experimentation in psychology still retains a fundamental artificiality for the subjects must participate in a preset paradigm designed by the experimenter. This method of data collection ignores the study of experience as it naturally occurs. Rather, the preset procedures are preferred because the subjects are restricted in their response options, and the data can be analyzed in a simplified manner. This reductionistic method of study essentially defines the scientific approach to psychology.

Wundt and Titchener's school of structuralism was attacked by Watson (1924), the first behaviorist, when he realized that trained introspection was an artifice of the experimenter. Watson proposed a simple solution to the dilemma of how to understand experience: he banished the study of consciousness from the range of legitimate psychological inquiry. It would have been a much more reasonable option had the subject been allowed to describe the experience in his own words. However, Watson wanted to study only observable behavior, not attend to verbal reports. By restricting his attention to the study of non-verbal behavior, Watson offered a radically new approach to understanding; and his pioneering effort soon dominated experimental psychology.

Before Watson's writings there were important nineteenth century studies of personal experience such as those of Purkinje. He recorded his own experience that the perceived brightness of colors shift when daytime changes into twilight (Boring, 1963). This difference in perceived brightness was labelled the Purkinje Phenomenon and later in the twentieth century was explained as due to a physiological shift from cone to rod vision. Purkinje's observations embody a method of study that is central to what is now existential psychology. Existentialists consider it vital to first carefully observe and report on one's own personal experiences. Out of such personal observations tentative generalizations can then be made which may ultimately prove useful in understanding the experiences of others.

The use of this process of careful personal observation can be seen in the writings of William James (1890). In his text *Psychology: The Briefer Course*, James labelled his study of the human experience "the study of consciousness." He described the four main characteristics of consciousness, paraphrased as follows: (1) Every state of consciousness is part of a personal consciousness. Therefore it is always "my" consciousness that I experience; (2) My consciousness is always changing and can be likened to a stream; (3) My consciousness is sensibly continuous since it contains transitional links exemplified by words such as "but," "and," "or;" (4) My consciousness is always choosing; it always knows where it is going.

Since James was attempting one of the very first descriptions of consciousness, it seems logical that it was obtained by his careful attention to his own experiential world. It is likely that James, adopting the method of Purkinje, described his own experiences, the personal nature of consciousness, which he then attributed to people other than himself.

In a comparable vein, Brentano's (1874) definition of psychology was also most likely initially based upon study of his own personal experiences. Brentano defined psychology as the study of *acts*. Human acts included judging, ideating and feeling. Consequently, the mental activities of a person could be understood as purposive or as having intentionality. Both James and Brentano recognized the directional movement of human conscious activity and therefore both implicitly acknowledged that mental processes were intentional rather than simply random.

These nineteenth century pioneering psychologists were primarily concerned with understanding human experience. Existential psychologists also focus their attention upon studying a person as an experiencing process. Therefore, when defining the discipline of psychology, existential psychologists fundamentally reiterate the views of the aforementioned nineteenth century theorists. According to May (1958), existentialism centered on the existing person and emphasized the "emerging" and "becoming" nature of the person. Bugenthal (1965) considered an existential orientation as a way of looking at the human experience. Current existential psychologists differ from some of their earlier predecessors primarily in their emphasis upon the changing nature of the human being. However, even this focus is not totally new for this position was also advanced by James (1890) during the nineteenth century.

The Opposing Camps in Early Psychology

Psychology began to emerge as a separate field in the nineteenth century due to the confluence of two very different disciplines. The need to understand the nature of bodily experiences by measuring people's reactions to different stimuli was a task first posed by physiologists. These physiologists are best characterized as scientists who decided to study restricted aspects of human experience in order to better understand the nature of the human body. They could help create and participate in this new field of psychology only if it were a scientific discipline.

Other individuals attracted to the new discipline of psychology saw it as a potential embodiment of applied philosophy. Husserl (1965), for example, wished to discover how humans were able to acquire knowledge, a concern leading him to investigate the new *empirical* science. Early psychology, as practiced by Wundt, James and Brentano, was primarily directed toward discovering the nature of consciousness; and for philosophers, this newly emerging discipline or psychology was a potential source of additional information to increase their understanding of the full range of human experiences. These philosophers believed that psychology could become a vital discipline if it remained strongly connected with the rich knowledge and theories they advanced.

When current day psychologists dispute to what degree psychology is an art or a science and when they disagree over the importance of theory to psychology, they basically are reenacting the two opposing points of view that in combination founded psychology. Philosophy and science have played central roles both in the creation of the discipline of psychology as well as in the advancement of understanding the behaving, experiencing human. The writings of existentialists such as Jaspers (1955) particularly acknowledged the necessity of drawing upon the insights of both philosophy and science for the fullest understanding of humans.

More recently van Kamm (1969) proposed to utilize existential insights in order to integrate science and philosophy. He considered current day psychology to be constituted of three different bodies of knowledge: (1) subjectivism, personal experience is the only valid data; (2) objectivism, scientific observations provide the only valid data; and (3) situationalism, the social environment is the only source for valid data. Like Brentano, van Kamm characterized the human as "intentional." To possess intentionality the individual must at least implicitly acknowledge that a real world exists. A person experiences intentions toward the real objective world. Consequently, the essential intentionality of the human must assume an objectively existing world where people behave and where they are subject to social forces. According to van Kamm, the intentionality of the person is the central existential concept which, when fully understood, will enable psychologists to integrate the sciences of subjectivism, objectivism and situationalism.

The writings of van Kamm focus upon achieving a conceptual

integration, a concern shared by many existential thinkers, especially those with a strong philosophical allegiance. Because most existential psychologists maintain a firm tie to their philosophical forefathers, their writings are often steeped in lengthy discussion of both philosophical and intellectual issues (see, for example, *The Review of Existential Psychology and Psychiatry*). Such concerns are often foreign to many of today's psychologists who were trained primarily in the science of psychology and who remain fundamentally ignorant of both the historical and current bonds between psychology and philosophy.

Current existential psychologists consider it imperative to maintain a significant alliance with philosophy and with the insights it has provided into the human condition. Their interest in maintaining both a historical and current relationship with philosophy makes the existential psychologists' viewpoints rare within psychology. However, the American Psychological Association's Division 24, Theoretical and Philosophical Psychology, offers a forum for the continued study of the relationship between philosophy and psychology.

Whereas philosophers such as James were crucial in helping to create psychology, the philosophies of knowledge proposed by Locke and by Kant (Rychlak, 1987) provided the basic outlines for the creation of the different theories of personality. Rychlak documented how an understanding of these philosophical theories better enables psychologists to evaluate the different concepts of human functioning. Major contributions of Husserl (1965), Kierkegaard (1957), Nietzsche (1968), Heidegger (1962), Jaspers (1955) and Sartre (1956) have all provided the impetus for the creation of existential psychology.

In addition to significant existential contributions to philosophy and psychology, the talents of writers such as Sartre and Camus have graced literature and theater; further existential perspective was added to religious theory by the contributions of Tillich (1952) and Buber (1958). Existentialism spans many different disciplines even though much disagreement remains about what existentialism actually involves. The insights of writers in each of these disciplines have important bearings upon the development of existential psychology, the particular focus of this book. It is therefore necessary to discuss some of these major contributions in order to understand more fully the compositions of existential psychology.

Initial Forces Affecting
Existential Psychology

The potential relationship between the new psychology of the late nineteenth century and classic philosophy was a primary concern addressed in the writings of Husserl (1965). Husserl was a philosopher particularly interested in "the new empirical psychology" which studied human experience. Because Husserl believed that philosophy had as its task the understanding of knowledge, he also believed that philosophy needed to account for and to deal with the ways in which knowledge was being studied in empirical psychology. In order to fully understand the process of knowing and knowledge *per se*, Husserl believed that three separate disciplines needed to be utilized.

The first of these disciplines was the newly emerging empirical psychology, defined by Husserl as the natural science of consciousness. This psychology attempted to understand the consciousness of an empirical being in the real world. Husserl himself focused upon developing a phenomenological philosophy which was to be the second discipline for understanding knowledge. Phenomenological philosophy's goal was to understand pure consciousness. It was Husserl's contention that a new third discipline was also needed, and he labelled it phenomenological psychology. The task of phenomenological psychology was to examine the essence of consciousness in its relationship to the outside world.

Husserl stated that the phenomenological philosopher, in order to understand pure consciousness, must attempt to eliminate attending to the real world and instead focus exclusively upon his own consciousness. However, the phenomenological philosopher immediately discovered that his consciousness always focused upon specific objects. He experienced not pure consciousness but rather a consciousness of "something." These experiences clearly demonstrated to Husserl that consciousness is an intentional process, for consciousness is always directed.

Husserl hoped that a phenomenological psychology could be developed which would understand the intentional nature of consciousness as well as its directing ego. Such a phenomenological psychology has still not been created. However, Husserl did advance the concept of phenomenology, and phenomenological study has become the central method of attaining existential insights.

The concept of phenomenology has been taken by psychologists to mean the understanding of another human by suspending one's self and experiencing the world as if one were the other person. In psychology the purest example of the phenomenological method is practiced in the client centered approach of Rogers (1951). Rogers contended that the best way of accepting and helping others is by sharing their experiential world without superimposing one's self or one's own views upon the other. Rogers can best be categorized as the descendant and therapeutic practitioner of Husserl's phenomenology.

Even though European philosophy and psychology remained closely allied well into the twentieth century, these two disciplines moved apart in the United States in the early part of the century. Once James abandoned psychology for philosophy, American psychology quickly disentangled itself from its philosophical roots. Instead, the new psychological theories of behaviorism and psychoanalysis were advanced, and neither theory acknowledged a connection with philosophy. Each of these two viewpoints captured the attention of large numbers of American psychologists.

Watson's (1924) approach of behaviorism negated the value of any experiments which purported to study human experience. Instead, Watson called for psychologists to concentrate exclusively upon studying observable behavioral events. Watson viewed the experiments of Wundt, which involved trained introspection and the description of conscious experience, as outside the area of relevant psychological inquiry. Watson may well have been correct to attack the method of trained introspection, but the exclusion of consciousness from psychological inquiry made the human experience an alien concept to the discipline of psychology.

For those psychologists interested in a global understanding of the person and of psychopathology, attention was turned to the intriguing new concepts of Freud, Jung, Adler and the subsequent neoanalysts. These psychotherapists advanced radically new ideas about personality and psychopathology and proposed new systems for treating mental illness.

As a result of the appeal of both behaviorism and psychoanalysis,

American psychologists fundamentally renounced the study of experience for the first half of the twentieth century. There were only a few noticeable exceptions, such as Allport (1934, 1960) who created theoretical concepts including the "proprium" which recognized intentionality and free will in the personality structure.

Despite the fact that American psychologists had virtually abandoned the study of the person as an experiencing process, the European psychologists Koffka (1935), Kohler (1947) and Wertheimer (1945) engaged in experimentation which documented that humans as well as animals could immediately perceive totalities or Gestalts. These psychologists disputed the theories and experiments of Wundt for radically different reasons than did Watson and in the process, created the Gestalt school of psychology. Central to the Gestalt position is the recognition that all experience is immediate and indivisible. The Gestaltists asserted that the process of perception was not composed of simple underlying small elements which produce the immediate Gestalt, or wholeness, in perception. The "aha" phenomenon, in which one immediately sees the solution to a problem, was considered a process, non-dissectable. They believed the solution to problems was immediately experienced; it was not an additive phenomenon.

The writings and experiments in Gestalt psychology were primarily focused upon studies of perception and simple problem solving tasks. When Gestalt psychologists immigrated to the United States in the thirties, their ideas presented a major challenge to the dominance of behaviorism in America. The Gestalt viewpoint was ultimately extended into a large scale theory of human psychopathology and psychotherapy, documented in the writings of Perls (1969). The Gestalt school has a fundamental historical alliance with the existential position for they both focus upon the experiencing process by using the phenomenological method. However, the existential point of view also has a deep connection with a philosophical viewpoint, a connection which is alien to Gestalt psychology. According to Perls, the Gestalt therapist aims to change the nature of the immediate experiencing of the patient. In contrast, the existential psychologist draws upon important philosophical concepts to understand the dilemma and reasons for the person's constricted experiential world.

Much of what we know that is called existential philosophy was written by Europeans during the first half of the twentieth century. The nineteenth century writings of Kierkegaard (1957) and Nietzsche (1968) were rediscovered and reexamined, and the contemporary writings of Jaspers (1955), Heidegger (1962) and Sartre (1956) offered a wealth of insights for understanding the experiencing process that is the "person." These writings were largely unknown by American psychologists, and many books were not even translated into English. Only with the publication of *Existence* (May, 1958) did American psychologists begin to reexamine experience as a legitimate topic of inquiry and to acquaint themselves with the writings of existential philosophy.

Exposure to these European philosophical and psychological writings led American psychologists to develop existentially-based psychotherapies. The most prominent of these treatment methods are described in the writings of Burton (1974), Bugenthal (1965) and May (1958). New journals such as *The Review of Existential Psychology and Psychiatry* and *The Journal of Humanistic Psychology* appeared primarily to disseminate these new existential ideas in the United States.

However, by the mid-twentieth century American psychology had moved so far in the direction of being a science that its philosophical roots were virtually ignored in its graduate school training programs. Textbooks referred to Wundt as the "Father of Psychology," stating that he had created the first psychological laboratory. Earlier inquiring individuals were called "armchair theorists," and both their procedures and conceptualizations were considered woefully inadequate for the "science" of psychology. This academic position placed predominant value on experimentation and minimized the importance of theory. No credence was given to personal observation, phenomenology or to holistic integrative thinking. Even more so, these destructive characterizations disparaged the clinical psychologist who sat in an armchair conducting psychotherapy with his patients.

This very narrow perspective which disputes the value of theory was directed upon graduate students in clinical psychology. Assigned readings were almost exclusively restricted to the works of psychologists or psychiatrists. Philosophy was an alien body of knowledge for most psychology students unless they had studied it as undergraduates or acted upon personal needs to acquire such information. As a result, American psychologists were not prepared to attend to the message of existential psychology, with its philosophical roots, for they were encountering a language which was foreign to their psychological training. In addition, because the concepts of philosophy were not created to be reduced to observable laboratory data, they were an anathema to many mainstream psychologists. Consequently, only a small number of psychologists became interested in even exploring the existential point of view.

The problems of effectively disseminating the existential viewpoint are additionally aggravated in large part by the lack of any comprehensive textbook on existential psychology. Consequently, confusion abounds over the content of existential psychology, and the disagreements occur among existential psychologists themselves. I have been somewhat reluctant to describe my own work as existential because existential means different things to different people and has always posed a problem in hermeneutics. However, existentialism also espouses that all labels and language simultaneously both increase and restrict one's understanding. As both a psychotherapist and a theoretician I, therefore, describe my own approach with the term pragmatic-existentialism.

Two:
Central Themes of
Existential Psychology

Existential Philosophy
As It Relates To Psychology

The term existentialism was first used by Sartre to describe the plight of the human condition, a viewpoint expressed in his novels, plays and books on philosophy and psychotherapy. Later, Kaufmann (1975) in particular used the term existentialism to include the philosophical writings of Kierkegaard, Nietzsche, Heidegger and Jaspers.

Since the label existentialism has been affixed *ex post facto* to the writings of different individuals, it is not surprising that disagreement occurs among the different catalogers as to what comprises the basic existential beliefs. Individuals endorsing widely disparate beliefs have all called themselves existentialists. Frankl (1960) at times considered himself existential and at other times vehemently dissociated himself from an existential position particularly when he identified the term existentialism exclusively with Sartre. In American psychology, Maslow, Allport, Rogers, May and Ellis have all described themselves as existentialists.

The body of existential writings is varied, amorphous and vulnerable to the idiosyncratic interpretations of any reader. An American psychologist would have to independently read these writings and then evaluate the degree to which these ideas were congruent with her own position. It is, therefore, quite understandable that psychologists reading different authors arrive at different interpretations of what constitutes existentialism.

The aforementioned American psychologists drew upon their own understandings of the works of Kierkegaard, Jaspers, Heidegger and Sartre. Each of these authors attempted to elucidate the human condition rather than provide a description of psychopathology. With the notable exception of Jaspers, who had previously written a text on psychopathology (1963), none of these writers was familiar with or particularly concerned about mental illness; they were philosophers rather than psychologists.

Heidegger's philosophy, however, was later adapted for use in psychotherapy in the writings of Binswanger (1963) and of Boss (1963), making these individuals pioneers of existential psychotherapy. Jaspers was a psychiatrist before he became a philosopher, and Jaspers' philosophical writings certainly reveal his understanding of the psychological pain that can lead to mental illness. Sartre ventured outside of philosophy and literature by writing *Being and Nothingness* (1956), a critique of Freudian psychoanalysis, which offered a new model of psychotherapy based upon existential principles. More recently, Ramsgate (1989) applied the nineteenth century writings of Kierkegaard to the practice of psychotherapy.

At this point in time, there are psychotherapists whose direct study of existential philosophy led them to create therapeutic systems (Binswanger and Boss). Still others recognized a similarity between their own views and the writings of existential philosophers and subsequently called themselves existentialists (Maslow, Allport, Rogers, Ellis). Both May (1958) and Yalom (1981) have written major works on existential psychotherapy describing how they apply existential concepts in their therapeutic work.

However, no effective consensus has been reached which documents the essential components of existential psychology. The philosophical descriptions of the human condition certainly can be extended to the realms of psychopathology and psychotherapy. Still the process of abstraction from one discipline to another is fraught with many difficulties. Even an attempt to apply only one philosophical system to the practice of psychotherapy evokes significant disagreements. Boss (Hall, 1968), for example, claimed that Binswanger had misapplied Heidegger's theory and quoted Heidegger himself to prove that Binswanger was in error.

A psychologist may individually decide that she is existentially oriented based upon her own acquaintance with certain writings. It is quite likely that her own particular conception of existentialism will significantly vary from the ideas of other psychologists or philosophers. It is very difficult to determine which aspects of each philosopher's theories are most applicable to the understanding of psychopathology and to the process of psychotherapy. It becomes easy to ascertain why so many disagreements and misinterpretations occur among psychotherapists who call themselves existentialists.

The term existential psychology is used in this text to encompass all of the attempts to apply existential philosophical writings to the field of psychology. Existential psychology here also includes all of the historical writings in psychology which are allied with the ideas of existential philosophy and which focus upon the person as an experiencing process.

Major Ideas of Existential Philosophy

The following outline represents one integration of the major universal ideas shared by different existential writers. These authors depicted what they believed to be the essential truths of the human experience. It is vitally necessary to review these truths because they function as the necessary prelude for understanding how psychopathology can become manifest in humans.

The person is an experiencing process

The experiencing person is described by existential philosophers as a *Verb* rather than a *Noun*. Describing the human as a *Verb* implies that the human is a process of change. To designate *change* as the basic characteristic in the human experience, existential writers used words such as "becoming" (Allport, 1960) and "being" (Maslow, 1968) in the titles of their books. These authors also emphasized the emerging and growing nature of the person throughout their writings.

Sartre (1956) defined all humans as "existence" (Verbs) which are attempting to become "essence" (Nouns); furthermore, humans cannot escape the uncomfortable fact that they exist as *Verbs* even though they spend lifetimes trying to become beings of permanence or *Nouns*. A description of the human as existence-trying-to-become-essence is an alien concept to the mainstream psychologists who utilize a reductionistic framework for understanding people and who prefer molecular to molar concepts.

If psychologists are to focus upon the changing nature of the person rather than upon human constancies, they will need to make a radical shift in their orientation. By defining the central nature of the person as a changing process, existentialists have launched this different type of psychological inquiry. In the simplest logical terms, if the fundamental hypothesis states that the basic nature of humans is to change, then those individuals who do not change should be considered unusual or aberrant. If this hypothesis is accepted, psychology will no longer be interested primarily in understanding the constancies in humans but rather will attempt to understand the nature of change as the basic human condition.

When taken to its extremes, existentialism asserts that constancy is not only unusual but is also indicative of a problem within a person who fails to change. Indeed, psychopathology is often described by some existentialists as the presence of constancy and the very lack of change. It is fundamental basic human nature to be ever-changing. Consequently, existentialists regard mainstream psychologists' refusal to focus upon change as a monumental obstacle blocking their understanding of basic human nature.

This changing nature of the human is conveyed by Heidegger and in the derivative systems of Boss and Binswanger by the German word *dasein*; literally, *dasein* means "being there," although it is more commonly translated as "being-in-the-world." Of all the existential philosophies Heidegger's is the most phenomenological. He stated that humans exist only as they experience. In other words, when we do not experience, we do not exist. In fact, the world only exists in the immediate experiential process of the person. Consequently, Heidegger hyphenates being-in-the-world as an indivisible unit. To speak of the person abstracted from the person's experience is to create a fiction. Heidegger might be tempted to label psychology as a discipline which studies a fiction.

Heidegger's view of experience can be taken as an implicit and very powerful critique of mainstream psychology. If individuals are viewed as ever-changing experiential processes, it would be an exercise in futility to study human experiences at any given moment, as people change from moment to moment. The ongoing changes in people render their past historical responses irrelevant to each new moment. This very radical existential position affirms that we are not what we were a second ago, but we are new creatures at each new moment. This revolutionary position of Heidegger also asserted that people only exist as experiencing processes. The tree that falls in the forest makes no sound when no one is around; indeed the tree does not even exist. However, the tree does make a sound whenever I experience the tree falling, and I do not have to be physically in the forest to experience the fall of the tree.

To study the ongoing experiencing process that is the person, therefore, requires the student to focus upon the immediacy of the *here* and the *now*. When people are asked if they perceive changes in themselves over time, they usually respond with resounding affirmative answers. However, most psychologists do not recognize this ongoing change as a fundamental human process. Hence, rather than study the immediacy of experience these same psychologists study constancies across time and people. They then view such constancies as the fundamental data in psychology.

In contrast, existentialists attempt to discover what the person is experiencing "at the moment" as well as how that experiencing occurs. The existential psychologist prefers to question *how* the experiencing is occurring as opposed to *why* the experiencing is occurring. To ask *how* is to focus upon a phenomenological understanding of another person. The *why* question, typically raised by analytic psychologists, attempts to look underneath the immediate experience in order to discover the hidden unconscious psychodynamics. By their inquiries these depth psychologists are asking what has produced the overt experiences of the moment. They regard the overt experiences simply as clues which will enable them to find the *real* underlying data. Existential psychologists believe that such thinking abandons the study of what is real and immediate and, instead, substitutes theoretical fictions.

The person can best be understood phenomenologically

If the human is to be understood as an ongoing experiential process, this description must be equally applicable both to the psychologist and to the person whom the psychologist is studying. Consequently, psychological inquiry involves 1) an experiencing process, the psychologist, who is trying to understand 2) another experiencing process, the patient or the subject. Of course traditional scientific psychology defines humans in non-experiential terms and therefore avoids this particular complexity. "Scientific" psychologists believe that they can study other people from an objective vantage point—a viewpoint that existentialists consider a deceptive and destructive illusion. Because psychologists are human experiencing processes themselves, they can only understand their patients through the filter of their own experiencing. Thus, no human can fully know another.

Consequently, the therapist's understanding of the patient is tempered by her own experiencing process. She is not the simple mirror of reality that objective science demands. Instead, a psychologist is a complex process who immediately understands many phenomena in a host of diverse ways. Boss (1963) described this fundamental human participation in the world as a "meaning disclosing encounter." We humans immediately make sense of our world; at times, as Boss pointed out, it may be the wrong sense, but we still immediately "know" or apprehend whatever surrounds us.

The task of the existential psychologist is to discover how the patient is making sense of her world. Binswanger (1963) discussed the use of different meaning categories which individuals use to apprehend their world. Meaning categories are evaluative concepts which individuals possess and then use as the way to make sense of all situations; Binswanger labelled this as the *a priori* ontological structure. According to Binswanger, the experiences of other humans make sense to us once we know the meaning categories they use at any given time. Because there are many meaning categories which can be utilized at any moment, individuals will see their world in very different ways depending upon which categories are utilized. For example, you, the reader, will read these words differently one way if you view them as written by a male, and another way if you view them as written by a female. Although Binswanger did not attempt to write an exhaustive list of meaning categories, he saw them as dimensions to evaluate experience which could then be classified by attending to both ends of the dichotomy. In the classic case of Ellen West (May, 1958), a patient of Binswanger's, he explained her choices as a consequence of the meaning categories she possessed. After splitting her world between the ethereal world and the tomb, she chose to commit suicide.

Psychoanalytic theory also pays particular attention to the inappropriate uses of meaning categories; however, it describes such processes with the special terms *transference* and *countertransference*. These terms imply that both the patient and the therapist, respectively, will misunderstand each other. Both can misperceive and react as if the other individual were a figure from their historical past instead of recognizing the present unique person.

However, a patient may be free of transference in the classical sense of the term but still misinterpret her therapist. That distortion can occur whenever the patient uses a meaning category which is excessively restrictive. For example, if the patient perceives the therapist as old, *i.e.*, out of touch with today's standards, then she may pay little attention to what the therapist is saying. However, if the patient perceives the therapist as old, *i.e.*, wise and experienced, then she may be more attentive to the therapist's communications.

Understanding another human being is and always will be enormously complex. We can effectively perceive some aspect(s) of another person or even apprehend the immediate intentions of the other, but no one human can fully apprehend or perceive another human.[1] Since each human is a changing and emerging process, any understanding of another human can only be valid for one fleeting moment. As soon as one might grasp how the other person is at any particular moment, the moment passes and the other person is again changing. Even though full understanding of another is impossible to obtain, the most complete understanding of the other is achieved by fully attending to his experiencing process.

---

[1] I follow other existentialists in using the word *apprehend* rather than *comprehend*. Apprehend implies that there are many possible ways of knowing; comprehend implies knowledge gained exclusively through the use of the intellect. This distinction can be better understood by turning to Jung (1946) who described four different functions that produce knowledge: thinking (using reason); sensing (objective recording of data); feeling (knowing through emotion); and intuition (knowing through unconscious processes).

In acknowledging that the fundamental existential task is to apprehend the process of the other, it becomes apparent that *knowing* occurs through the use of any or all of the four functions cited above. Psychologists trying to understand their therapy patients are using, at different times, each of these different functions. It is impossible to ascertain if one of these functions is better than another at any point in time. However, most psychological theories consider the only acceptable scientific ways of knowing to be via the functions of either sensing or thinking. Psychologists who consider cognition the only valid dimension for understanding will attempt to restrict their ways of knowing patients through the exclusive use of thinking and sensing.

In trying to understand the ways in which individuals make sense of their worlds, Boss's (1963) concept of *dasein* is invaluable. Our ways of being-in-the-world, or *dasein*, necessarily shift and change at different moments. At certain times individuals are highly focused or attuned to understanding their world, while at other times they are unfocused or inattentive. Boss's term *pitch* conveys these varying degrees of receptivity. The concept of *pitch* helps us to better understand therapy patients as it describes their quality of participation in the therapeutic dialogue. The concept also can be quite helpful in assessing the psychotherapist's variable effectiveness. The psychotherapist may be more tuned in to the patient at some moments than others; and she also can understand and empathize with some particular patients more than with others.

The fundamental and most effective way to grasp the other as an experiential process is to try to see the world as she does and to experience the world as she would. This method of understanding was termed "phenomenology" by Husserl (1965). In order to effectively utilize the phenomenological method, one must suspend one's own self and personal needs and empathically move into the psychological world of the other person.

Heidegger was perhaps the most successful philosopher to utilize phenomenology in describing the human experience. He considered the experience of the person as the only valid data and, consequently, dismissed the use of traditional objective anchors to apprehend experience. Even the most basic parameters of objective science, the dimensions of time and space, were described by Heidegger as experiential processes. Humans only exist in whatever space they feel they inhabit. When people describe their world only by using the language of science, they then become exclusively restricted to the realm of objective facts. Following Heidegger's existential philosophy, a person does not necessarily exist in the physical space that her physical body inhabits. People exist as they experience, so that I am "on the beach" and not in this room. "Scientific" psychologists dispute this position and would counter that I am simply fantasizing being on the beach. The "scientists" believe it is within their province to specify what is objective reality and what is fantasy. Following Heidegger, I am "on the beach" whenever I am in that experience. However, having been raised with twentieth century dictums, I have been taught to say that I am experiencing the "fantasy" of being on the beach. Such language may deprive me of the richness of my personal experiences; the beach felt warm and now that I am "in" the cold room, I long to be back at my beach.

In a similar manner, following Heidegger's argument, I am "in" the time period of my immediate experience, and I am not in the time frame specified by the scientist who focuses upon the objective world. Consequently, my existence spans centuries, even millenniums, even though "objective" science limits my existence to the twentieth and, hopefully, the twenty-first century.

As one accepts the experiential world of the other, it becomes extraordinarily difficult to dispute the accuracy of what the other person sees. If I can be on the beach, then the patient can be Napoleon. This kind of logic taken to radical extremes poses major dilemmas for individuals attracted to an existential position.

I have personally dealt with this dilemma by recognizing that patients indeed have experiences which are very real to them. I understand that the kinds of experiences they have are a result of the meaning categories which they are bringing to bear upon their experiences. I ultimately encourage patients to question the meaning categories which they use at particular moments in order to give themselves a richer and fuller understanding of the world.

However, the position that I assume implicitly, and at times explicitly, disputes the accuracy of the patient's experience of the world. There are other professional psychologists who may believe that my position is unacceptable, that the patient's experience is the only reality to be understood. Such attempts to understand the patients by exclusively focusing on them as experiential processes is called *radical phenomenology*. Since this method of understanding was present first in Husserl's writings and later in the works of Heidegger, any psychologist who practices the radical phenomenological method is fundamentally allied with existentialism. For this reason Carl Rogers can quite legitimately claim to have created a form of existential psychotherapy.

It was Rogers' (1980) contention that he could grasp the experiential world of the other only by suspending himself, as the therapist. Hence, his early writings on client centered psychotherapy prohibited the therapist from asking questions or giving any interpretations or advice to the client. Rogers believed that to ask questions or to give advice necessarily demonstrated that the therapist held a different viewpoint from that of the patient. Rogers felt that it was impossible for him to simultaneously evaluate and listen to his client. In fact, Rogers believed that clients could most effectively become healthy by receiving warmth and positive regard by the therapist. Only after therapy sessions had ended would Rogers listen to tapes and describe the process in terms other than those used by the client.

Understanding the patient in non-phenomenological terms

When therapists attempt to apprehend the experiential world of the other, they are aware that only some of the patient's experiences are directly expressed verbally. The work of Gestalt psychologists such as Perls (1969) has particularly demonstrated the significance of nonverbal communication in psychotherapy. Most therapists acknowledge that patients are able, for a variety of reasons, to directly verbalize only part of their experiences. The therapists also know that patients often express emotion in nonverbal ways which, at times, contradict their overt verbal communication.

Effectively trained psychotherapists know the varying ways in which people feel, express or do not express their anger. Consequently, these psychotherapists can "read" the presence of anger in a patient when the patient may deny or only minimally own these feelings. Other emotions have a range of nonverbal expressions as well. Therapists can detect the sad, anxious or depressed patients by physical stance and voice tone. Psychotherapists are not the only individuals who can discern such emotional clues. Part of our effective participation in the world necessitates "reading" the other person, especially when the other may not be directly and/or honestly communicative with us.

Since a therapist will also conceal information from others at certain times, she can draw upon her own personal experiences to anticipate the ways in which her patients may also be reticent in revealing certain information. The therapeutic ideal calls for the patient to be fully open and self-disclosing. However, the ideal is rarely if ever seen in practice. Therapists must be particularly wary whenever patients appear to be fully compliant and expressive as they are likely to have a hidden agenda.

Unfortunately too little has been written documenting the ways in which therapists listen to and understand their patients. In previous material (Potash, 1981) I described universal and general elements of understanding which therapists regularly utilize to apprehend their patients. These elements operate in conjunction with the four functions of thinking, feeling, sensing and intuiting as outlined by Jung (1945).

The universal elements of understanding include: (1) formal knowledge, *i.e.*, drawing upon theories, research, techniques and facts that psychologists acquired during their professional training; (2) problem solving strategies, *i.e.*, listening to the patient's difficulties by remembering techniques that the therapist has either personally used or known as effective ways of dealing with the world; (3) personal values, *i.e.*, standards for living which are part of the therapist's own moral code; (4) emotional responsiveness, *i.e.*, feelings activated in the therapist during the dialogue with the patient; (5) interfering personality dynamics of therapists, *i.e.*, countertransferential distortions; (6) knowledge about communication, *i.e.*, the therapist's interpretations of the intentions and feelings of the patient, based upon the therapist's knowledge of nonverbal communication patterns.

As therapists interact with their patients over time, they also acquire two general elements of understanding which can alter the ways in which they listen to the patient. These include: (7) a general understanding of the patient gained through prior dialogue; and (8) a sense of how the patient sees the therapist.

When therapists listen to their patients by drawing upon their own general (prior) understanding, they may have stereotyped their patients in some fashion and are not listening very attentively to the immediate communications. Additionally, when the therapist hears the patient's communications as based upon the patient's transferential feelings, the eighth general element of understanding, she may not give the patient's communication full credibility.

The particular functions and elements of understanding that are used by the therapist at one given moment will create radically different apprehensions of the patient. Consequently, what the therapist understands to be the process of the patient at that specific moment is produced by the particular elements and functions the therapist utilizes at that particular moment.

One of the most important insights that existential theory offers to psychotherapists is the realization that the ways in which they understand their patients are the most important keys to ultimate therapeutic success. It is crucial for psychologists to reflect upon the diverse ways in which they personally listen to and process the extensive communications of their patients. An expanded study of how to apprehend patients would, therefore, be central in an existential model for training psychotherapists.

The distress of being human

Many individuals think exclusively of Sartre when they hear of existentialism, and many of Sartre's writings are very depressing. Sartre describes inevitable and inescapable pain as a necessary and at times a seemingly primary component of the human condition. All of the existential philosophers and psychologists have their own special ways of focusing upon the distress of being human, and readers of these tracts find it difficult to disagree with their major arguments. However, there are important differences in the context and extent of the pain as described by the different authors.

The earliest existential philosopher, Kierkegaard (1957), focused upon the parable of Adam and Eve in order to redefine the nature and causes of human anxiety or, as he chose to label it, *dread*. For Kierkegaard, the loss of innocence created *dread*. When Adam and Eve were told not to eat an apple in the Garden of Eden, they first faced the possibility of making a meaningful choice. Before they were first given a taboo by God, they were incapable of engaging in wrongdoing because they were innocent. That is, they did not know that there was the possibility of wrongdoing or evil. If they had simply eaten an apple from the tree of knowledge before they had been told to avoid the tree, there would be no rationale for punishment or for banishment from the garden of Eden.

Consequently, Adam and Eve lost their innocence once God prohibited them from eating fruit from the tree of good and evil. It then became possible for Adam and Eve to commit a sinful act. The taboo led them to the anticipation of possibly committing a wrongful act and of facing unknown but likely negative consequences. This anticipation of potential, negative consequences is what Kierkegaard described as the experience of *dread*.

Psychologists can expand upon the arguments of Kierkegaard and easily describe such *dread* as the essence of neurotic symptomatology. If Adam and Eve became fearful that they might eat the prohibited fruit impulsively without stopping to think about it, they might have restricted their movements to only certain areas of the garden; this is the behavior of individuals who suffer from phobic reactions. One might predict that Adam and Eve could have created specific rituals in order to avoid the temptation of eating an apple; these are the actions of individuals who suffer from obsessive compulsive disorders. It is also possible that Adam and Eve might have become generally tense because of the possibility of violating the taboo, but at the same time they would not wish to know the source of their anxiety; the behavior is an example of an individual suffering from anxiety disorder.

Kierkegaard considered *dread* to be an inescapable human experience because humans are not innocent. Consequently, all people must make choices and be responsible for their actions. Even when humans live what Kierkegaard labelled the ethical life through obeying the dictates of God as written in the Bible, they still cannot escape making choices in their lives. There are times when we must transcend duty and the universal rules of ethics. We also will experience times when we behave in ways we believe correct, yet we experience massive pain. Individuals must agonize in choosing how to be. Ultimately they must recognize that some of their choices may indeed be quite wrong. Nonetheless, making choices which can never be validated is an inescapable and painful part of being human.

Perhaps the most blatantly depressing existential statement was offered by Sartre. He wrote, "Every human thing is born without reason, prolongs itself out of weakness and dies by chance" (Sartre, 1956). It was Sartre's contention that each human must accept the fact that there is nothing outside of oneself that is valid. He did not offer reassurance by stating that the "self" one created was valid. Rather, Sartre challenged the presence of any universal meanings or solutions to life's pain.

Sartre concurred with Nietzsche's affirmation that God was dead and consequently urged people to reevaluate their existence. Hence, all human existence was arbitrary and there could be no universal ethics, values or standards which, if followed, would provide for a meaningful existence. When a human accepted Sartre's beliefs, the inevitable experience that followed was aptly described by one of Sartre's book titles, *Nausea* (1962).

Sartre's earlier statement that humans are *Verbs* trying to become *Nouns* also very much describes the universal pain that people experience. There is a strong wish in all humans to attain the fixed and non-changing state of safety and security. To have a permanent, unchanging identity with firm beliefs and values would provide us with a solid frame of reference to guide our lives. According to Sartre, however, such permanence can never be attained.

Jaspers (Wallraff, 1970) described the inevitability of human pain through his concept of *ultimate situations* which include struggle, guilt, death and suffering. Humans cannot escape these feelings. Everyday life naturally produces suffering, for each person's existence is in some way an inconvenience to others. My food could go to other people, my job could have been performed by someone perhaps more needy than myself. Even my ideas may antagonize other people as I do not endorse their opposing beliefs. I also struggle within myself as I experience inner conflicts and attempt to control myself, be it with my penchant for eating chocolate bars or simply in trying to decipher the best decision to make among many appealing alternatives.

Guilt also is inevitable according to Jaspers, for the human's actions have unknowable consequences. Whenever I drive a car, I might hit a pedestrian. I may say and do offensive things without being aware that my remarks will hurt another. I cannot be sure that I behave correctly as a parent, for I do not know all the correct behaviors. Furthermore, I can feel guilty, and I cannot avoid having these negative feelings.

Additionally, I know that I am going to die and that all others whom I know and love will die as well. It is very painful to face the inevitability of death as well as the immediate reality of the death of other people. For all of these aforementioned reasons, I will, therefore, suffer. Life includes pain, and we can never successfully escape the pain of being human.

Bugenthal (1965), an existential psychologist, offered another extensive description of the inescapable pain of being human and identified this pain as different forms of *existential anxiety*. In his writings Bugenthal spoke of four ontological "givens," or truths, about the human condition. To face these truths entails corresponding subjective experiences. Facing each of these four painful truths will activate a different form of existential anxiety. Finally there is a particular ultimate form which this existential anxiety will assume in all humans.

Bugenthal's first ontological "given" is whatever degree of awareness that we humans may attain, it will always be insufficient or less than we would like it to be. We will never know all that we could or should know. To experience this unavoidable fact is to have a feeling of *contingency*—a recognition that there will be times in our lives that we will be victimized by events beyond our knowledge and control. The anxiety we feel when we recognize this truth is the sense of fate. The ultimate existential anxiety that this recognition assumes is the dread of death. Death is the ultimate victimization that awaits us all.

The second ontological "given" described by Bugenthal is humans do behave or do take action. Since we are active behaving creatures, it stands to reason that our actions have consequences. When we recognize this truth, our subjective experience is a feeling of *responsibility*. The recognition of the unknowable consequences to our actions generates a particular form of existential anxiety, which Bugenthal calls guilt. The ultimate form of existential anxiety associated with our sense of having poorly managed our responsibilities is the dread of condemnation.

Bugenthal's third ontological "given" is humans are always able to make choices. Although it is certainly true that we must often select among undesirable options, we still are compelled to make choices. Even not choosing is a choice. When we experience this truth and recognize that we are indeed subjects rather than objects, we have the subjective experience of *autonomy*. However, because we have incomplete knowledge and always face unpredictable consequences, we again will experience existential anxiety as we face the inevitability of being creatures of choice. The particular form this anxiety assumes is the fear of emptiness, to be living each day with no significance or purpose. In its ultimate form we experience the dread of meaninglessness. It is impossible for humans to have choices validated, for there is no one to state what is right or wrong. Therefore, it is inevitable that we face the possibility of living a life without meaning.

The final ontological "given" which Bugenthal outlined is humans are both separate from and simultaneously connected to others. We experience this truth as a feeling of *a-part-ness*. People can never be fully connected with others. Hence we each are alone regardless of important relationships with other people. The existential anxiety which is associated with this truth is the tension of loneliness. The ultimate dread this produces is the anticipation of complete isolation.

The existential writers mentioned above offer very powerful statements about the inevitable pain of the human condition. It is indeed very depressing and often overwhelming for us to own these insights. Sometimes the despair over our human fallibility can be so crippling that some of us do not recover from the pain felt by facing one's own humanness. However, the existentialists state that even greater destruction will be wrought by self-deception. We must come to terms with our human limitations. In fact, different existentialists propose a most ironic solution for our anguish: Only through first facing our fallibility with its concomitant anxiety and pain can we then live our fullest and most authentic form of existence.

Three:
Existentialism
and Psychopathology

Self-Deception and
Stunted Growth

A central theme in existential literature is the awakening of the sleeping human. Individuals who lead lives of blind conformity, or simply the "good life" as embodied by societal values, are seen as underdeveloped and full of denial. When these people confront the imminence of their own demise, as in Tolstoy's *The Death of Ivan Ilyich* (1960), they see the emptiness of their past existence. Some people are then able to find significant meaning and importance before death while others remain powerless. According to existential thinkers, the most dreadful human condition is the refusal to face an inherent fallibility and subsequent failure to create a life which might be personally meaningful.

Conformity is often interpreted by existentialists as a primary way in which individuals negate themselves. For several reasons individuals also deny their power to act or to make choices. Because it is painful to admit to one's general sense of powerlessness, many people become workaholics; they keep themselves very busy in order to avoid such self-awareness. However, despite incessant attempts to remain occupied, there are periods when individuals cannot find sufficient diversionary activities in order to remain oblivious to their fundamentally empty lives. This syndrome most likely occurs on non-work days, and Frankl (1967) designated it "Sunday neurosis." The term describes the symptoms of anxiety and depression which appear when people cannot find satisfactory preoccupations.

Fromm (1941) realized that the difficulty in accepting one's human limitations was a large scale societal issue. His main theme in *Escape from Freedom* is that people avoid developing their own individuality by endorsing totalitarian regimes. People find safety and security by allowing their life styles and values to be dictated and defined by others. Through such a strategy, they avoid the anguish of making choices and falsely believe that they can escape the possibility of guilt. They find it too lonely and too risky to become individuals who create themselves, functioning in what Fromm later called the "being mode" (Fromm, 1981).

Many existential psychologists believe that by stunting the expression of his own personal individuality, a person creates psychopathology within himself. May (1972) acknowledged that an individual's refusal to accept the inevitability of existential anxiety produced additional psychological pain. People who repress their existential anxiety will ultimately experience neurotic anxiety and neurotic symptomatology. These individuals are viewed by May as deeply afraid of facing their human fallibility. Even though they deny the inescapable truth of their inherent human weakness, they, nonetheless, still remain fundamentally afraid because they sense that this denial will fail. By relegating such conflict to the level of unconsciousness, they have compounded their pain and now have symptoms of generalized anxiety. The symptomatology reflects the underlying tension associated with maintaining this kind of self-deception.

Sartre (1956) developed the above theme quite eloquently by stating that any individual who engaged in a purposeful self-deception was living in "bad faith." One must necessarily recognize a painful event, at some level, before one can decide to repress it. Therefore, such people are lying to themselves. Sartre criticized psychoanalytic theory for postulating the presence of a lie, *i.e.*, repression, without acknowledging the presence of a liar, the person telling the lie. In other words, repression is a purposive act of self-deception. People who utilize repression and who lie to themselves are still responsible for their actions.

In contrast, Freud postulated that repression occurred at the unconscious level, and he seemingly absolved individuals from being responsible for their unconscious processes. Sartre disagreed with Freud (1966) as Sartre believed that when individuals utilize repression, they still remain responsible both for creating repression and for continuing such self-deceptions. The fundamental messages in Sartre's writings demand the end of self-deception, the recognition that societal and religious standards do not provide universal truths, and the subsequent acceptance and development of individuality, whereby humans create their own selves and their own lives.

The existential psychologists engage in many more discussions about the positive consequences of confronting one's humanness than do the existential philosophers. For the literary person it is much more dramatic to describe anguish and pain than to describe the resolution of such pain. Furthermore, it is the primary business of psychotherapists to assist patients in attaining mental health. As a result, existential psychologists are invested in describing positive resolution to this universal human pain. Certainly, philosophy may have important applications for human living, but clinical psychology in particular describes its primary focus as application to the clinical situation

Endorsing Existential Values

Of the different existential philosophers, Jaspers (Wallraff 1970) offered the most positive outlook regarding the human condition. He acknowledged that we humans primarily live as empirical existences in the world. Our behavior follows basic psychological principles, as we do not usually function as if we were primarily in charge of our own lives. Fortunately, this is not an immutable condition as we could potentially function at Jaspers' level of *existenz*, which is a totally different way of being. When functioning as *existenz*, humans achieve their highest form of individualistic being. They experience the freedom to choose and thereby to create themselves. They are the choices they make. The person lives as *existenz* only insofar as he chooses. Once he stops making meaningful choices, he returns to the level of empirical existence.

Jaspers believed that he could not simply explain *existenz* to an individual who had never functioned at that level. Instead, he used analogies and approximations to help such a reader understand *existenz*. He said that *existenz* was not a state of being but rather a "being able." It was labelled the polar opposite of the "persona" or social mask that most people wear when dealing with others. Jaspers attempted to inspire his readers to strive for *existenz*, and he pointed out the extreme difficulty of sustaining this full form of self-expression. Rather, humans will regularly fall back to functioning as empirical existences in the world and then once again move forward to the heights of *existenz*.

May's (1979) distinction between functioning as an object or as a subject paralleled Jaspers' distinction between existence and *existenz*. May stated that we humans simultaneously possess the qualities of subjects, in charge of our lives, as well as objects, creatures without power who are manipulated by the external world. May believed it is vital for us to recognize that we function in both modalities, for this enables us to more fully "own" the subject pole of experience. In other words, we can realize there are times when we are powerful, just as there are times when we are powerless.

Existential psychologists frequently point out that individuals can take fuller charge of their own lives. For example, Maslow (1961), who is identified as more of a humanist than an existentialist, considered self-actualization the highest form of self-expression. In Maslow's schemata, when individuals do not attain self-actualization, it is because they are still focused upon satisfying lower level needs. When people must struggle for survival, love and self-esteem, they are unable to develop their latent potential for self-actualization. The development of the full range of one's human potentials is possible, according to Maslow, only when the most basic conditions for effective living have already been met.

Rogers (1951) also wrote that individuals who do not receive unconditional positive regard or fully unqualified love are blocked from fully developing their individuality. Instead they experience conditions of worth. In other words, they deem only certain feeling states and behavior as acceptable in lovable humans. As a result, these people distort their awareness of themselves and others in order to view themselves as fundamentally lovable. According to Rogers, this conditional positive regard is the essential cause of all forms of psychopathology.

Jaspers, May, Maslow and Rogers each discussed universal conditions which produce the milder forms of psycopathology. These authors all affirmed that conformity is an essentially destructive behavior as it deprives people of their individuality. Furthermore, they all believed that a full development of one's potential represents the highest level of functioning. Each of them hoped to inspire their audience to acquire what Tillich (1952) called *The Courage to Be*. Authors of any theoretical persuasion necessarily want to affect their audience; the particular intent behind most existential writings is to encourage people to develop a highly individualized and fulfilling life style.

Each existential writer had special terms to describe what he considered the best approach to living. For Jaspers it was striving for *existenz*, while for Rogers, it was actualizing one's experience. Binswanger considered it most desirable to utilize many meaning categories in order to enhance one's understanding, and Boss considered it vital to be open to experiencing. Bugenthal advocated striving for authenticity, and Maslow urged self-actualization. Finally, Yalom (1981) advocated that we confront death, freedom, meaninglessness and isolation.

Existential psychologists and philosophers fundamentally agree that the best way for people to live is by taking effective control of their lives. For a person to do this, he must first recognize that he alone can best choose how to be. Existential therapists overtly acknowledge that their patients can make the authentic choices which most deeply express their own particular values.

In most if not all instances, therapists do not have the right to impose their own views or to tell their patients what are the "right" or correct choices to make. If a therapist were to render such opinions, he would be imposing his own values upon the patient. Even when a therapist does not verbalize opinions about the patient's choices, he may still know that some of the choices the patient makes may prove to be disastrous.

Nonetheless, existential psychotherapists, like all other humans, have personal values as well as particular professional values which guide their own lives. When deciding to become a psychotherapist, the existential psychologist, like the psychologist allied to other theoretical frameworks, endorses the belief that good mental health is a desirable human value. In meeting with patients all therapists are making a professional commitment to help these patients change in ways that will further their mental health. If therapists were unconcerned about patients changing, they would have no reason to practice psychotherapy. Therefore, therapists cannot be neutral about their patients, and they cannot be indifferent about the degree of progress their patients exhibit. Some therapists may believe it is counterproductive to directly reveal their involvement, and they therefore may remain non-verbal about the patients' progress. However, therapists of any and all theoretical persuasions cannot truly be unconcerned about their patients and still remain effective responsible professionals.

Because the fundamental task in all forms of psychotherapy is to assist patients in moving toward greater mental health, no therapist can afford to lose sight of this goal. By their implicit endorsement of furthering the patient's mental health, existential therapists, like all other therapists, are endorsing professional values which guide their work.

Attaining Authenticity and Health

To effectively move toward greater mental health, one must face the aforementioned existential truths and feel the pain associated with being a transient and inevitably flawed human. Therapy patients who are trying to become healthy must be willing to acknowledge the self-deceptions they have been practicing. It is overwhelming to most people to confront oneself and feel the enormous pain created by self-deception. When a person sees the effects of his life-long lies, he usually becomes very depressed; he may also acknowledge that his entire life has been empty and meaningless. It is indeed appalling for any of us to realize we have practiced self-deception, been cowardly and inauthentic, and have let time slip away, knowing it is time we will never be able to recapture.

Existential psychotherapists know that some patients do make a wonderful leap away from their despair and feelings of personal meaninglessness. When a patient accepts the fact that he has the capacity to take control of his life, make choices and carry out the awesome responsibility of being a fallible human, the patient often does make progress. Such growth is not easy; and when it does occur, it is usually after a long struggle. Nonetheless, when growth does happen, it transforms people's lives for the better.

Gaining control of his life does not make a patient free from anxiety, for healthy individuals must recognize that anxiety is an inevitable part of life. After allowing themselves to take the full responsibility of their lives, patients begin to like and eventually love themselves. They finally feel proud of who they are and what they are doing. Existential psychotherapists will rejoice at seeing their patients begin to feel so empowered.

When patients work successfully in making such personal transformations, they soon discover that other people develop high regard for them. They receive signs of affection and love which further encourage them to pursue honesty and self-expression. By taking control of their own lives, these individuals begin to create very full and rich lives for themselves.

Because existential psychology has been able to assist people in making such broad, sweeping, positive changes, it is therefore a very optimistic viewpoint about the human condition. Many individuals embrace the tenets of existential psychology once they fully understand how its message empowers them. As people discover they have the capacity and the skill to take effective control over their lives, they feel exhilarated.

When Existentialism Works

It is an exhaustive and enormous undertaking to confront one's own self-deceptions. The issues that need to be resolved will differ depending upon the amount of constriction. As a general rule, the greater the degree of self-deception that one has practiced, the harder it will be to face oneself honestly and to recognize one's current inauthenticity.

Individuals who have been basically psychologically healthy and who have practiced only minor degrees of self-deception will usually be able to hear the messages of existential psychology and begin to apply them to their personal lives. For example, it has been common for undergraduate students to state that a course in existential psychology has transformed their lives in far-reaching ways. When a person begins to challenge his self-deceptions, this process of self-confrontation seems to become an ongoing part of life. The positive results encourage individuals to become even more self-expressive and more in charge of their lives which, in turn, elicit more positive reactions from other people.

Expanding Upon Existential Truths

To be able to confront long practiced self-deception, cope with the feelings of emptiness, and resolve both to change and to implement such changes requires tremendous underlying personal strength. Consequently, a therapist cannot be simplistic and tell a patient who has been institutionalized for a long time that he has always had the capacity to make correct choices and can now transform his life. Theoretically it may be true that such patients might be able to do something about their immediate condition. However, patients must first believe that they can change before any small change may actually be implemented.

The description of the inevitable pain, struggle and joy inherent in the human condition does not have the same powerful effect on individuals suffering from extensive psychopathology as it has upon healthier individuals. To be able to grasp the totality of the human condition and the anguish which people face requires the capacity to effectively abstract and conceptualize oneself in relation to the world. When an individual is riddled with major problems making it enormously difficult to cope with the demands of everyday life, he is rarely able to suspend his immediate pain and pose higher level questions about the nature of existence.

Basic existential ideas can, nevertheless, be quite useful in helping very troubled individuals. Existentialism requires a phenomenological understanding of the patient as an experiencing process, and this method of apprehending another can be used with both the deeply troubled as well as with the highly functioning individual. As therapists attend to the experiential process of the other, they can understand how amenable patients are to exploring alternate ways of making sense of their worlds. The message that all humans have choice and responsibility will threaten the essence of some patients so deeply that they will not be able to process this message correctly.

Individuals feel much anguish and self-recrimination when they ultimately acknowledge that they have and have always had the power to make changes in their lives. Many people have practiced such massive self-deception and have so restricted their self-awareness that they must strongly resist acknowledging they indeed have this personal power. Realizing the presence of massive self-deception over the course of a lifetime can produce intolerable pain and guilt from which some patients may never recover. For this reason, it is vital that the therapeutic relationship provide strong support and comfort (see chapter 7).

In contrast, it is easy to recognize why the ideas of existential psychology have ready appeal to bright, high-functioning, college-educated 22 year olds. Young adults want to hear that they can undo their past, that they can transform themselves into whatever they want, and that authority and religious institutions only have legitimacy when they give them legitimacy. At this point in life these people are most receptive to productive changes, and the existential theories are very consistent with their needs.

However, it is an entirely different matter to give the same message to a 65 year old who has spent a lifetime in a job he hated, in a loveless marriage he was afraid to leave, and who has been cold and punitive to his children with a "spare the rod and spoil the child" attitude. For such people, any heightened self-awareness means recognizing the enormity of long standing, past self-deceptions and confronting the probability that they have spent the major portion of their lives in a very confined and destructive manner. It is highly unlikely that this new level of self-awareness would subjectively be judged worth the pain of confronting one's historical self-deceptions. Patients can face such ugly truths about themselves only when they sense that they can ultimately change this pattern for the better.

First Application to Personality Disorders

It is neither cowardice nor neurotic fear of making poor choices that lie at the basic core of serious forms of psychopathology. For example, when therapists treat patients who exhibit a profound fear of expressing their individuality, it soon becomes apparent that these people were terrorized as young children whenever they exhibited the most basic forms of self-expression. Individuals whose symptomatology corresponds to what is broadly labelled a "personality disorder" suffer from such pervasive and primitive fears. The case histories of these patients demonstrate that their very existence was constantly threatened by destructive parental figures. These patients were both physically and psychologically brutalized for exhibiting basic human needs. For such a person, survival required that he develop a distorted view both of himself and the world. If we describe such people as practicing self-deception, we miss the essential problem which begins with their underdeveloped sense of self. Self-deception can only be practiced when there is a self to deceive; in many of these personality disordered people little sense of self is present.

The psychological growth of such individuals first requires that a self be constructed, long before the enhanced satisfaction of basic needs can be an issue. First they must be able to better recognize the world of objective reality and begin to see that they can navigate themselves through it successfully. An individual must experience at least a minimum of underlying strength before he can directly face the universal pain of being human. It is the underlying strength and belief in ourselves that enables most of us to withstand psychological pain.

For example, it as at best a half truth to tell an individual with low level skills that he has the capacity to convince an employer to hire him. Until he knows how to dress appropriately, how to make good eye contact, how to respond to questions or how to fill out a job application, he lacks the necessary power to convince a potential employer of his desirability. A therapist may certainly need to tell patients that they have underlying power. But even more importantly, the therapists must help these patients develop the necessary skills so that the inherent power becomes a reality rather than remains a verbal fiction.

Many different strategies can prove useful with such patients, and the remainder of this book will address how best to help personality disordered patients by using an existential perspective. The existential therapist must first address the extensive psychological damage present in personality disordered patients, and then find ways to help the patients desist from engaging in further self-defeating and self-destructive behavior. Once patients have effectively learned survival techniques and experienced fundamental personal gratification, they then can deal with the universal pain associated with being human. Clearly, the task of understanding the patient as an experiential process takes precedence over dealing with issues of uncertainty and suffering.

Existentialism for the Psychologist

When psychologists endorse the validity of existentialism, both their personal and professional lives are affected and thereby changed. They find that certain existential insights enable them to see their patients in a different manner. The special task for the existential therapist in professional practice will be to decide which existential insights are most relevant for each particular situation.

Existentialism also has a major impact upon the psychologist at the level of personal living. As the tenets of existentialism are applied to oneself and the psychologist scrutinizes his own self-deceptions, he, too, feels more empowered. Existential insights help psychologists make positive changes in their personal lives as well as reinforce the notion that existentialism can benefit their patients as well. First and foremost, existentialism provides a framework for living one's own life. In a secondary but still very important way, existentialism functions as a useful philosophy for understanding psychopathology and for conducting psychotherapy.

As he hears and believes the ontological givens of the human condition, previously cited by Bugenthal, the psychologist is necessarily humbled. These truths demonstrate the folly of assuming a position of superiority over a patient. When we confront the universal pain of the human condition, we may view our psychotherapy patients as fellow humans who are also in pain. Simultaneously, we recognize that some pain is inescapable for both our patients and for ourselves. Therapists and patients alike will always have to contend with anxiety and guilt and will always struggle with their inherent, human limitations.

However, the psychotherapists do have certain knowledge and skills that their patients do not possess. These existential psychologists maintain: 1) a fuller recognition of the human condition and its pain; 2) an awareness that confronting one's humanness is a necessary and inevitable task for healing to occur; and 3) a level of skill in understanding psychopathology and interpersonal relationships which can be shared with the patient and used to assist the process of growth and change in the patient.

Existential therapists' specialized knowledge does not transform them into better or more valuable people. It does not provide license for assuming a position of superiority, and patients must also understand these truths. One way I communicate this message to my patients is by describing myself as simply another service professional. Just as patients can assess the effectiveness of the plumber and the electrician, so, too, the patient has both the right and the capacity to assess the level of assistance provided by the psychotherapist. When a person believes that a plumber is inefficient or charges too much money or does not respond quickly enough, he discharges the plumber and finds another. It is part of a patient's inalienable right to be able to assess the psychotherapist in the same manner. When this message is given to the patient, a fundamental underlying existential message is provided as well. By telling my patients that they have both the power and the responsibility to evaluate me, I am affirming their capacity as choosing, capable human beings.

Relinquishing false superiority and replacing it with the perception of psychotherapy as a dialogue with one's fellow human frees the therapist of unnecessary encumbrances. For instance, the psychotherapist sheds the illusion of being fully responsible for the patient's welfare. Therapists are responsible for trying their best to be helpful, but no one can accept the fundamental responsibility for another human's life. This does not, however, provide license for irresponsible passivity on the part of the therapist. If a patient is overtly suicidal, it is the therapist's responsibility to have the patient hospitalized. No therapist can conduct 24-hour suicide watches, and that vigilance is the job of a full service hospital.

The task of the existential therapist is to help the patient see himself and others more accurately and to help the patient recognize that he has the ultimate power to be in control of his life. All existential psychotherapists will also encourage patients to recognize themselves as processes of experience.

Misunderstanding Existentialism

It is relatively common for psychotherapists to combine the existential outlook with other psychological theories, especially existential-humanist and existential-analyst. Professionals who define themselves thus believe that the messages of existentialism provide important insights into the human condition. However, these individuals also believe that other theoretical constructs are necessary in order to practice psychotherapy most effectively. Unfortunately, when existentialism is blended with other viewpoints, the existential message may become diluted or overshadowed by the other theoretical constructs.

Existentialism is a practical philosophy for living, and existential psychotherapists attempt to apply these ideas directly in the consulting room as they work with patients. Existential psychotherapists first abstract what they consider to be the essential ideas of different philosophers and psychologists and then apply these ideas in their behavior and interactions with their patients. Since different individuals are each making their own abstractions and applications of existential principles, it is not surprising that the descriptions of existential psychotherapy will radically differ among psychologists.

For example, a therapist who reads Yalom (1981) learns that the central themes of existential therapy are death, freedom, isolation and meaninglessness. If he were to approach treatment with a strong need to be systematic, he might insist that a patient engage in deep discussions about mortality and ultimate death. While one's eventual death is certainly a legitimate psychotherapy topic, the time and frequency of such discussions will differ among patients. Superimposing an agenda upon the patient and insisting upon a discussion of the patient's mortality violates the person as an existential process. Therefore, psychotherapists must avoid taking the ideas of existentialism and transforming them into techniques or weapons which negate the individuality of the patient.

Once it is recognized that the patient is an experiential process, it quickly becomes apparent that psychotherapy can never be practiced as a set of techniques which the therapist routinely applies to the patient. Techniques are artifices which erode the genuineness and spontaneity of the interaction. Psychotherapy is closest to the classic existential process when it occurs as one being-in-the-world responding to another being-in-the-world.

Pragmatic-Existentialism

The message of existential psychology will lead therapists to gain a fundamental understanding of the human condition which can guide effective therapeutic work. Because existentialism involves a set of beliefs and is a particular philosophy, application of its messages will vary among therapists in their practice.

Through my years of conducting psychotherapy I have developed my own interpretations of existential insights, particularly for the treatment of personality disorders. Clinical psychology is a pragmatic discipline, and I believe that pragmatic principles must always be basic in the work of psychotherapists. My work as a psychotherapist may be defined as a blend of the existential understanding of the human, coupled with a pragmatic approach and healthy therapeutic parenting. Consequently, my approach to psychotherapy is best classified as "Pragmatic-Existentialism."

Four:
Pragmatism in Psychology
and Psychotherapy

Clinical psychology is an applied discipline. It differs from the larger body of psychology as it does not pursue knowledge purely for the sake of knowledge but rather for particular pragmatic goals. Clinical psychologists' intentions are to understand people in order to help them develop. The forms of assistance that can be provided are multidimensional. Although traditionally they were involved in assessment, clinical psychologists have broadened their role to become agents of change as well as providers of education and other services. The clinical psychologists who describe themselves primarily as scientists rather than as therapists were, nevertheless, trained in graduate programs which required them to learn the skills of both science and practice. Although clinical psychologists are fundamentally committed to understanding humans, such understanding is expected to be put to good practical use.

The aims of clinical psychology are, therefore, pragmatic. The expert's understanding of a human needs to be utilitarian. However, the dual training in science and practice has made clinical psychologists divided in their loyalties. Recently, the overall discipline of psychology has split itself into two distinct professional organizations, representing the camps of science and practice, respectively. Clinical psychologists themselves remain in conflict over the degree to which they should assume the role of scientists and perform research or function exclusively as practitioners.

Even when the clinical psychologist works only in private practice settings conducting psychotherapy, it remains necessary to read research reports to guide the professional practice. The route to effective practice is expected to be provided by the scientific camp, rather than by theorists or by one's personal experience in conducting psychotherapy.

The dual training in science and practice has become a part of the more recent Psy.D. programs which were purportedly designed to train practitioners. These programs increasingly require students to complete lengthy projects which approximate the research-based dissertations in Ph.D. programs.

When clinical psychologists are trained to search for scientific answers, they have usually been taught the nineteenth century models of science which are highly reductionistic in scope and have been discarded by most of the physical sciences in the twentieth century. Hence, even the "aha" problem solving solutions described by Gestalt psychologists are considered deficient strategies by those individuals who adhere to a very narrow conception of what constitutes effective scientific explanations.

This form of scientific thinking hypothesizes that complex phenomena are composed of simple underlying elements. Once these elements can be identified, the relationship between the elements is believed to produce the complex psychological phenomena. Such assumptions are the core of structuralism; these reductionistic assumptions have also remained central to mainstream psychology. This theory is evidenced in behaviorism where human action is attributed to a stimulus (S) which precedes a response (R). Sociological factors have also played a large role in affecting the development of psychology for the discipline of psychology is primarily American and therefore reflects much of the American ethos.

American Ideals of Pragmatism

It is more than pure happenstance that clinical psychology has emerged and flourished particularly in the United States, for Americans have always had a strong affinity for using applied skills. The overwhelming majority of clinical psychologists are American, and only in the United States does one see a significant number of doctoral level psychologists practicing psychotherapy. As a result, the particular form of pragmatism evident in clinical psychology is largely a reflection of long-standing, particularly American values and ideals.

American folklore places a high premium on the concept of individualism. Our mythology is replete with instances of the person who seizes an opportunity and turns it into an enormous personal success. Grammar school children are taught that America is and always has been the land of opportunity. The Pilgrims came here for a better life as did all the other waves of immigrants. The United States is often considered a country founded by pioneers who created full and successful lives with few initial resources other than their willingness to work very hard. Many technological advances of the past two centuries have been invented by Americans, and the phrase "American know how" is an important part of the American identity.

Americans much prefer the image of the self-made man to that of the baby born with a silver spoon in its mouth. American folklore is full of tales of fiercely independent individuals, determined to achieve success. The sweeping popularity of the early twentieth century Horatio Alger stories attests to the American belief that change in social class is always possible whenever one has sufficient personal drive.

The American ethic has traditionally demanded that one work hard in order to be successful. However, success does not occur simply through the sweat of one's brow. The hard working individual is also expected to think with vision, be aware of opportunities that loom on the horizon, and take the necessary risks that will produce financial success. Consequently, the most admired Americans have made the leap from dire poverty into enormous prosperity, the John D. Rockefeller myth retold in countless ways.

Success by American standards is frequently measured financially rather than through other values. The scholar, researcher, artist and teacher do not command the respect in our society that is typically given to the person of wealth. Most Americans distinguish social classes primarily by the amount of money that people possess rather than by their intellectual or creative achievements.

The most popular film at Christmas time, *It's a Wonderful Life*, also epitomizes America's preoccupation with financial success. It is only an angel who can save the hero from committing suicide because of financial ruin. Although the ultimate moral of the story is that interpersonal connectedness is of the highest value, such humanitarian concerns often are given a low priority in daily living.

The American pursuit of financial success has certainly affected the curricula of its institutions of higher learning. Many universities have adopted the philosophy that a major purpose of education is to make a person more successful, and success remains closely wedded to future income level. This preoccupation with material success has changed the patterns of higher learning in the past twenty years. The single-minded concern with obtaining a good job immediately after college has produced massive shifts in undergraduate specializations. The preponderance of college students now majors in business rather than in the liberal arts. Even when students remain in the liberal arts, the popular majors have become computer science and economics; it is the rare student who studies the humanities. Few American college students wish to obtain a broad-based liberal arts education as most view college as a career training path. Many universities have reshaped their curricula to offer this more "practical" training.

While pragmatic learning remains the form of education most valued in the United States, purely intellectual pursuits are often downgraded and even ridiculed. When an author proclaimed *All I really need to know I learned in kindergarten* (Fulghum, 1988), his book became a best seller. Even prominent Americans (Agnew, 1969) have labelled intellectuals as "effete eggheads." The word "professor" is commonly associated with "absent minded" by most Americans. Consequently, the fact that the current college students eschew the pursuit of pure knowledge reflects a basic mistrust of intellectualism, long in the mainstream of American thinking. The latest form of derision of the pursuit of intellectual knowledge has been the outcry against studying the writings of D.W.E.M.'s, the acronym for dead, white European males. Many of today's college students prejudge the intellectual concepts developed by men of previous centuries as inapplicable to their personal lives.

The notion that effort and hard work are desirable motives remains quite popular in American culture and is currently embodied in the recent television commercial for sneakers which proclaims "Just do it." There is enormous allure to the concept "Just do it." Certainly, when one applies this idea to the practice of psychotherapy it would be wonderful if it could simply be "done." The deep-seated power of the American ethic and particularly of behaviorism has fostered the mentality that "Just do it" is, indeed, possible both in psychology and in psychotherapy.

Pragmatism in American Psychology

Because psychology has thrived in the United States more so than in any other nation, the American ethos has necessarily affected and indeed pervaded mainstream psychological thinking. American psychologists have typically maintained the strong anti-intellectual stance that is popular in this culture. The distrust of complex intellectual thinking has its particular manifestation in a strong bias against any theory offering contradictory possibilities or not advocating firmly entrenched pragmatic goals.

Structuralism, which many label the first school of thought in psychology, had only a short life in the United States for it did not ask pragmatic questions. Because structuralists sought to discover the basic units of the mind without focusing upon the possible practical utility of this knowledge, it was fundamentally inconsistent with the American pragmatic ethos.

The first distinctly American school of psychology was labelled Functionalism, and it developed as a reaction against structuralism in the latter part of the nineteenth century. Functionalists focused their inquiry into the human condition by asking questions regarding a person's purpose and intention. The actions of people were thought to be best understood when they were viewed as goal directed. Functionalism was, therefore, closely related to the "act psychology" that had been proposed in Europe by Brentano. Even though functionalism was short-lived, it nonetheless had major impact upon American culture through its influence upon Dewey (1899) who initiated the progressive education movement.

I earlier referred to the anti-theoretical stance of the introductory psychology textbooks that espoused experimentation and decried armchair speculation. Conceptualizations that did not lead to measurement were considered inappropriate psychological endeavors in these texts. Therefore, it is not surprising that when Watson, the first behaviorist, pronounced he could make any infant into a doctor, lawyer or Indian chief, he found a most enthusiastic American audience. Watson embodied the American argument that anything was possible with enough hard work and inventiveness. By adding the dimension of situational controls, it would be possible to shape human behavior. Behaviorism offered the promise of quick, far-reaching results through the use of simple, scientifically-based principles.

A review of the theoretical models taught in personality courses easily demonstrates that most of these theories were borrowed from psychiatry. The most popular approaches were proposed by American psychologists Rogers and Skinner; both models utilize few theoretical constructs in contrast to the conceptions developed by the psychiatrists. Skinner (1971) advocated collecting facts through research before creating any theories, and he wanted to keep theory as simple as possible. Rogers (1961) strongly disagreed with the content of Skinner's arguments; his own theory considered warmth, genuineness and empathy sufficient for behavior change.

Rogers essentially believed that therapists who provide unconditional positive regard were the catalysts for the client's personal growth. Because "caring" is the most central therapeutic element, little formal training would be needed to teach people how to "care" for others. The Rogerian prescription for effective therapy embodies the deeply American "if there's a will, there's a way" philosophy. Because he believed the basic tendency of individuals is to self-actualize (Rogers, 1984), the simple process of full acceptance by a therapist would enable clients to revert to their inherent self-actualizing tendencies. When such an appealing therapeutic philosophy is adopted, it becomes very difficult to justify requiring six to seven years of graduate training before one is allowed to practice psychotherapy.

Rogers' system of therapy has not become the predominant treatment approach. Nonetheless, his belief that therapy can be effectively conducted without intense professional training has been adopted by many graduate programs. Some schools send first semester students into clinics to perform psychotherapy before they have even completed a course in therapy. Training in theory or factual knowledge is not considered a prerequisite for therapeutic work by those educational institutions which endorse simplified models of psychotherapy.

These graduate schools are, unfortunately, reenacting certain phenomena of the 1960s and 1970s. During that time many individuals who lacked formal training in any graduate mental health program could and did lead marathon encounter groups. These group facilitators argued that the group process by itself was therapeutic, and they knew how to harness the power of the process effectively. Accelerated training in group techniques often was provided in the matter of a few weeks, and these encounter groups proliferated. Mainstream psychology at that time disagreed with this position and rushed to establish licensing laws restricting untrained individuals from conducting psychotherapy and providing therapeutic services.

The concept that effective therapy can be administered by individuals who are not trained in clinical psychology has more recently been advanced by some behavioral psychologists. Some experimental psychologists who have received no clinical training argue that they are ideally suited to teach courses in behavior modification, for a behavioral model enables them to generalize across species. These experimentalists insist that the same fundamental principles apply to all organisms; therefore, experimental psychologists are perfectly capable of modifying the behavior of humans who emit undesirable behavior, just as they can modify the behavior of organisms ranking lower on the phylogenetic scale.

The belief that lengthy professional training is not essential for the effective practice of psychotherapy is also endorsed by other mental health professions. Social workers must complete only two years of academic course work before they are able to function independently as therapists. Nursing now has "clinical specialists" who conduct psychotherapy in hospitals with minimal course work in psychotherapy and with limited formal training in models of psychopathology. Even some psychiatrists conduct psychotherapy with little formal course work in psychopathology, personality theories and psychotherapy.

A newer and even more alarming trend is now practiced in many general hospitals. These facilities hire B.A. level people to staff their emergency rooms and make clinical decisions. Even with the very minimum in professional standards and training, these hospital employees independently assess patients, deciding which are to be evaluated by psychiatrists and which should be discharged with no psychiatric consultation.

Far too many people believe that effective mental health treatment can be dispensed by individuals with little formal academic and professional training in psychotherapy. This attitude stands in marked philosophical opposition to schools of depth psychology which demand four years of post doctoral analytic training before certifying analysts. Given the American predilection for achieving quick results, it is not surprising that these time consuming training models have fallen into disfavor and have been replaced by therapy approaches requiring little formal training.

Despite the wish to abbreviate professional training, it is impossible to effectively short circuit the process and still produce very capable professionals. Therapists need a great deal of theoretical and practical information in order to understand the complexities of humans. Therapy patients are experiencing, behaving creatures with pertinent developmental histories, who operate in diverse social settings. All of these dimensions need to be fully understood by professionals before they can choose the most effective intervention strategies. Training in psychotherapy is a multidimensional process which would be woefully inadequate if it involved only the acquisition of intellectual knowledge. It demands much work on the personal level where psychotherapists must study themselves and understand the interaction between their personal needs and their theoretical preferences. Consequently, it is crucial for trainees to receive extensive supervision so that they can ultimately develop into efficient psychotherapists.

It is only through such lengthy training that psychotherapists acquire enough knowledge and skill to become effectively pragmatic in their practice. A traditional long-term training model is the best way to teach psychotherapists which issues can be addressed in a most forthright manner, gently and diplomatically over time.

The necessity to look behind the immediate verbalizations of a patient to discover hidden issues is demonstrated by the following case. During the first session, a patient stated that she wanted assertion training, claiming she was too passive in her behavior. If the therapist had simply complied with the patient's request, she would have immediately initiated structured assertion training. Yet only through an ongoing dialogue did the therapist realize that the patient did not need assertion training at all; rather, her most immediate experienced problem was that sometimes she lost arguments with her spouse. She thought she needed to be able to win all these arguments, as she considered a 90% "success rate" intolerable. This patient's problem was overdeveloped narcissism, not her poor assertion skills. Therapists must fully understand their patients before they implement treatment techniques. A simplistic use of technique without an extensive understanding of the patient can prove disastrous. When the training of the therapist is abbreviated and narrow in focus, errors of this kind become more and more commonplace.

Pragmatism as Short-Term Treatment

A more recent manifestation of the belief that "quicker is better" has been the increasingly popular notion that psychotherapy can be effectively administered as a short-term treatment for all forms of mental disorders. Here, cost containment has become the new synonym for pragmatism. State and local governments increasingly favor short-term treatment programs for inpatients, and insurance programs correspondingly are only willing to reimburse for short-term therapy. As a result, the typical length of psychiatric hospitalization ranges from two to six weeks. The exact numbers of days that patients will be hospitalized is largely dictated by their insurance policies and not by the severity of their symptomatology. Current mental health practices are now commonly dictated by both personal finances and by the terms of insurance policies. The length of treatment and hospitalization is no longer decided primarily by the mental health practitioner's assessment of the nature or extent of the patient's problems.

In the supposed interest of efficiency, federal and state laws now demand that treatment plans be immediately formulated for the newly hospitalized patients. Lists of treatment goals must be written in the first few days of hospitalization; and a few weeks thereafter, more documentation is required which describes how effectively these treatment goals have been met.

These regulations have essentially diverted one third of each mental health professional's work week into the generation of paperwork. Worse still, in order to maintain continued funding of treatment programs, mountains of documents have been written which declare that seriously disturbed hospitalized patients show marked improvement in symptomatology in a matter of a few weeks. Such documents proclaim that effective treatment of serious mental illness requires only minimal time. The fact that most of these patients are eventually hospitalized again with the same symptomatology is not part of the documentation of these "effective" treatment plans.

Unfortunately, only the most extreme psychotic symptoms diminish during brief hospitalization, usually as a direct result of medication. Fundamental changes do not occur in a patient's personality structure or her essential psychopathology within a few weeks. Nonetheless, by complying with the demands for goal setting and for "positive sounding" documentation, mental health professionals have now been coerced into legitimatizing all forms of short-term treatment. The multitude of treatment plans written in hospitals and clinics is followed by discharge summaries which specify that these patients were significantly improved. With all this written documentation in place, it is now logical for insurance companies to state that ten sessions of outpatient psychotherapy is sufficient treatment time. Since short-term treatment "works" with psychotics, it certainly should be able to work with less disturbed patients.

Pragmatism and Managed Care

The most recent manifestation of the demand to abbreviate psychotherapy and to produce quick results has been the movement into the managed care model. Here, insurance companies and managers, who have minimal or no training in psychopathology, diagnosis or psychotherapy, state which are the most efficient and therefore the "fundable" treatment methods for emotionally disturbed patients. Because of many financial pressures, certain models of psychotherapy, namely short-term, are viewed as the most desirable forms of treatment. Long-term models of psychotherapy are deemed inefficient because they are costlier. Consequently, these long-term therapy models will be increasingly less likely to be funded by insurance companies. Such thinking moves the United States back to the time when only the wealthy could afford to stay in "therapy as long as needed."

Long-term psychotherapy is certainly very expensive. However, successful therapy profoundly changes people's lives for the better. Their quality of life significantly improves, and they typically become much more productive in their work. These positive changes in a patient's behavior will ultimately make her much more desirable to her employers. In that sense alone, the funding of long-term psychotherapy would, in fact, be cost efficient.

Benefits of Pragmatism

Because clinical psychology is a pragmatic discipline, it certainly must be concerned with increasing the effectiveness of the therapeutic services it supplies. The current crisis over the cost of health care extends to psychotherapy, and practitioners need to carefully evaluate the services they provide and attempt to increase their efficiency. Patients deserve effective psychotherapy, and all mental health professions need to focus much more upon quality control. Psychologists need to maintain a sensible pragmatic approach to the delivery of psychological services. However, such pragmatism does not at all mean that simplification of psychopathology is the way to maximize the delivery of effective services.

Even when clinical psychologists attempt to make the practice of psychotherapy more effective, it remains a very difficult and complex task. Curtailing the number of sessions that patients receive will not specifically produce better psychotherapy; rather it will make treatment focus upon one issue alone at a time.

The demand for focused treatment of specific symptomatology may, in fact, be counterproductive in itself because such a strategy assumes that the specific symptoms are the patient's only problem.

Although consistent with both the *Diagnostic and Statistical Manual of Mental Disorders* (DSM) and with a behavioral framework, this strategy is not universally accepted. In my own private practice, patients have frequently reported changing maladaptive behavior patterns that were never a topic of discussion within the therapeutic hours. In such instances the therapeutic process itself has enabled these people to feel confident about making other changes in their lives. As patients undergo a shift in their self-images, they can make important changes without the direct input of the therapist. Of course, a focused discussion of problems is often the best strategy, but it is not exclusively the optimal treatment procedure.

Effective psychotherapists modify their intervention strategies to fit the patient's particular needs as they change over time. As stated in chapter 2, existential therapists first must understand the patient as an experiencing process. Attending to the uniqueness of each patient enables detection of each patient's needs and intentions. Understanding the patient as a process of intentionality will help guide effective psychotherapy.

Patients enter therapy with varied needs and expectations. Some people will only consult a therapist if they are in a state of crisis. For these patients the therapist best responds by utilizing some form of crisis management. This entails a quite different manner of interacting than with a patient who enters psychotherapy without a sense of immediate crisis. For patients in crisis it may be important to quickly inform them of one's availability outside of the scheduled therapy hour. However, to make the same comment to a patient who is not in crisis may foster unnecessary and unhealthy dependency by the patient.

Existential psychology encourages understanding the patient as an experiencing process which can best be accomplished by focusing upon the patient's intentionality. Therapists need to understand that the experiences of the person are an outgrowth of her purposes. Often a patient may not be immediately able to acknowledge what her intentions are, but the direction of wishes is evident in her conduct during the therapeutic dialogue. When a therapist grasps the intentionality of the patient, she can see what the patient will accept and what the patient will resist. Knowledge of the patient's intentionality will lead the therapist to adjust her interactive style to match the patient's immediate needs and purposes.

The inexperienced psychotherapist will often directly respond to patients who plead for behavioral suggestions. Such a therapist will soon discover that her suggestions are routinely criticized by her patients. The patients will tell their therapists that these strategies were tried in the past and failed then and will fail now; or they will say these strategies would never work. The intentions of such patients are to prove both that their therapists are inadequate and that their life situation is hopeless. Their intention is not to change, even though these patient may verbalize, very often, that they indeed want to change their life situations.

Eclecticism

Many American psychologists disagree with aspects of all the models of personality theory, psychopathology and psychotherapy. Rather than fully accept a controversial theoretical position, they instead label themselves "eclectic." This term means that they borrow from different theoretical viewpoints and utilize the approach which works best at the moment. There is certainly a freedom in being eclectic for the therapist does not have to accept any one particular theory as valid. Such an approach also fits into the American predilection toward individual creativity. In eclecticism the therapist selects whatever approach work best with each patient.

However, eclecticism is necessarily unsystematic. The way an eclectic therapist makes sense of a particular patient is supposedly guided by the spontaneous, theoretical mixture concocted by the therapist. It is highly unlikely that another therapist would come up with the same amalgam of theoretical constructs when working with the same patient. Since such a therapist does not systematically present her eclectic theoretical systems, it becomes unreplicable and essentially beyond verification. Furthermore, a mixture of theoretical systems which are philosophically in conflict cannot be sensibly blended in long-term therapeutic work. Not only does eclecticism promote an ephemeral uniqueness in theory and in practice, but it also enables therapists to proceed without a systematic theoretical plan for therapy.

When the individual is viewed from an existential perspective and characterized as an experiencing process, the strategies used by the therapist are very much based upon theoretical understanding. The flexibility proposed by eclecticism can still be present, but it becomes wedded to a comprehensive theoretical approach. The strategic problems of eclecticism can be solved through a pragmatic-existential viewpoint.

Pragmatism From an Existential Perspective

An example of existential theory leading to practical interventions is demonstrated by the concept of *pitch* (Boss, 1963). Boss stated that individuals regularly change the ways in which they process experiences. Sometimes people are very perceptive and effectively make full, complete sense of their worlds. At other times, they are not very attuned and misperceive both themselves and their worlds. The concept of *pitch* describes the degree of one's perceptivity at particular moments. It is vital to understand not only the *pitch* of the patient but also the *pitch* of the therapist.

Consider what occurs when a therapist interacts with a patient who is extremely depressed. The patient demonstrates a low energy level and shows little interest in attending to diverse meaning categories. Instead, the patient is flat in affect and is very difficult to engage in meaningful dialogue. For effective dialogue to occur, the therapist must find some way of energizing the patient. Understanding the patient's powerlessness and simply reflecting these feelings back to the patient will not be helpful. The therapist typically will expend a great deal of energy and assume a very active stance with such a patient to counteract her depression. In such situations the therapist's high expenditure of energy can be described as the "loan" of ego strength. The patient, by participating in the dialogue, will begin to draw upon the therapist's source of power in order to ultimately connect with her own underlying strengths.

To work effectively with depressed patients the therapist needs to have a high personal energy level to draw upon. It is certainly far less taxing to work with individuals who are able to spontaneously and actively participate in therapy than it is to work with depressed patients. An ideal psychotherapy working day would rarely involve consecutive sessions with depressed patients. Given the opportunity, one would alternate patients who require more effort with patients who require less therapeutic activity. If therapists could arrange their schedules in such a manner, their energy would be replenished rather than depleted. Unfortunately, logistics typically prevent therapists from arranging their hours in such a fashion.

When a therapist attends to the patient as an experiencing process and apprehends the level of pain the patient feels, she begins to sense what intervention strategies are likely to be effective. She will offer a tentative comment or hypothesis and see how it is received. If the response is unfavorable, she tries a different tactic until she finds a style of interacting that engages the patient.

For example, when working with some highly anxious patients, the best intervention strategy may be to remain essentially quiet and reassuring. These patients may need a place and person who will allow them to ventilate feelings without comment or direction. Other highly anxious patients may need the therapist to be more structured and authoritative. These patients feel so lost that they need the therapist to function first as a strong but reassuring parental figure. The initial tentative understanding of the patient leads to the use of certain styles of interacting with each particular patient. Following the ideas of pragmatic-existentialism, one would assess how the patient responds to different therapeutic strategies and then make adjustments in style to increase rapport.

Sullivan (1953) stressed that all humans change their style of interaction as they deal with the different people in their lives. He thought that we were a different social self with each major figure in our lives. In extending this concept to the psychotherapeutic relationship, it would follow that therapists also behave quite differently toward each of their patients. Therapists need to be particularly sensitive to the patient's feelings and find the most effective ways of responding to different patients. Pragmatic-existential therapists will exhibit radically different behaviors throughout a working day as they adjust their interactive style to match each patient's needs.

Sometimes the needs of a patient require a radically different approach by the therapist. One of my patients, who was a practicing psychotherapist, needed to expand his understanding of his early formative years. We did not talk about his current life situation at all because his immediate interpersonal life was quite satisfactory to him. However, he needed to understand how his early years were currently affecting his professional work. In contrast, most other patients enter psychotherapy to alleviate an immediate pain. Consequently, therapeutic dialogue needs to focus upon the immediate situation rather than upon past histories.

Pragmatic-existential therapy requires the therapist to gain a sense of the patient's most pressing needs and then create particular intervention strategies based upon a recognition of those priorities. A graduate student described the difficulties she was having communicating with her first psychotherapy in-patient. This male patient could not maintain attention on any topic and exhibited rambling, haphazard and illogical speech patterns. The student felt quite frustrated because she could not keep the patient focused on any topic. I suggested she tell the patient that she was going to behave as if she were his partner on a television quiz show. Whenever the patient changed topics, she would make a loud, buzzing noise. She was going to be his "buzzer lady," and he would hear the buzzing sound each time he changed topics in conversation.

I had never personally used any such intervention strategy with a patient before, nor had I read about a "buzzer technique." However, I sensed it was likely that the patient was a TV watcher, as it is a frequent activity in mental hospitals. It seemed that an intervention technique treated as a game might arouse the patient's interest. It was necessary to talk to this patient as well as other patients by using ideas and concepts that are consistent with their experiential worlds.

The patient became enchanted with the buzzer game, and after a few sessions he made the buzzing sounds himself. He soon adopted this technique to monitor his own behavior so he could recognize whenever he began to lose focus. In fact, several sessions later when the therapist made a buzzing sound, the patient told her he had not lost focus at all and continued to explain how his apparent new train of thought was related to the topic he had previously been discussing.

This use of a buzzing sound could also be described as a simple behavioral technique applicable to different situations. However, it was created as a strategy designed to be meaningful in this particular patient's experiential world. While it might indeed prove to be a useful strategy elsewhere, effective therapy does not simply proceed as the straightforward use of different techniques, however efficient they may prove to be. Rather, capable therapists will adjust their interactive styles to be compatible with the experiential world of their patients.

The use of a buzzing sound was essentially a pragmatic intervention strategy, based upon the recognition of this particular person as an experiencing process. This patient had been communicating in an illogical manner and was personally unaware of his unfocused attention. Approaching the patient with this new way of attending to his personal experience made it possible for him ultimately to feel and to act empowered. He gained control over his attention deficit and could thereby begin to feel more capable in his interactions with other people.

Some psychologists might argue that the above strategy is a violation of an existential position because the therapist directly guided the patient. Such critics could say existentialism is supposed to recognize that all individuals have the power to ultimately take control of their lives and that this patient, too, could focus his attention through his own efforts without being directed. This critic might suggest that simply telling the patient that he is not focusing his attention would suffice to enable the patient to change his behavior.

This kind of reasoning represents an overly simple yet erroneous application of existentialism. The existential psychologist will recognize that in serious psychopathology the patient does not own a real sense of personal power. To tell such a patient that she has the power to change is synonymous with telling a person with broken fingers that she can play the piano. The pianist can play only after the fingers are healed, just as the patient can assume power only after major psychological healing has taken place.

Trained clinical psychologists do not simply assume that people are able to develop their inherent human capacities without the aid of education or support. Individuals suffering from serious psychopathology are diverted from owning and developing their positive potentialities. It is especially true that psychotherapy patients who suffer from personality disorders have experienced such major psychological damage. They have been traumatized, victimized and suppressed in many ways they cannot readily identify. Such individuals must struggle a great deal before they can begin to recognize their potential power. Often these patients must also learn a set of skills that will enable them to manifest this power.

Consequently, pragmatic-existential psychotherapy demands therapists be willing to interact with patients in several ways that will include structured training as well as passive listening. Understanding the patient as a process and responding effectively to the patient's needs cannot be done in a prescriptive fashion.

Psychotherapy patients have often been deprived of a sense of real power throughout their entire developmental history. In fact, their psychological survival may have been predicated upon their full retention of a passive, infantile role. People who have never felt a sense of power cannot believe they are powerful, just by being told that they are. These individuals need repeated and long term affirmation, coupled with encouragement and training in the exercise of personal power.

Correspondingly, it would be futile to tell psychotic patients who, by definition, have retreated from the interpersonal world that they can be effective in dealing with other people. First of all, therapists are inconsequential entities to such patients who are likely to ignore whatever each therapists might say. Therapists assigned to work with psychotic patients need to recognize that their major task is not to provide insight; rather, their prime therapeutic goals are to establish meaningful contacts with these patients. It is extraordinarily difficult to achieve meaningful contact with a psychotic patient, for such affiliation reverses the patient's intended retreat from the interpersonal world. Attempting to make meaningful contact with the psychotic patient may be the best long-term goal of therapy, while similarly making meaningful contact with non-psychotic patients often is accomplished during the very first psychotherapy session.

Again, when the therapist understands patients as experiential processes, she will create the most effective pragmatic therapeutic strategies. Understanding the person as a process is the primary existential goal. Finding effective strategies based upon this understanding is the pragmatic dimension of psychotherapy.

Pragmatic-existentialism involves the use of both methodologies.

The psychologists who are most committed to defining the discipline as a reductionistic science will oppose the approach of pragmatic-existentialism. These "scientific" psychologists seek universals in the understanding process. For them, the ability to formulate a diagnosis should at the same time enable the practitioner to create a prescriptive approach to psychotherapy. If one believes it fully viable to characterize individuals by diagnostic labels, such as paranoid schizophrenia, then one would also reason that it is ultimately possible to treat all paranoid schizophrenics through the same therapeutic approach. Such a prescriptive and restrictive approach neglects the ongoing process that is each person. One loses the uniqueness of the patient in the search for generalities. This argument for nomothetic as opposed to idiographic study has been effectively disputed by Allport (1960).

Differences in orientation between the pragmatic-existentialist and the nomothetically-oriented psychologist can be seen in their probable responses to specific therapeutic questions. For example, should a therapist touch a patient's arm when the patient appears to be in distress? A universal rationale for touching a patient would be that touching represents an attempt to reassure and comfort a person who is currently in deep pain. The "touching" is an attempt to make a nonverbal connection with the patient. Consequently, touching could be considered an appropriate strategy when the patient is hurting a great deal.

Following this line of reasoning, psychologists who favor universal strategies would teach "touching" as a technique, to be used on a regular basis in response to profound pain exhibited by patients. However, if such a "touching" technique became a prescriptive strategy, the pragmatic-existentialist would argue that the therapists were committing a significant error. Some neurotic patients will see any physical contact as intrusive, frightening and potentially sexual while other neurotic patients might feel deeply reassured by such contact. Similarly, touching might help create a deep bond with some patients suffering from personality disorders yet it might also totally undermine therapy with other personality disordered patients who cannot tolerate closeness.

To decide whether to "touch" a patient or to make other

interventions requires understanding the patient as an experiential process. Therapists must sense both how receptive particular patients are and how threatened and fragile others feel. This knowledge of patient accessibility is gained through the informal assessments therapists make of their patients, as well as through the occasional formal assessment of administering and interpreting psychological tests. When pragmatic-existentialists sense it will be helpful to touch the patient's arm at a particular moment, they can trust and act upon that feeling because they are attuned to the patient as a process. (Obviously, therapists who are personally uncomfortable with making physical contact should never touch their patients because their discomfort would be subliminally communicated.) The best way to thoroughly understand how to be with a patient can again be ascertained by focusing upon the process nature of the patient.

Even though clinical psychology is deeply rooted in the assessment process, assessments have, unfortunately, typically been confined to an understanding of the patient's pathology. Rarely do assessments describe the patient's interpersonal style or comment on the patient's receptivity to different patterns of interaction. However, psychologists ideally need to know which patients need overt strength, which ones need quiet warmth, which need confrontation, and which need a myriad of interactive styles. Careful attention paid to the patient's interpersonal style, along with the fundamental psychopathology, will indicate what style of approach will be most beneficial and therapeutic.

The closest clinical psychology has come to addressing this issue has been an acknowledgment that therapists need to be able to trust their own instincts in deciding how to respond to patients. One hopes that all therapists' sensitivities will have been sharpened and increased through the process of professional training. Effective training coupled with a personal sensitivity to the needs of others will indeed enable the therapist to make the correct assessments and to choose the best intervention strategies with patients. In those cases where the therapist lacks a sufficient understanding of how to proceed, or at those times when significant countertransference issues are present, such problems should be dealt with in the therapist's personal psychotherapy. This procedure is the basic rationale used by the typical clinical psychology training model.

Effective therapists are indeed sensitive and adjust their responses to patients based upon what their patients need. It seems patently obvious that the way a therapist can be most effective with a four year old will be radically different from the way the therapist can best affect a 25 year old. Comparably, the therapist cannot utilize the same strategy when dealing with all 25 year old patients if she wishes to be maximally effective. Common sense dictates that therapists must be very concrete when working with mentally retarded patients, making sure that their word choices will be easily understood. However, if therapists acted this way when working with very bright patients, the patients would probably feel patronized and would most likely terminate treatment. As the therapist shifts modalities of treatment from working with individuals to working with families, her style of interaction will necessarily shift as well. Any therapist who attempts to utilize the same pattern of interaction with all patients will negate the process that characterizes each individual.

Not only will pragmatic-existential therapists use fundamentally different intervention strategies with each patient, but they will also adjust the ways in which they interact from moment to moment. As was stated earlier, the therapist's *pitch* will change just as the patient's *pitch* changes. Because existentially-based therapists respond to the immediacy of the patient as a process, they attend to the patient's verbal and nonverbal communications and the underlying intentionality. The therapist's understanding at each particular moment will dictate the manner of her response.

Psychotherapy is an interactive process where therapists must first thoroughly listen to and then respond in ways that are most helpful to their patients. Too many therapists utilize only a narrow range of responses to patients, mainly because of the nature of the training they received. The most frequently used models of psychotherapy were developed to deal with a neurotic population. Yet, patients who experience neurotic difficulties are fundamentally quite different from all other psychotherapy patients and are very rarely encountered in therapists' offices today.

Neurotics are, by definition, individuals with a fundamentally strong personality structure. They usually are capable of withstanding much frustration and are able to direct their own therapies quite effectively, according to both the psychoanalytic and client centered models. These underlying personality strengths of neurotic patients have enabled psychotherapists to be successful practitioners even when the therapists were extremely passive. Therapeutic passivity may be very effective when the patients have the basic strengths to heal themselves.

Therefore, when graduate students first learn about psychotherapy, they are taught the therapeutic models that were created to work with the neuroses. Unfortunately, few extensive models of psychotherapy were created for the treatment of more severely disturbed patients. By following the models for treating neurosis, students of psychotherapy will come to believe that detachment and passivity are effective therapeutic strategies. However, these approaches will be quite inappropriate when working with patients who are depressed and who suffer from the more severe forms of psychopathology, *i.e.*, personality disorders and psychoses. The fundamental weaknesses in the personality structure of these patients require much more direct and active intervention by the therapist. One cannot simply trust that the innate life force of these patients will guide them toward health. Usually therapists have to first acquaint these patients with the premise that they possess such a life force. It is only after patients can recognize their untapped latent power that they can develop and harness this personal force to achieve a more fulfilling life style.

Psychotherapy with more seriously disturbed patients often involves direct teaching because these patients have neither an effective frame of reference to organize their world nor the fundamental behavioral skills to manifest interpersonal power. Sometimes it becomes necessary to be a directive teacher, not because the therapist wants to run the patient's life but rather because the therapist has crucial knowledge which the patient lacks. The decision to be directive at these times is based upon the recognition that the patient is desperate for some behavioral successes.

However, to make the categorical decision to be directive in working with all very disturbed patients would be counterproductive. Some of these patients may need a great deal of support and psychological hand-holding without being pressured to make changes. An attempt to move these patients toward behavioral change would fail and concurrently undermine the therapeutic relationship. Psychotherapists must decide which is the better strategy by relying upon their understanding of the patient as an experiential process.

All patients need to be understood in a multidimensional manner, meaning therapists must apprehend them in the immediacy of the moment as well as understand them as individuals entering treatment with a significant historical past. The therapist must acquire a sense of how the patient's difficulties arose and how they continue to be manifested in the current situation. It is vital to understand both how patients interact with the world and what pressures are exerted upon them by the significant others in their lives. In order to maximize the effectiveness of treatment, the therapist must assess the patient's strengths and weaknesses and determine how open or closed the patient will be to different forms of assistance.

Experience in conducting psychotherapy is often the best teacher, but one must be inclined to learn so that new experiences prove helpful. Recall that being a process person, the heart of existential thinking, involves an ongoing willingness to grow and develop. Therefore, therapists who are open to new experiences and who can see their work and their patients in new and different ways will also be affirming themselves as existential beings.

Despite whatever styles of interaction the therapist may develop, it is ultimately and always the patient's decision whether and to what degree the professional assistance is accepted. The patient continually has the right and the power to disagree with the therapist and in pragmatic-existential therapy is, in fact, encouraged to do so. A number of patients may decide that they do not wish to use psychotherapy for behavioral change. Therapists need to accept the fact that patients can and will make these decisions independently without feeling that they themselves have failed to fulfil their professional responsibilities.

Depth of Therapists' Participation in Therapy

As treatment continues over time, psychotherapists regularly become aware of many of the intimate details of their patients' lives. They work diligently to increase their patients' sense of personal satisfaction. One cannot make a commitment of such time and effort toward helping other humans without also caring about them in a fundamental way. While many models of treatment advocate that therapists assume an overt position of objective detachment from their patients, it would violate basic human nature if these therapists did not care about the people with whom they worked. Therapists who are emotionally detached from their patients would have to be individuals suffering from schizoid personality disorders. It is healthy to be involved in one's work and to gain a sense of satisfaction from a job well done. When one's work involves helping other people to make significant changes in their lives, one must have a sense of pride and satisfaction when a patient exhibits such positive growth.

Caring for a patient in a highly professional manner is an essential part of effective therapy. Therapists can exhibit their caring for patients through unconditional acceptance and encouragement. Caring can also be expressed by challenging patients and sometimes even through the expression of anger. Through each of these behaviors, the therapist's overt responses do not negate but rather affirm an underlying care for the patient.

Distinguishing Pragmatism From Eclecticism

The pragmatism advocated here is, therefore, quite different from both eclecticism and the historical American pragmatism cited earlier. The pragmatism proposed is fundamentally and systematically based upon the theoretical concepts of existentialism. In contrast, eclecticism represents attempts by therapists to do whatever seems most useful, and evolves through the unsystematic borrowing of concepts from different theories and techniques. Although both approaches are based upon formal and informal assessments, the pragmatic-existentialist is systematic because existential theory guides the way toward understanding and intervention.

The writings in existentialism provide a framework for understanding and treating mildly disturbed neurotic patients as well as the more seriously disturbed characterological and psychotic patients. Neurotic patients refuse to accept themselves as changing because they wish to avoid the pain and underlying anxiety associated with acknowledging their inescapable human limitations. They need to deal with the truth of what it is to be human, which means facing one's inevitable fallibility and death. The best way these patients can accept this humanness will be through establishing a deep connection with a therapist who is their fellow human.

Characterologically disturbed patients were severely damaged in their earliest years. Many of these individuals sensed that to become individuated, or to be a changing and choosing human process, would lead to psychological abandonment and eventual death. These cognitions are not verbally formulated or owned by these patients but rather represent the cornerstones of the patients' basic postures in the world. Being damaged in this manner fundamentally stunted the development of basic coping skills. Personality disordered individuals lack personal power and a sense of self; both are necessary in order to lead substantially satisfying lives.

Pragmatic-existential psychotherapy is designed to assist neurotic and personality disordered patients to recognize and to feel they can become the active, choosing and directing agents in their own lives. The multilevel assessment, an ongoing part of the therapeutic interaction, informs the therapist of the manners in which patients exhibit their inability to take control of their lives. An existential understanding of how the patient keeps herself from moving forward in the world leads the therapist to select different types of dialogue and interventions with the patient. The chosen therapeutic strategies are then ultimately connected with a recognition of the process nature of the human, with the understanding that people are capable of choice and must experience existential anxiety.

The pragmatic-existential therapist's methods of interaction with patients will reflect the basic equality between the therapist and the patient. The only dimensions of superiority in the relationship are the therapist's greater knowledge of psychopathology and her awareness of multiple strategies for behavioral changes. Patients enter therapy to acquire this expertise.

I am, therefore, advocating the use of a pragmatism that is well connected with the fundamental existential descriptions of the human condition. In contrast, eclecticism lacks a systematic theoretical base, and the eclectic therapist proceeds to work with patients with only a vague, unspecified model of what is healthy and how to best promote it for each particular patient. Eclectic psychotherapy is haphazard and unreplicable for it is based upon unsystematic thinking.

Even when therapists understand the patient as an experiencing process, they can still accept the concepts of other theoreticians and recognize, for example, that some patients will manifest symptoms reminiscent of an Oedipal Complex. A pragmatic-existential psychotherapist may even speculate that the ways in which this particular patient was treated historically could have produced the rivalry-fear-sex-repression complex so well documented by Freud. On the other hand, pragmatic-existential therapists can also understand the patient's reactions as experiential processes without necessarily invoking a psychodynamic model of causation. One can accept the validity of an Oedipal problem in a particular patient while simultaneously disputing that such feelings are universal. One could take such a stance and correctly be described as functioning as a typical eclectic psychotherapist. However, to describe the patient as an experiential process, who is rigidly and repeatedly using restricted meaning categories, is to speak from the vantage point of pragmatic-existentialism. Beginning with these concepts, it becomes possible to understand how a particular patient can experience the different feelings associated with an Oedipal Complex from an existential rather than from a traditional psychoanalytic framework.

In a similar vein therapists may encounter patients who struggle to replace feelings of inferiority with feelings of superiority. To help such patients one does not necessarily have to understand them exclusively from an Adlerian point of view. It is possible to utilize Adlerian thinking to gain some insights into particular patients, but we must still understand these individuals mainly as experiential processes.

The theories of personality, psychopathology and psychotherapy, experience in assessment, knowledge of relevant research and personal experience in conducting psychotherapy all are useful in helping therapists to understand the patient as an experiential process. These forms of knowledge can be used to guide interactions with patients to provide maximal assistance. Extensive knowledge still remains the best guide for effective psychotherapy.

Pragmatic-existentialism draws upon all the above factors. It recognizes the patient as an experiential process and attempts to assist patients in owning their capacity to choose, to create and to improve their own personal lives. This approach is quite different from American eclecticism which substitutes individualistic for systematic, replicable conceptualizations. In fact, pragmatic-existentialism furthers the best ideals of early American psychology as it proposes that therapists should be practically effective in their work with patients. Even more importantly, however, pragmatic-existentialism advocates a broad- based theoretical model will provide the most effective strategies in psychotherapy.

Five:
Personality Disorders:
An Existential Perspective

Existential psychologists characterize a human as a *Verb* - an ongoing, changing process. This viewpoint stands in marked contrast to the position of most other schools of psychology which describe a human as a *Noun* or a constant, fixed entity. The two philosophical positions are opposed, as the one considers change to be central and the other believes constancy to be the most important quality of humans.

It is certainly true that humans exhibit both of these qualities. That is, we change and we do not change; it is impossible for us to do otherwise. The problem that each psychologist faces is to decide which viewpoint is more accurate. I endorse the existential position because it offers the fuller explanation of the nature of human functioning.

When adopting the existential viewpoint, one has to account for the fact that often humans appear to be rigid and unchanging even though change is hypothesized as an essential part of the human condition. In contrast, the changing nature of the human is not given much credence by many other psychological schools of thought, particularly the psychoanalytic camp. While implicitly acknowledging that people can change, they view such changes as a result of the interventions of the psychologist and particularly of the therapist. Whatever changes occur in people that are not a result of professional intervention are considered unimportant and rarely are the topic of their psychological inquiries.

Even though the school of behaviorism prefers not to be characterized as owning a philosophical position, it is, nonetheless, in the same camp as existentialism in that it asserts that change is an essential characteristic of organisms. Behaviorists describe change as new learning, and all organisms are seen as capable of acquiring such new behaviors. However, because behaviorists avoid discussions of human nature, they are not interested in questioning why changes do or do not occur.

For the existential psychologist it is vital to understand how and why people do or do not change, as this knowledge leads to effective psychotherapy. Existentialists begin to answer this question through the recognition that humans experience their worlds dialectically. That is, we see our world in terms of polar opposites. We comprehend the concept of good only because we comprehend the concept of evil. One could not act in a "good" way if one did not know the opposite of good. It would be impossible to make a significant choice of one direction of action if one did not recognize the alternative possibilities. Therefore, we know what it is like to change because we know what it is like not to change.

The existential psychologist also recognizes that humans could not function if every experience was totally different from every previous experience. People would feel overwhelmed if they experienced incessant change as there would be no frame of reference to help make sense of their experiential processes. Binswanger (1963) described this overwhelmed feeling as *dasein* or being thrown into experiencing. He believed the way to surmount these overwhelming feelings was by producing a constancy in ourselves, enabling us to feel empowered. Maintaining a certain degree of constancy within ourselves provides an anchor from which we can also experience changes. Therefore, people can change while remaining constant.

Even as we humans attempt to maintain some constancy in our experiences, it is true, nonetheless, that our experiences at any one particular moment cannot be totally identical with our previous experiences. Since we exist over time, we keep having new experiences which necessarily change us, if even imperceptibly. You are now reading a new text for the first time which makes it a different experience. However, this current process of reading is similar to the process of reading which you have engaged in over your lifetime, which makes it in some ways a familiar experience.

The dialectic truth that we simultaneously change and do not change requires an existentialist to focus upon two opposing alternatives. The human is understood as a person who fluctuates between two poles; the task for the existentialist is to apprehend how and when such movement occurs. In contrast, other schools of psychology prefer to use demonstrative reasoning rather than dialectic. In demonstrative reasoning only one condition or dimension is accepted as valid, and its polar opposite is thereby rejected. Consequently, the human is considered a constant, unchanging entity.

The English language offers many more words to express demonstrative rather than dialectic reasoning. When one begins a sentence with "the person is," the sentence affirms only one possibility and therefore reflects demonstrative reasoning. To write the sentence in dialectic language it would have to read "the person is ... and the person also is not ...." When a psychological theory is based upon demonstrative reasoning, it significantly reduces the number of accountable alternatives in its explanation of the human. Demonstrative reasoning allows for reductionistic theorizing; this does not occur in dialectic reasoning.

Psychologists who study constancies across human behavior typically seek the universal qualities of people and subsequently pay little attention to individual differences. The problems in this search for universals were well explained by Allport (1960). He stated that all humans are (1) in some ways like all other humans; (2) in some ways like some other humans; and (3) in some ways like no other humans. When the search for constancies is linked with the search for universals, only the first two conditions cited above are given sustained attention. Allport's third observation of the essential uniqueness of each person would also become lost in the search for universals. However, existential psychology considers uniqueness very important and views the human both as a process of change and as a process of non-change. Therefore, the existential position describes the person as endless possibilities rather than as a fixed, unchanging entity.

Existentialists pay crucial attention to how and why people do not allow themselves to change. They recognize the person's experience of discomfort in being a changing, emerging process because change is experienced as a loss of security. To know where one stands at a particular moment and to be able to predict the actions of the significant people in one's life provide a sense of familiarity. To change one's perceptions, behaviors and sense of self is to rush into the realm of the unknown and become susceptible to feelings of dread. For these reasons, abused spouses often stay in destructive relationships because the known pain is implicitly judged safer than the unknown pain. Although all humans are reluctant to change and lose the security of the immediate moment, they differ in the degrees to which they are willing to take such risks. We humans create personal constancies, enabling us to feel secure because a change of perception will evoke feelings of insecurity. Accordingly, people develop and maintain a consistent frame of reference which they use to understand their worlds. They develop specific values, beliefs and attitudes which they repeatedly bring to bear in different situations.

This constancy in experiencing, values and behaviors, coupled with the individual's reluctance to change, is viewed by some existentialists as a violation of the basic human (changing) nature. When people do not change over time, constancy is viewed as a primary manifestation of psychopathology, as described by certain existentialists such as Binswanger (1963). Such constancy prevents individuals from accepting the fact that they live in an ever-changing world.

Existentialists view human constancy in a manner radically different from other psychologists. They do not believe that any human quality, value or behavior has an inherent permanence. Fixed responses and experiences are understood as immediate methods of escaping the anxiety and pain of being a human process. Consequently, the consistent, unchanging experiences and behaviors do not express the essential nature of any person as these qualities negate the fundamental human tendency to continually change. According to existentialists, any psychological description of humans that attends only to their constancies is grossly deficient. Such descriptions omit the possibilities of change and yet, ironically, all schools of therapy must accept the implicit existential belief that change is possible in people.

When mental health professions recommend psychotherapy to treat psychopathology, they are implicitly affirming that the patient's observed qualities, which prompted the diagnostic classification, are open to change. The psychiatric classification system describes supposedly fixed conditions, but the use of intervention strategies affirms the existential position that constancy and permanence in humans are artificial and temporary conditions.

The existential realization that the human is a changing process was also used by Boss (1963) to demonstrate a fatal flaw in the psychoanalytic theory of psychopathology. According to Boss, if unconscious determinism is the universal causative factor behind all human experience and behavior, then psychoanalysis cannot work. The fact that Freud's patients were able to evidence significant changes demonstrated that determinism was not universal, as it could be reversed; therefore, the Freudian theory of psychopathology was in error.

Psychiatric Diagnosis and Existential Thinking

When psychologists become involved in the diagnosis and treatment of psychopathology, they typically must work with the *Diagnostic and Statistical Manual of Mental Disorders*, known as the DSM. This manual and its several revisions have been written primarily by the psychiatric community, who primarily endorse a medical model of psychopathology. The essential rationale of the medical model is that a consistently identified overt cluster of symptoms is indicative of an underlying disease state or illness. When a consistent pattern of symptoms is detected, a search is then launched for the basic disease. The diagnostic task is to find the crucial clusters of characteristics present in patients, which will lead to the particular psychiatric diagnoses.

The diagnostic categories in the psychiatric classification system describe fixed, unchanging characteristics in people which stands in marked contrast to the existentialist view of the human as a changing process. The psychiatric model of psychopathology is based upon demonstrative reasoning, and it does not allow for the dialectic view of the person as both changing and not changing. As a result, existentialists will strongly disagree with any characterization of psychopathology that describes states of abnormality as fixed qualities in people, as this ignores the person's essential capacity to change.

Because psychiatric diagnoses focus upon fixed as opposed to changing human qualities, many existentialists prefer not to participate in this method of classifying people. However, existential psychologists, just like all other therapists, still do distinguish the broadly healthy and self-affirming human activities from the unhealthy and self-negating human activities. By conducting psychotherapy, existentialists overtly endorse the value of positive change. Furthermore, by functioning as psychotherapists, existentialists help their patients acquire and strengthen desirable and self-affirming qualities. Therefore, existential psychologists do distinguish between what is healthy and what is unhealthy, although they generally prefer to avoid voicing these distinctions.

Despite the fact that existentialists strongly disagree with the philosophy behind the DSM as well as with its particular manner of making diagnoses, they must make a pragmatic concession and use this diagnostic system. To receive financial reimbursement for therapeutic services, the existential therapist has to conform to the demands of insurance companies by providing a psychiatric diagnosis for each patient. The system puts existentialists in the awkward position of implicitly affirming the very psychiatric diagnostic system which they explicitly consider invalid. The existential therapist usually cooperates with the flawed diagnostic system, just as all humans must participate in social systems and organizations they consider deficient (see Jaspers, 1954).

The Psychiatric Classification System

The existential psychologist, like every other clinician, will use the *Diagnostic and Statistical Manual of Mental Disorders*. Therefore, it is important to understand how this classification system works, its historical development, and its strengths and weaknesses. A description of how psychiatric classification is currently used makes it easier to explain the alternate ways that psychopathology can be understood, using an existential viewpoint.

The successive revisions of the DSM each present a broad based model for cataloguing all forms of mental disorders. While the different versions of the DSM all are based upon a medical model, classifying clusters of symptoms as separate forms of disorders, little or no attention is paid to causation in this psychiatric classification system. Rather, the fundamental notion behind this form of classification is that the overt symptomatology, the phenotype, reflects an underlying universal condition, the genotype.

Our focus upon personality disorders will be sharpened by a review of how this particular category of classification is described in the different versions of the DSM. Each successive revision of the classification system has offered major changes in the numbers and types of personality disorders that are catalogued.

The first type of personality disorder historically detected was designated the "psychopathic personality." The classic psychopath was characterized as devoid of both anxiety and guilt, could not learn from experience, and had an undifferentiated sexual drive as well as poor impulse control. This description of the psychopath, which appeared in the first version of the DSM, did not have much behavioral specificity, a perceived flaw which later versions of the DSM attempted to rectify.

When one reads the latest version, which is the DSM III R, it becomes apparent that the manual now uses particular behaviors as the criteria for specific diagnoses. The defining characteristics for psychopathic personality disorder, which is currently called the "antisocial personality," have been made much more operational as they now involve specific overt actions. In fact, patients must have exhibited at least three out of 12 possible antisocial behaviors prior to age 15, and must exhibit at least four of 12 possible anti-social behaviors after age 18, in order to qualify for this diagnosis.

When the mental health community first attempted to diagnose the different forms of mental disorders, the term psychopathic personality acquired two distinct meanings. The term psychopath was used to describe the person who behaved in very antisocial ways, but this term was also used as a more general designation for serious defects in the fundamental personality structure of individuals. Two different meanings of psychopathic had then evolved: "psychopath" described the specific antisocial person who evidenced no anxiety, no guilt and who had poor impulse control; "psychopathic" also described the range of fundamental disorders of personality. In order to reduce this confusion, the specific antisocial person became designated as a "sociopath." The sociopathic label was created to describe only individuals who consistently acted against societal norms. The use of the term psychopathic as a general label was subsequently replaced by the term "personality disorders."

By the time the initial *Diagnostic and Statistical Manual of Mental Disorders* appeared in 1952, the term psychopath had disappeared and personality disorder became the general all-inclusive term for "developmental defects or pathological trends in the personality structure, with minimal subjective anxiety, and little or no sense of distress" (DSM 1952, 34).

In this 1952 version of the classification system, four types of personality disorders were catalogued. They consisted of personality pattern disturbances (inadequate, schizoid, cyclothymic and paranoid personality), personality trait disturbances (emotionally unstable, passive-aggressive, compulsive and other), sociopathic personality disturbances (antisocial reaction, dyssocial reaction, sexual deviations including homosexuality, drug and alcohol addictions), and special symptom reactions.

"Personality pattern disturbances" designated certain types of personality structures believed to be highly resistant to change by any form of professional intervention. "Personality trait disturbances" described individuals who regressed under stress and whose personality had never developed properly. "Sociopathic personality disturbances" were described as the failures to conform with the predominant milieu of the culture. The "special symptom category" was a miscellaneous term which included sleep walking, tics or bed wetting.

The second revision of the *Diagnostic and Statistical Manual of Mental Disorders*, in 1968, included several new classifications. Specifically, explosive, obsessive-compulsive, hysterical, and asthenic were the newly designated personality disorders. Homosexuality remained a diagnostic category until 1973 when the membership of the American Psychiatric Association voted to delete this condition from the manual. However, when the third version of the DSM appeared in 1980, ego-dystonic homosexuality was a new diagnostic category. In the 1980 DSM, homosexuality was classified as a psychiatric problem only if it produced significant distress in the patient.

The third version of the *Diagnostic and Statistical Manual of Mental Disorders* appeared in 1980 and was revised in 1985. In both the DSM III and the DSM III R, personality disorders are treated in a radically different manner than in the previous diagnostic manuals. The personality disorders were separated from the other mental disorders, catalogued in a different way, along a separate Axis. This diagnostic decision by the American Psychiatric Association made it possible to assign multiple diagnoses to patients. Individuals could be classified as having a personality disorder as well as a major psychosis. This newest form of classification no longer attempted to limit its categorization. Furthermore, individuals could be assigned more than one type of personality disorder. According to the DSM III and the DSM III R, "personality disorders" were to be diagnosed whenever individuals exhibited inflexible and maladaptive traits which produced either major impairments in functioning or significant distress.

The latest form of diagnostic classification, the DSM III R, contains several major changes in the conceptualization of psychopathology. This classification system is free of both etiological and theoretical dimensions. Hence, the system was designed to be all inclusive, providing the diagnostician with maximum flexibility.

Problems With the Philosophy of the Classification System

Overall, the DSM III R focuses much more upon behavioral expression of symptomatology than did the earlier versions of the manual. This diagnostic system, by concentrating upon overt behavior, pays too little attention to how patients experience their world. Consequently, this method of classification is an anathema for existentialists. How one behaves certainly is a necessary topic of psychological investigation, but to describe behavior without discussing feelings is to divorce the person from his behavior.

Furthermore, the use of a frequency count to define a disorder is, at best, arbitrary as it eliminates an understanding of the non-behavioral qualities of any person.

Despite the manual's language to the contrary, this latest version of the DSM certainly and implicitly does endorse a fundamental theoretical position because the system was not a random creation. The DSM III R's system is based upon a medical model that favors behavioral descriptions of psychopathology. By focusing upon overt symptomatology, it is far more consonant with the behavioral approach than with any other theoretical viewpoint. It gives little credence or attention to the nature of the patient's experience, and it avoids a view of psychopathology that attends to personality dynamics or unconscious forces.

Psychodynamic thinkers would not accept the validity of multiple diagnoses of personality disorders, as it violates the notion that separate disturbances have separate etiologies. This new classification system offends the existentialist as well. Not only does an existentialist prefer a non-reductionistic view of people and their problems, but also the existentialist believes that the totality of the person is lost when the diagnostic system focuses on non-experiential characterizations of the person.

The *Diagnostic and Statistical Manual of Mental Disorders* has always been very brief in its description of psychopathology. Each classification has roughly one page of text; etiology is barely mentioned, and theoretical explanations of causation are avoided. The DSM III R draws heavily upon the concept of personality types for its classification system, despite the fact that there is considerable disagreement among psychologists over the validity of typologies as an effective way of describing personality.

Because of the brief descriptions in the different DSMs, it is often difficult to make effective diagnostic decisions. Many hospital case conferences become preoccupied with finding the correct diagnosis and are hampered by a manual which provides only two or three line descriptions of classifiable conditions. It is, therefore, not surprising that the research literature on the diagnostic process has regularly shown that psychiatric diagnoses have proven to be notoriously unreliable (Schroder & Livesley, 1991).

Only a few of the personality disorders described in the DSMs have been given enough attention to become the topic of separate books. Nonetheless, individuals are diagnosed with specific personality disorders which do not appear elsewhere in the literature on mental disturbances. As a consequence, disorders are classified which have unknown etiology, little experiential description, and no specified psychotherapeutic models for treatment. Even though the medical model adherents assert that the designation of clusters of characteristics as diagnostic entities is an effective way to understand disease, it is highly questionable whether any positive function can be accomplished through such a sparse classification method.

The Diagnostic Problem of Lack of Constancy

During my internship, I interviewed a patient who appeared to have all the qualities of a hebephrenic schizophrenic. The DSM description of inappropriate affect which was central to this diagnosis seemed to be unfolding immediately before my eyes. Not only did this patient show disordered thinking, but he fluctuated between laughter and tears, all in the matter of a few moments. The patient seemed to be in a hallucinatory state, paying little attention to my questions. Several days later after I had presented my findings in the diagnostic case conference, the patient was brought into the room and interviewed by the professional staff. None of the hebephrenic symptomatology which I had seen earlier was apparent in that second interview. The patient behaved appropriately, was relevant and rational in his speech, and exhibited no strong emotional reactions.

This patient taught me an important lesson. The diagnostic classification system cannot and will not explain the fundamental person. Psychiatric symptoms do fluctuate over time, even over a very short time; and if one's attention is focused exclusively upon understanding the psychopathology, one will overlook the patient's strengths and, as a result, will make deficient treatment recommendations.

The fact that severely mentally ill patients can and do exert significant control over their symptomatology was repeatedly demonstrated in a series of studies (Braginsky & Braginsky, 1969).

When psychiatric in-patients were told that they were to be interviewed in order to gain grounds privileges, they did not exhibit psychotic symptomatology. However, when they were told that they were to be interviewed for possible discharge, many patients spontaneously described ongoing hallucinations. Consequently, psychiatric patients can and do manipulate their degree of apparent symptomatology in order to attain specific goals from the hospital staff. Intentionality is indeed present, even in supposedly severe psychotic states, which makes a classification system based upon constancy in behavior highly suspect. The Braginsky research clearly indicates the danger of assuming that a psychiatric diagnosis of psychosis describes an immutable condition.

Problems in Making a Definitive Diagnosis

The different versions of the DSM each describe specific human qualities that are abstracted from the total person. For example, in diagnosing a patient as having a schizoid personality disorder, one finds that the DSM III R categorizes such patients as emotionally cold and aloof and states that they lack warm and tender feelings toward others. It is then necessary to decide if and to what degree an individual can have any warm feelings and still qualify for a schizoid diagnosis. In other words, diagnosticians must decide whether the presence of *any* warm feelings in the past or in the present contraindicates the use of a schizoid diagnosis.

Diagnosticians must also evaluate the degree to which non-schizoid qualities are present and whether there are strong enough signs of different forms of pathology to override the schizoid diagnosis in favor of a different diagnostic label. Because the diagnostic task is to attend simply to the pathological qualities of the individual, the non-disturbed or healthy parts of the person are disregarded for purposes of psychiatric classification.

When the clinician looks beyond the immediate language of the DSMs, it becomes possible to raise insightful questions that will lead to better diagnoses. For example, clinicians know that the presence of certain behaviors or symptoms can result from a multitude of factors. In psychodynamic theory, the lack of warm feelings in a patient could either be a particular defensive maneuver or it could be a repeatedly used characteristic which describes the person's primary method of interaction. Only if the latter description is accurate will the diagnostician be warranted in using the term schizoid personality.

Nonetheless, even when correctly assigned a schizoid diagnosis, the person is still, like all other humans, a process of change. If the qualities which define a schizoid personality disorder were, in fact, immutable, then any and all forms of therapeutic intervention would be contraindicated. It would make no sense to assign such a patient to psychotherapy because schizoid patients are supposedly unable to connect with other people. Psychotherapy is fundamentally predicated upon the development of a meaningful connection between patient and psychotherapist, a connection that could not take place with an irresolutely cold person. Since schizoid patients are assigned to psychotherapy, mental health professionals implicitly do believe that personality disorders can, in fact, be changed.

Problems with the
Science of Classification

Few designated psychiatric clusters of symptoms are universally accepted as true and homogeneous forms of mental illness. The DSM III R does not even consider personality disorders to be pure, mutually exclusive conditions. Sound psychometric principles demand there be high reliability in any classification system before its validity can be demonstrated. Research studies on the reliability of psychiatric classification have frequently demonstrated poor agreement between judges in the classification of specific subheadings of psychiatric disorders (Mezzich & Mezzich, 1979, Schroder & Livesley, 1991). Reliability was quite low in studies with the DSM II, although it improved somewhat with the DSM III (Scheftner, 1980). Nonetheless, because of problems with reliability many psychologists do not consider subclassifications of the DSM III valid, and many professionals dispute their utility.

To directly establish the validity of a psychiatric classification system, some proof needs to be found that these designations are accurate. At the very least, some common agreement among professionals regarding the causes of a disorder could be a first step toward establishing the validity of classification. However, mental health practitioners strongly disagree among themselves about the nature and etiology of psychopathology.

A second and even better way of validating the classification system would be through the presence of a consistent, successful differential treatment method for particular diagnostic categories of psychopathology. This, too, is still sadly lacking, especially for personality disorders.

Even the very term "personality disorders" may ultimately be abandoned as psychopathology in general becomes better understood. Nonetheless, today's pragmatic concerns require all clinical psychologists utilize this psychiatric classification system which has low reliability and questionable validity, is biased toward a medical model, and does not acknowledge the process nature of humans.

The existential psychologist in particular faces a major dilemma in deciding how to deal with diagnostic classification. Despite all the flaws of the *Diagnostic and Statistical Manual of Mental Disorders*, many of the clusters of symptomatology described in the DSM III R manual do exist in some measure in certain humans. Clinicians need to be familiar with the different patterns described in the diagnostic manual, as there will be a few patients who appear to personify specific DSM descriptions. However, patients who possess only classically defined characteristics of one disorder are extremely rare. Most patients exhibit mixtures of the different diagnostic typologies. Because diagnostic typologies only approximate an effective description of any one patient, existential psychologists would not accept the DSM system as a suitable means of understanding patients.

The most tolerable, or the least offensive, forms of psychiatric diagnosis would, therefore, be those with the least amount of specificity, according to existentialists. Existentialists are more comfortable using the broadest psychiatric headings, such as personality disorders, psychotic disorders and anxiety disorders rather than the specific subclassifications such as avoidant personality disorder. The subdiagnoses of particular personality disorders are most problematic for existentialists as they involve specific behaviors. People are best understood by existentialists in non-behavioral terms.

Theoretical Conceptions of
Personality Disorders

At the beginning of my career, along with my fellow psychology interns, I agonized over whether to assign a psychotic diagnosis to a particular patient. At that time both interns and staff members often equivocated in making such diagnoses, and as a result we usually assigned the label of "borderline" to such people. The word borderline then described someone with mixed symptomatology whose problems fell somewhere between a personality disorder and a psychotic state. Individuals given this classification manifested at different times the symptomatology of each of these two disturbances. The use of this label in the 1960s and early 70s was a conscience-salving mechanism rather than a refined homogeneous diagnosis.

Over time, the borderline designation has become understood in a fuller and richer manner. Now an analytically based theoretical model offers an etiological explanation for this particular disturbance. Because such a theory has been advanced, the category of "borderline personality disorder" is better understood than most other personality disorders. Analytic literature considers the genesis of the borderline personality to lie for the most part with the unsuccessful resolution of "splitting," due to fundamental disturbances in the small child's relationship with parental figures (Masterson, 1972).

Nonanalytic practitioners do not accept this particular explanation of the disorder. However, the presence of such a fully developed theoretical model offers a substantive position which can be challenged, altered or extended. Because the borderline designation is one of the few personality disorders which has an accompanying model of etiology and treatment, this diagnosis is assigned to too many patients and often loses its specificity through such sloppy diagnostic procedures. Diagnosticians, being human, are more prone to diagnose a condition that has an explanation of causation and treatment than to diagnose a condition which is poorly understood and lacks a method of treatment.

In order to diagnose an individual as suffering from a Borderline Personality Disorder, the DSM III R requires that the individual exhibit at least five of the following eight characteristics: (1) self-damaging impulsive behavior; (2) extreme fluctuation in interpersonal relationships; (3) anger which is out of control; (4) major problems with identity; (5) radical shifts in emotion which last no more than hours or days; (6) desperate need for the presence of others; (7) self-destructive behaviors; and (8) ongoing feelings of emptiness and boredom.

The analytic conception of "splitting" offers important insights into the behavior of the patient who has a borderline personality disorder. In splitting, certain feelings are isolated and unconnected with other feeling states of the person. This condition is seen in the classical borderline patient who responds negatively to warmth and positively to coldness and anger. These patients' emotional reactions are opposite to those of healthy people. As a result, therapists who work with borderline patients will routinely feel frustrated because they must invert their normal reactions to these patients in order to be effective.

One particular patient I worked with warranted the borderline diagnosis. Therapy with this patient was very difficult, but we eventually made significant progress and reached the point where the patient felt that he had made sufficient gains in order to discontinue therapy. However, in the final session this patient turned to me and said he believed that therapy had not helped him at all. At the time when most patients feel good about the connections made with the therapist and acknowledge the potential loss of the relationship, this patient had to invert the process and disparage therapy in order to sustain his separateness from the therapist.

Along with the important defining work on the borderline personality disorder, significant contributions have been made to the understanding of the etiology and treatment of the schizoid personality (Arieti, 1974, Laing 1960). The overt symptomatology of aloof detachment, which characterizes the schizoid personality disorder, is explained somewhat differently by both writers. Nonetheless, they do agree that major problems in the early parent-child relationship create longstanding developmental disturbances which in turn produce a schizoid personality disorder. Arieti described the intense anxiety, generated by parental rejection, as an intolerable state for the young child. The only protection then available to the child was a massive psychological withdrawal. This pervasive pattern of interpersonal withdrawal describes the schizoid personality structure.

Laing believed that schizoid individuals had a split or divided sense of self. They admit to or "own" an inner or designated real self which they hide from other people. They acknowledge that the world sees a different self -- the person that interacts with other people. However, these patients designate the outer self that is seen by others as a fake self. People with this divided sense of self necessarily must be detached from their ongoing life experiences. A schizoid patient feels untouched by other people because he hides his "real self," and any negative reactions elicited by the "fake self" do not have any validity or importance. Such types of dissociation frequently occur among personality disordered individuals. These patients do not have a clear, well developed sense of a personal "I" which could integrate all of their experiences and behaviors. The division of the self described by Laing may be a particular manifestation of splitting, but it is the sense of a personal self that is arbitrarily subdivided. Most individuals who suffer from personality disorders do exhibit one of many possible forms of splitting.

Since the classical schizoid patient is perceived as fundamentally cold, the therapist may feel unable to make a meaningful connection with that patient either in the present or the future. However, if the therapist met a patient who had schizoid defenses but was not fully schizoid, he would sense that a meaningful relationship might ultimately develop once these defenses had been lifted.

The distinction between the classical schizoid patient and the patient with schizoid defenses can be compared to different types of ice covered mountains. In order to climb any mountain, one must be able to find or to create toeholds. The patients who have schizoid defenses may be likened to an ice covered mountain that has small crags and crevices; and the patient who is classically schizoid would be the mountain of sheer ice with no toeholds. From an existential perspective, a classical schizoid would be quite rare; he would have ceased functioning as process, becoming so rigid that he was beyond intervention.

The distinction between specific "classical" personality disorders and the presence of defensive maneuvers can be applied to virtually all of the different personality disorders. Another way to understand this distinction is to recall the existential insight that people are changing processes who sometimes develop characteristic ways of being-in-the-world, called defenses in psychodynamic theory. Individuals are still capable of shedding these defenses and again becoming changing processes. When the therapist recognizes the inherent capacity to change that characterizes all humans, he will facilitate the patient's movement in that healthy direction.

The Existential Method of Study

Few theories explain the etiology and effective treatment of the full range of personality disorders. However, it is possible to broaden our knowledge of these characterological difficulties through a phenomenological understanding of the experiences of individuals suffering from such disorders. Until one knows how such patients experience their worlds, it will be impossible to enter into meaningful dialogue with them. This phenomenological understanding leads to important generalizations about the essential qualities of personality disordered people. Pragmatic-existentialists can also draw upon their knowledge of psychopathology and their own interpersonal expertise to increase understanding of particular patients.

To best understand the patient's interpersonal world, or *mitwelt*, pragmatic-existential therapists can function as the generalized other, utilizing their own personal reactions to their patients. By knowing how these patients affect them personally, therapists will hypothesize their reactions as likely to be the same as the reactions evoked in most other people. By trusting that his own emotional reactions were induced by the patient's actions, the therapist can anticipate the patient's interpersonal successes and failures.

Even if one grasps the experiential world of the personality disordered patient, it is extremely difficult to sustain such a view of the world. The patient's experiences are full of inconsistencies and contradictions which frequently makes his interpersonal skills quite ineffective.

The patient's interpersonal difficulties can be better understood by studying the experiences of individuals who utilize the particular defensive maneuver of denial. People who deny will know a particular fact, then, through denial, no longer know this fact; later they may know this same fact once again but now in a distorted manner. The inability to retain knowledge in consciousness transforms the patient into a victim. When one does not remember being hurt, then one will be unable to avoid being hurt again.

Consider a wife whose face is slapped by her husband. If she practices denial, she may only momentarily experience "my husband hit me." Soon she will no longer acknowledge that she was slapped. In the next few days she may again recall being slapped but now will have reinterpreted the interaction. She may say that she was accidentally slapped or that she was responsible and provoked her husband into slapping her. She may continue to vacillate in her perceptions of the abuse, at times remembering that she was victimized and at other times denying that such an event took place.

The experiential world of such an individual is, therefore, quite amorphous and chaotic. Therapists often discover that a patient can no longer remember incidents of abuse that had been discussed in the preceding therapy session. Consequently, it is difficult and sometimes impossible for a therapist to remain within the experiential world of such patients as it is confusing and frightening.

Individuals who frequently utilize denial have an underdeveloped sense of self. When they apprehend that it is psychologically necessary to deny basic events in their lives, they ignore or minimize their basic perceptions of the world. They do not know essential truths about themselves and others and, as a result, they cannot find the best self-enhancing behaviors. One must first be able to perceive without distortion in order to be able to choose the most effective course of action. One cannot simultaneously know and not know and concurrently be fundamentally self-protective. Most personality disordered people learned at a young age that it was dangerous for them to act in self-protective ways; therefore, they did not develop such skills. One of the most basic ways of being self-protective is reflecting upon one's behavior or, in other words, using introspection. It is rare indeed to find a personality disordered individual who has been able to introspect without transforming the self-knowledge into self-blame.

If an individual has not developed good self-protective skills, he will not be able to participate in a fully healthy way in his interpersonal world. To be able to have good relationships with others, it is necessary to have a fully developed sense of one's self and one's needs. When the self is underdeveloped, the connections with others will fluctuate between extremes and cannot be based upon mutual self-respect. Some individuals with personality disorders enter into symbiotic relationships with others, and their sense of personal self disappears in the union with the other person. Still other individuals with personality disorders both dread and avoid any deep and meaningful connection in order to protect the fragmented sense of personal self. A different pattern shows marked fluctuation in interpersonal connectedness; sometimes the personality disordered patient is highly connected, and sometimes he is very isolated.

For many personality disordered individuals, relationship problems are very central, preventing effectively participation in their interpersonal worlds. Other patients, not so pervasively hampered, are able to relate well in certain specific life situations. For example, they may be able to successfully interact in the business world but lack satisfying personal lives. Relationships can be constricted in many different patterns; individuals may relate to only one sex, or only to older people, etc. Personality disordered patients are impaired in their capacities to relate to others in healthy ways. These problems are perpetuated because most personality disordered people are rarely able to use introspection as a way to make effective changes in their lives.

Personality disordered patients rarely distinguish among different levels of consciousness. Rather, they usually view each and every experiential state as having equal validity. Whatever they feel at any particular moment is deemed to be fundamentally accurate. Healthier people are able to discriminate between different transitional states. For example, if I find myself grouchy and irritable I can usually recognize, at least later, that I was tired and the fatigue created irritability. I may then apologize for my grouchiness. This kind of minor self-evaluation rarely occurs in personality disordered individuals. Instead, internal feeling states, which often should be discounted or minimized, are assigned inappropriate validity.

I have treated patients who frequently, perhaps several times a day, experienced internal commands to hurt themselves, *e.g.*, to jump out of a window or to stab themselves in the heart. Under questioning, these patients usually acknowledged that they did not want to act upon these self-destructive thoughts; but rarely would they independently label these commands as especially unusual or "sick." They were so accustomed to having their private worlds dominated by self-hatred that they considered these thoughts routine rather than aberrant.

Although personality disordered patients may be accustomed to the presence of destructive thoughts, the familiarity does not preclude feelings of extensive psychological pain. Their pain experience may come in many forms, such as overwhelming anxiety, depression, sleeplessness or self-destructive commands. Nonetheless, all forms of the pain are continual, extensive and seemingly impervious to the patient's attempts at self-control. It is very difficult for personality disordered patients to understand how and why their pain exists; however, they usualy do consider their pain to be warranted. All too frequently they believe their pain is justified because they view themselves as deficient individuals.

Neurotic and personality disordered patients differ significantly from each other in the ways they cope with their personal pain. Neurotics fundamentally believe they can or should be able to control and eliminate their psychological pain. Even when they avow personal responsibility for pain and feel guilt for transgressions, neurotics still believe they should have anticipated the negative consequences and thereby prevented their happening. This sense of potential self-control is absent in personality disordered people. These patients may hate themselves for their transgressions and say they should have acted differently, but they do not have an underlying sense of personal power. Pain for them is a routine way of life, especially the pain that is self-inflicted.

The basic reason for many personality disordered people's avoidance of psychotherapy is their belief that pain must remain as a fundamental condition of their lives. Other personality disordered individuals may be able to acknowledge that their pain is "abnormal," yet they continue to believe that change is beyond their power. Consequently, they, too, do not seriously consider using psychotherapy.

At first glance it may appear that many personality disordered people can and do engage in behaviors designed to avoid immediate pain, *e.g.*, substance abuse to alter the immediate psychological state. The use of escapist tactics to minimize pain is ultimately self-defeating. When facing difficulties, individuals who do not take constructive action are likely to experience higher levels of pain in the future. Consequently, what appears initially as self-protective is actually self-punitive.

In a comparable vein, many individuals who initially appear self-indulgent or narcissistic may also be courting pain. By living at a superficial level, they do not experience deep gratification. Instead, their high self-preoccupation often leads them to behave in ways that are offensive to others. Because they do not carefully examine their own behavior, they are likely to feel unjustly victimized and criticized; therefore they feel frequent pain. They do not let themselves realize that if they repeatedly engage in behaviors that cause pain, they must have a need to be in pain.

As a result, it is logical to believe that the pain experienced by most personality disordered individuals is intentional and purposive. The sociopathic individual may be an exception to this hypothesis, but rarely do therapists encounter such a person. Those therapy patients who initially appear to be sociopathic are usually pseudo-sociopathic in their character structure. That is, classic sociopaths are able to use their intelligence to strike out against the world without feeling guilt or ambivalence about engaging in such actions. As they are not in conflict over their antisocial activities, these individuals should successfully manipulate the world and escape punishment. Furthermore, they would have no reason to seek therapeutic assistance for they would not feel any pain.

The therapy patients who appear to be sociopathic are, in reality, those individuals who engaged in antisocial activities that were actually designed to fail. These individuals undoubtedly have hidden motives for their behavior which they do not immediately understand. The purpose behind self-destructive actions appears to be the need for punishment, personal pain and suffering. I designate these patients as pseudo-sociopathic because their acting out behavior is designed to evoke ultimate pain and punishment for themselves.

The Nature of Pain in Personality Disordered Individuals

The hypothesis that the pain experienced by personality disordered patients is purposive can easily be affirmed by examining certain patients. When these people discuss their experiences, they describe ongoing, vicious, internal self-attacks. Such self-criticism, and at times suicidal ideation, is rarely connected with any significant behavioral transgressions. Rather, it appears to be an extreme form of self-hatred.

For another group of patients their need to be in pain can only be deduced from their actions. They do not verbally berate themselves but instead regularly act in ways that are self-destructive. They are unaware their behavior will cause them pain. These patients hurt themselves through their deeds rather than their words. When these patients are asked to account for such self-destructive behaviors, they frequently state that they lack self-discipline. However, anyone who repeatedly engages in behavior that has massive negative consequences must be continuing this behavior because of an intention to re-experience pain. The patients' rationalizations that they are living life haphazardly disguises the fact that they are purposively courting pain and self-destruction.

It is much easier to understand and effectively assist the first group of patients described above, those who verbally attack themselves, rather than those patients who do not experience a loud self-critical voice. When patients become phenomenologically oriented and can describe the inner world of experience, the presence of an internal self-attacking mechanism becomes immediately apparent to them. Phrases such as "you deserve to die," which have been subliminally uttered along with many other vile epithets, can now be questioned. Even though such negative thoughts intrude into the patient's consciousness seemingly without warning, they are, indeed, purposive. These destructive thoughts rarely appear after the patient has done poorly or failed at an important task, but rather seem to follow quickly upon the patient's successes.

I have worked with patients in psychotherapy who hated themselves for not having cured themselves 20 years ago. I have also treated patients who hated themselves simply for existing. While the patients in this last group often seem to be repeating parental comments uttered decades earlier, not all forms of self-hatred can be so easily traced. Nonetheless, pervasive forms of both self-destructive thoughts and actions are at the core of the personality disordered patient.

The Inner Voices

All humans engage in some form of dialogue with themselves. For example, one voice in me says "I will have a second helping of dessert" and another says, "No, you won't." Whether one prefers to use the terms ambivalence, opposites or approach-avoidance, each concept conveys the fact that different, conflicting tendencies reside in the experiential world of humans. I prefer to describe this phenomenon as the presence of *inner voices* because this terminology has helped my patients to identify when and where their voices first arose. That is, these different voices apparently represent the internalization of the viewpoints from significant figures in their lives. Once a patient can identify the historical antecedents of these voices, he can then make more studied decisions as to which of these voices to heed and which to ignore. While mundane dialogue over whether to do the "right thing" is common among healthy people, the inner dialogue in personality disordered individuals assumes a radically different form. Because the personality disordered individuals each have an underdeveloped self, their healthy and self-preservative tendencies rarely speak in opposition to the voices of self-attack and self-hatred.

When many personality disordered patients describe their inner dialogues, at least one loud, critical, self-hating voice can be readily detected. It is rare for a counterbalancing, self-protective voice to speak out and attempt to stifle the self-hatred. Some positive self-affirming tendencies must exist within these patients' personality structures; for if the self-hating force was the only voice present, the patient would have died years ago. The belief in the presence of self-affirmation is a deduction from basic knowledge of human nature. This belief or recognition is one way an existentialist can know that a process is present within the patient even though the process is not directly evidenced through the patient's verbalizations.

The extreme self-abuse and self-hatred in personality disordered patients will propel them into life patterns and interactions which produce intractable pain. Therapists cannot hear about these difficulties without feeling deep compassion for these patients. It is dreadful for people to live routinely with unrelenting, vile feelings about themselves. When such self-hatred is omnipresent, it dominates the patient's personality structure. This negative force attacks the patient at the most basic level, for its intent is to punish and ultimately to prevent the person from experiencing any healthy individuation and self-affirmation.

This self-hating voice is often diabolically disguised and is identified by the patient as the internal voice of rational self-evaluation. Personality disordered patients regularly state that all the negative feelings they have about themselves are, indeed, deserved. They regard the self-attacking voice as their own legitimate conscience. They contemplate various forms of self-punishment because they see themselves as loathsome, having committed unpardonable transgressions. Careful scrutiny of each patient's behaviors will reveal that such negative feelings are not warranted at all. Nonetheless, it is extremely difficult to convince the patient of his innocence.

Self-Hatred as a Major Psychological Concept

The aforementioned description of personality disordered patients as experiencing powerful, self-destructive tendencies echoes the thinking of several theorists. Freud (1955) first described the presence of masochism and later posited a death drive (Thanatos) which acted in opposition to the life drive (Eros). Guntrip (1968) described the presence of an "anti-self" which acted against the interest of the self. Fairbairn (Buckley, 1986) discussed the internalization of "bad" objects including destructive parental figures, which the child subsequently represses. Winnicott (Buckley, 1986) described the universal threat of "annihilation of being" which all infants experience. These analytic descriptions of self-hatred differ, however, from the pragmatic-existential explanation because they remain steeped in the psychoanalytic theory of psychodynamics, psychic energy and object introjects.

The pragmatic-existential therapist believes that self-hatred can readily be detected as a conscious voice that speaks loudly in the patient's experiential world. In contrast, analysts relegate self-destructive tendencies to the realm of the unconscious. The analytic therapist leads the patient to believe that it is impossible to directly detect self-hatred and teaches him to use indirect methods, like dream analysis, to increase self-awareness. In pragmatic-existential therapy, the patient is encouraged to detect the presence of his self-destructive voice so he can become more empowered.

The first therapeutic task I assign to personality disordered patients is to listen to their internal dialogues and then recognize the particular manifestations of their own self-hating voice. If the patient is unable to identify the negative internal voice, I ask him to imagine how other people might experience such an internal dialogue. If a patient states that his day was ruined because he arrived five minutes late for work, he is asked if his co-workers would feel the same way about their own late arrivals. By asking patients to describe the probable reactions of others to the same situations that generate negative affect in themselves, the stage is being set for a later challenge to the dominance of the patient's self-hating voice.

The particular manifestations of the self-hating force are quite intricate and, consequently, vary a great deal from patient to patient. In some patients self-hatred is manifest as obsessive, suicidal thoughts. In other patients self-hatred is expressed by gross misinterpretations of the intentions of others, which then evokes the patients' anger and prevents them from sustaining positive relationships.

Self-hatred can be seen in a host of overt behavior patterns ranging from substance abuse to destructive interpersonal relationships. Defensive maneuvers, such as the regular use of denial, can also be interpreted as manifestations of self-hatred for they block the individual's ability to act effectively. The fundamental intention of the self-hating voice in all people is to prevent the exercise of healthy choices and to keep the individual in ongoing psychological pain. The inner voice does not intend total annihilation of the individual but rather maintenance of ongoing personal pain, misery and the blockage of healthy individuation.

Often the self-hating voice becomes most intense immediately after the patient has made healthy choices with interpersonal success.

Such internal dialogue makes it possible to differentiate between the neurotic and the personality disordered patient. Neurotics usually experience increased guilt and engage in self-attack after they fail, but personality disordered patients are usually most self-abusive whenever they succeed. The legitimate function of a conscience is to generate self-criticism whenever an individual transgresses against accepted personal values. Such a well developed conscience is rarely present in personality disordered patients. Instead these patients possess a self-hating force which fundamentally opposes any healthy self-interest.

Strengthening the Underdeveloped Life Force

Existential philosophers and psychologists understand the human as a process of being, emerging, and choosing. However, the presence of a strong self-hating mechanism in a human personality obviously opposes these movements toward growth. Personality disordered patients have an ongoing conflict between self-attack and self-affirmation. The self-affirming or basic life force in these people is underdeveloped and typically was seriously damaged early in their lives. As a consequence, these people are in significant pain; they enter therapy because they wish assistance in relieving or eliminating the pain so they can move their lives in more healthy directions.

The process of psychotherapy itself is fundamentally life affirming as it is designed to further the patient's capacity to make healthy choices and to counteract self-destructive tendencies. All models of psychotherapy attempt to eliminate a patient's self-hatred even though other therapy models may not consider self-hatred as the core of the psychopathology. Because self-hatred is present in all personality disordered patients, this negative force will oppose any psychotherapeutic process. The therapist attempts to strengthen the patient's life force; at the same time, the self-hating mechanism tries both to impede the therapist's work and undermine any positive manifestations of the life force.

The power of the self-attacking mechanism is clearly evident when one carefully attends to the experiential world of the personality disordered patient. These patients appear to lack the most fundamental forms of self-affirmation. Some of these patients seem to experience no personal wishes. If asked what they want, they cannot answer. To experience a personal wish, one first must own a sense of being a separate, independent person. In these patients a personal sense of self was not fully developed for they have not completely effected a psychological separation from their most powerful parental figure. Many of these patients do not have social lives, they do not go to movies, they do not care what they eat or how they spend their time. They never seem to have experienced joy.

Other personality disordered patients may appear to know and to act upon their wishes, yet, at the same time, they consistently behave in ways that block such wishes from being satisfied. Still other personality disordered patients successfully act upon their wishes but then hear an internal self-hating voice which demands they commit suicide. In all of these cases it is apparent that the entire process of "desire" generates excessive psychological pain.

People who do not "wish" do not own a healthy sense of a personal self. An individual who lacks passions, interests and needs can only function as an automaton and is well characterized as an empty person. Their closest approximation to a self is really a non-self, for it is devoid of the passions that healthy people experience when they live a full, rewarding life. These patients exist as psychological non-beings, *i.e.*, as non-feeling people. If they were to experience emotions, those feelings would jeopardize what little sense of self they do possess. Hence, existing with no feeling and no wishing is their most basic form of self-protection.

If these patients had risked emotional expression when they were young children, it would have jeopardized the very tenuous relationship that each had with a significant parent. Consequently, as they progressed into adulthood they continued to block emotional expression and remained interpersonally bland. If these patients were to wish, to deeply react and to own personal urges, it would profoundly threaten their psychological existence. They anticipate a kind of fundamental annihilation of the self, and they can only begin to understand this dread through a careful study of their own early interactions with parental figures. Individuals who have been damaged in this fashion have not been able to risk feelings or the development of an independent life force. Now as psychotherapy patients, they must trust and rely upon the power of the therapist and then ultimately draw from the therapist's own life force to create their own personal selves.

Therapeutic work with such patients is radically different from the work conducted with those who own a strong sense of a personal self. For these latter patients it is possible simply to encourage behavior change, and such changes will quickly generalize into the development of more healthy behavior patterns. However, patients who exhibit such accelerated growth are not personality disordered.

To attend to the personality disordered patient's experiential world is to recognize the existence of a significant and powerful internal force that opposes personal growth. This force is diabolically clever, for it has full access to all the strengths of the personality. Its voice advances arguments that will result in interpersonal failure, even as it convinces the person that these are logical and forward moving choices to make. For example, the inner voice will say "you have worked well in monitoring yourself and now you are entitled to a vacation from self-awareness." Once the person takes such a vacation and stops introspection, then the self-destructive voice resumes its dominance. The force which opposes growth in most personality disordered patients is initially more overt, and certainly more verbal, than the force which advocates healthy self-affirmation.

It is very helpful to the patient to have a label for this self-attacking, self-destructive, self-negating, and self-hating voice. Once a label is affixed to the process, it becomes easier for the patient to identify its presence. The patient needs to be able to discriminate between the voice of self-hate and the voice of self-love. The psychotherapist who listens carefully to the patient will quickly recognize that the self-hating voice does much of the talking in the initial phases of therapy.

Nonetheless, it is the underdeveloped healthy self that brought the patient into the therapy room, and it is this self that must be strengthened if the patient is to become healthy. The best way to accomplish this is to first help the patient recognize that self-hatred is prominent in his personality structure. Through the phenomenological method, the patient is taught to detect the different manifestations of the self-hating voice. Patients then begin to recognize that distortions pervade their personal experiences, and they discover how and why it is so difficult for them to see reality correctly.

Prior to entering therapy, the personality disordered patient is usually entrenched in rigidity and does not allow changes to occur. Even though such people may initially appear stationary and immutable, their capacity to move forward remains an essential part of their humanness. To study them as experiential processes is to understand the threat they feel at even the possibility of change. Since existential therapists apprehend people dialectically, they simultaneously acknowledge that both the processes of change and non-change characterize each person. Even so, the dialogue that the therapist holds with the personality disordered patient is directed toward the activation of the non-personality disordered parts of the person, *i.e.*, his capacity to change and move forward.

The initial reasons for these patients' difficulties lie in their early and ongoing developmental histories. To effectively free themselves and to become more fully changing processes, these patients first need to understand how and why they are so frightened to move forward, and then they need to affirm themselves. Common factors in the early experiences of these individuals generated their personality disorders. Both therapist and patient need to explore and counteract these factors as the way of moving the patient toward greater personal fulfillment and self-affirmation.

Six:
Historical Roots of
Personality Disorders

In the last chapter humans were characterized as *Verbs* or as ongoing, changing processes. That discussion focused upon the dialectic realization that change can only be understood when the possibilities of non-change are also considered. Further insights can be gleaned about the human condition through the existential description of the human as a changing process. To describe a person as changing is to focus upon transformations occurring over time. These transformations are conveyed linguistically by using the words *before* and *after*.

To understand that a person is "changing" requires that one distinguish between what the person was before this immediate moment and what the person has become at this immediate moment. Stated in dialectical language, one only understands the concept of *now* by distinguishing *now* from *then*. The existential study of the human, therefore, gives prime importance to the dimension of time. To apprehend the person at any given moment, the psychologist needs to know what the person is changing and emerging from. The person cannot be understood in the *now* without being understood in the *then*; this is the crux of dialectic reasoning.

When used to designate the experiential process, the term *then* can hold two very distinct meanings: one's historical past and one's anticipated future. In both cases the term *then* is used to contrast with the experiences of *now*. The following example clarifies this point. Now I am happy, but then (when I was 12 years old), I was unhappy, and then (when I pay my taxes), I will also be unhappy.

When the existentialist describes the person as changing, the term *then* exclusively refers to the person's historical past. Understanding the changing person requires that one attend to how that person was before the immediate moment. Such a reference to the individual's past may include events of many years ago, but it can also refer to how that person was just a moment earlier.

Even though many existentially-oriented therapists prefer to rivet the patient's attention to the immediate present, the dialectical perspective illustrates that the present has its fullest significance only through a comparison with the past. Humans understand and can appreciate *now* because they implicitly know what "not now" is. This point is further elucidated by recalling the distinction between reflective and prereflective consciousness. To think about or to reflect upon one's experiences is to distinguish between *now* and *then*. The process of reflection involves thinking both backward and forward in time. Prereflective consciousness involves knowing the immediate moment or the process of experiencing without reflection. When a patient discusses her problems, she is utilizing her reflective consciousness, a necessary requirement in psychotherapy.

Consequently, attending to a patient's historical past, even the past of five minutes ago, can provide a fuller perspective to the patient's experiencing of the immediate moment. While the past is relevant to the immediate moment, it is, unfortunately, also true that focusing on the past can detract from the significance of the present. Certainly, reflection upon the past can be useful, but it means that one is not taking action at this particular moment. Therefore, while a study of the past can enrich the present, it can also prevent full participation in the immediate moment.

Disadvantages of Studying the Patient's Past

Some existential therapists consider it counterproductive to seek historical explanations for their patients' difficulties. Recognizing that the search for historical answers calls for the use of reflective consciousness, they may prefer to focus upon the prereflective consciousness. These particular existentialists cite several reasons for keeping therapeutic discussions focused upon the immediacy of the moment.

One of these reasons revolves around the deficiency of the deterministic explanations of human behavior. Individuals who consider deterministic thinking valid believe that traumatic events, in and of themselves, may be sufficient to create psychopathology in people. This conclusion relegates humans to the role of victims as it assumes that people are and must always be powerless in the face of trauma.

Deterministic thinking has conspicuous flaws as many people have experienced dreadful childhoods and have yet been able to transcend their upbringings. In other words, these people were able to develop healthy personalities in spite of subjection to very unhealthy environmental conditions. Because such individuals were not crippled by destructive parents, even though they were trapped in noxious home environments, neither noxious environments nor destructive parents alone can be logically deemed responsible for creating psychopathology in children. Additional factors must be involved in order to explain why some children become healthy and others become emotionally disturbed. Existentialists prefer to use the experiential process to account for these differences.

Another reason many existentialists avoid seeking historical causes for their patient's difficulties is that many patients could use these explanations as excuses for prolonging their lifelong posture as victims. Even though these patients have, in fact, been victimized, they also have the potential power to undo the historically generated damage. It is vital for patients to understand this truth. Although patients may have excellent, rational reasons for being angry with their parents, they still have the ultimate responsibility of undoing that damage themselves.

Some patients will specifically use the therapeutic investigation of their past as a procrastinatory tactic, enabling them to avoid assuming responsibility for any changes in their current life situations. When psychotherapy encourages an intellectual exploration of the patient's past and yet avoids the pragmatic goal of improving the patient's current life situation, that therapy is basically nonproductive. In order to circumvent such an avoidance of responsibility, Boss (1963) suggested therapists ask their patients "Why not?" rather than "Why?" He believed that by therapeutically questioning "Why not. . . change?" the patients would be made aware of their inherent power to take significant action in their lives. By asking "Why do you not change?" therapists remind their patients that they always have the capacity to make choices in the immediate moment, irrespective of their pasts.

The Value of Studying the Patient's Past

Those existential therapists who do seek to understand the patient's historical past are attempting to expand the ways in which the patient can view her present situation and then fully participate in the moment. Most likely she has entered psychotherapy because of constricted experiencing; this same constriction constitutes her psychopathology. Consequently, the existential therapist attempts to assist her in acquiring a fuller and deeper apprehension of her world. This expanded experiencing is the most important therapeutic goal. When it is achieved, it will empower the patient. When the patient uses additional meaning categories to understand her world, she is expanding her experiencing. The existential therapist believes attempts to expand experiencing will prove to be much more beneficial to the patient than trying simply to induce behavioral changes.

Frankl (1960) believed that expanded experiencing would help a patient attain fuller meaning in life. In Frankl's system of logotherapy, patients expanded their experiencing through a search for meaning. Individuals find meaning either through behavior (action) or through experience (owning values and at times suffering). These different paths to meaning are quite useful as occasionally patients are in situations where behavioral changes are not viable. If a patient can reinterpret her life situations or change her experiencing, she is better able to attain full meaning in life. As one example, Frankl wrote about a man whose grief over the death of his aged spouse was made meaningful and tolerable only through his new therapeutic realization that his wife would have felt far more pain if he had predeceased her.

Because existential therapists attempt to expand the experiential worlds of their patients, they may appear to have goals identical to those of Gestalt therapists. Both systems do assert that it is important for patients to expand their ways of experiencing the world. However, Gestalt therapists are often active and directive and may prescribe exercises to immediately alter patients' experiences. In contrast, existentialists typically avoid such techniques and as an alternative, simply encourage their patients to develop a fuller conceptual understanding of themselves and others. Rather than the guided activities and exercises of Gestaltists, therapeutic dialogue and interaction are the prime methods existentialists use for expanding the patients' experiential worlds.

While some existentialists concede that past experiences may have shaped current behaviors, they also continue to stress that as the patient expands her awareness, she will be able to alter these undesirable current behavior patterns. The increased understanding of self is a central part of the existential therapeutic process. May (1979) believed that therapy can help the patient recognize that she often functions as an object in the world. This recognition prompts her to begin to act as a subject, *i.e.*, to take control instead of being controlled.

Even though a pragmatic-existentialist attempts to expand the range of the patient's experiencing, this increase in understanding is not the exclusive focus of the therapy. It is also very important for the therapy patients to reevaluate and consider changing some of their maladaptive behavior patterns. Existentialists believe that as patients expand their ways of experiencing their world, these new perceptions will lead the patients to change their behavior patterns. All forms of existential therapy assist patients in expanding and enriching the ways in which they view their world. Each theorist uses different terminology to describe such changes. Binswanger (1963) expected therapeutic dialogue to expand the meaning categories which patients utilize to make sense of their worlds. May, Angel & Ellenberger (1958) viewed therapeutic dialogue as beneficial in expanding the patient's biological, interpersonal and personal worlds (respectively, the *umwelt*, *mitwelt* and *eigenwelt*).

In my own experience, I have found that it is usually crucial to expand the patient's understanding of herself and others by discussing her own past. Patients need to apprehend how and why they see their worlds in their own particular ways. These discussions enable the patient to recognize that some of her unique ways of viewing others are based upon her internalizations of the views held by destructive parental figures. As she discusses the past behaviors of the major figures in her life, she can more fully understand how, if, or when she was mistreated or abused. A fuller understanding of her *then* will empower her to act more effectively in her *now*.

The patient's past does not need to be explored through a systematic or structured investigation. Because the patient is an experiential process, the therapeutic discussions need to flow spontaneously. Explorations of and references to the past will be most productive when they are natural extensions of the immediate therapeutic dialogue. Whenever a therapist insists upon acquiring a detailed psychosocial history from a patient, she is superimposing her agenda upon the patient. Furthermore, by taking a detailed history, the therapist is implicitly informing the patient that she needs such information. If therapists act in this directive manner, their patients will soon ask them how they plan or expect to use the information. Such questions would make most therapists uncomfortable for they would be unprepared to fully announce a treatment plan at that particular moment.

Investigation of a patient's psychological past can serve two different but very important functions. The exploration first provides the patient with a fuller understanding of her past, which offers her a different perspective upon herself as an emerging process. Second, she can use this new understanding to enhance her current experiences and to change her behavior in the immediate situation.

For example, a patient may recall specific incidents when her mother was excessively critical of her. After these events have been described, either the patient or the therapist is likely to label the mother's behavior as hostile and inappropriate. This new label enables the patient to see that she was not legitimately criticized but rather was victimized by her mother's aggression. She may recognize that she currently anticipates criticism from other people and has been quite defensive as a result of these dreaded criticisms. The patient can then change her expectations as she recognizes that other people have no need to be excessively critical of her as her mother was.

Psychologists do not yet know how large a role heredity or

biochemistry plays in the development of personality disorders. It would certainly be oversimplistic to assume that the human can be understood as a purely psychological creature, independent of physiology and genetics. However, even if important biochemical factors in personality disorders are ultimately discovered, psychotherapists will still need to assist patients in expanding experiences of themselves and others. Such enrichment occurs as a result of therapeutic dialogue and not through the administration of psychotropic medication. Consequently, existential psychotherapists are prudent in adopting the position advanced by Adler (1968) regarding biochemical and physiological factors. Adler believed that individuals can always compensate for their own physiological or genetic weaknesses. He concluded that people are capable of making significant choices and not simply helpless victims of inherited biochemistry.

Yet, individuals are born with certain response tendencies, and they live in environments which play a large role in shaping their earliest behaviors. Humans make differential responses to their environments, favoring some responses over others. The vast body of psychological knowledge repeatedly demonstrates that environmental factors and one's prior learning history significantly affect human behavior.

It is a somewhat difficult task to reconcile this body of psychological knowledge with the existential perspective that focuses upon choice and the experiencing process. However, the writings of Allport (1960) provide a possible bridge between these two different approaches. Allport stated that humans undergo a major developmental progression. As children they are all initially subject to the laws of learning and determinism. Later, as they move into adolescence, people develop what Allport labelled the "proprium," the new center of personality which eventually becomes the moving force behind human behavior. This proprium contains all human intentionality and is the seat of free will. Allport thereby accepted the powerful role that external forces play in the earliest years of people's lives and also recognized that people are capable of transcending these early shaping experiences as they move toward adulthood.

Therapy patients certainly need to become more aware of their immediate intentions and also need to better understand what their intentions were in different past situations. By encouraging patients to review their developmental history, pragmatic-existential therapy enables patients to better understand the actions of their parents as well as see the motives and intentions of all the significant figures in their lives. This kind of reconstruction and reconceptualization of the past is the precursor to any changes in the experiences and behaviors in the immediate situation.

While pragmatic-existential therapy encourages patients to recognize their own purposiveness, many patients find it quite difficult to accept the fact that they do, in fact, have intentions or that their behavior is, indeed, purposive. Even those passive patients are expressing their intentions, as their lack of assertion serves an important purpose. The function of such actions may be as basic as insuring survival, but it may serve other purposes as well. Individuals assume idiosyncratic ways of being in their worlds; usually they adopt these positions without engaging in much direct or conscious thought. Most people rarely question whether their particular ways of being are the most efficient ways to obtain need satisfaction. Therefore, it is important for patients to recognize that their ways of "being-in-the-world" were acquired through earlier interactions with significant others. This knowledge enables them to decide which of these patterns are valuable strategies they wish to retain for future use and which of these patterns they wish to discard.

One of the most important discoveries that patients make in review of their pasts is the recognition that they had a limited number of choices available to them when they were youngsters. Thorough discussions of their past interactions will enable patients to see that their parents would not tolerate certain behaviors or emotional expressions. Patients then begin to understand that in order to survive as children, they had to respond within definite and constricted parameters. These patients simultaneously begin to recognize they do have other and more extensive options available to them now.

Early History of
Personality Disordered Patients

The formal psychiatric diagnosis of personality disorder is applied exclusively to those individuals who have an extensively damaged character or personality structure. Pragmatic-existentialism, however, considers a diagnosis of personality disorder warranted for people who have not managed to attain healthy individuation. Both viewpoints imply that these individuals experienced major adjustment difficulties beginning in their earliest years of life.

Personality disordered patients were previously described as having extensive difficulties in their interpersonal relationships. Such relationship problems are usually the ultimate consequences of a deficient initial bonding with parental figures. The profound difficulties in early bonding block the development of healthy individuation and also prevent the person from learning how to behave with others in fundamentally satisfying ways.

The personality disordered individual has not experienced any deeply affirming relationships, either because she never met the right people or because her problems with basic trust prevented her from relating to others in a healthy manner. As a result, when this patient enters therapy she does not fully believe the therapist has her best interests at heart or even wants her to become healthy and successful. On the other hand, these individuals must have had some type of rewarding or satisfying interpersonal relationships in their past. If they only had experienced interpersonal pain, they would never have come to believe that another human could provide comfort or assistance. They consult therapists, hoping to find someone who can give them greater assistance than they have ever received before.

Personality disordered patients have major difficulties in their interpersonal relationships, and these problems are traceable to basic deficiencies in bonding with parental figures. Effective bonding begins when parents are attentive to the basic needs of their infant. A young infant is, essentially, a powerless creature who can only use screaming and crying to communicate discomfort and distress. In healthy parent-child interaction, the child's communication of discomfort is responded to in nurturant ways by parental figures. For example, the parents will feed the child, change soiled diapers, and provide warmth and comfort. By all of these actions, the parents are teaching their infant that it is acceptable to express one's needs as the parents are willing to be the source of need satisfaction.

In healthy parent-child relationships, the small child thereby learns acceptable ways of getting self-centered needs met in the interpersonal world. The child subsequently learns to modify her pattern of communication and later replaces screaming with verbal requests for attention and nurturance. Concomitantly, her parents no longer immediately gratify all her needs; soon they implicitly demand that she increase her frustration tolerance. As both parent and child modify their ways of responding to each other, the youngster begins to own feelings of being a separate person and starts to develop a primitive sense of a self. Parents are pleased to see such individuation and offer love and support for their child's increased psychological development. As a result of this parental support, the child begins to clearly know what she wants because she has learned it is acceptable to be needy. The child then can develop and refine her own sense of intentionality; eventually she will become an effective participant in the interpersonal world.

Personality disordered individuals do not achieve such healthy individuation. In fact, they are usually very ineffective in expressing their own needs in ways that will bring satisfaction from the interpersonal world. Many of these individuals neither seem to know nor communicate what their needs are. Other personality disordered individuals may know their needs, but their communication patterns are so deficient and ineffective that satisfaction will not be forthcoming. Still other individuals may know their needs but express them in antagonistic ways, *e.g.*, acting-out in antisocial ways which regularly produce retaliation and punishment.

Another group of personality disordered individuals is very aware of the wishes of others and also is effective in satisfying them. However, they do not seem to experience the healthy self-centered needs most people feel. Their repetitive caretaking behavior is reminiscent of the behavior of healthy parental figures who readily satisfy their own needy infants. These personality disordered individuals behave in such parental ways that it appears likely their relationship with the maternal figure must have been inverted during their earliest years. When still very young children, they must have assumed some of the maternal functions, normally performed by healthy parents. In such interactions, the child became the psychological mother; the mothering figure functioned as the psychological infant.

Some less disturbed, *e.g.*, neurotic individuals, also may nurture their own parents, but their manner of nurturance is quite different from the style used by personality disordered patients. These higher functioning patients regularly experience guilt and as a result feel obliged to take care of parents who used manipulation to elicit that nurturance. Often these neurotic patients resent having to succor and provide support to their parents. Neurotic patients are fundamentally separate from their parents and individuated enough to experience a substantial sense of a personal self. Since they have this more fully developed identity, they feel imposed upon whenever they experience inappropriate parental demands. These patients typically have well-defined boundaries, and they wish neither to be intruded upon nor to have their boundaries violated. They often feel angry over the guilt-inducing tactics of their parents, but their own guilt may still be too intense for them to be able to defy parental wishes.

Individuals who suffer from personality disorders may also occasionally feel resentful and angry at having to submit to their needy parental figures. They may correctly sense, even though they lack the capacity to verbalize it, that yielding to their needy parent diminishes what little sense of personal self that they do possess. These patients do not own the feelings of being truly independent people. Consequently, when they do feel angry, it is likely to be only for a short time. Personality disordered individuals lack deeply established personal values, as values usually are the expression of an integrated self. It is most common for personality disturbed patients to experience undifferentiated wishes rather than to own principles and beliefs that are the outward expression of a healthy core personality. Such patients were often forced to assume a submissive interpersonal role. Because they lack a fully differentiated self, they are unable to withstand the wishes or demands of other people.

A weak sense of self is characteristic of many personality disordered patients. If they initially assert a point of view which is at variance with the beliefs of others, these patients abandon their original beliefs and soon accept the views of the other. Yet personality disordered patients do differ in the degree to which they can maintain their own separate viewpoints when they are contradicted. Some patients will only temporarily abandon their original point of view while others appear to fully lose their own opinions and quickly accept the views of the other as valid.

The patients who cannot sustain their own opinions also do not fully experience the typical self-centered human needs. To have specific cravings, tastes and passions is to be a well-defined person. Individuals who have cultivated preferences are usually independent and separate from their parental figures. Such is not the case with many personality disordered individuals, as they relate on a symbiotic rather than on an independent level, both with their parents and with other people. These patients will most approximate independent functioning when they nurture other people. Such patients feel most alive when giving up their self, for at those times they psychologically fuse into a larger symbiotic unit. They have a foreboding of their possible psychological death if they attempt to function outside of the symbiotic unit; separation and individuation are life threatening. Such an experiential reversal, where one feels alive when serving others and feels deadened when serving the self, is a central dynamic in the borderline personality. The most prevalent characteristic in individuals who suffer from classical borderline personality disorder is inversion of all the usual patterns of human responses: they respond negatively to warmth and positively to rejection.

The universal struggle to function as independent beings has been eloquently described by Rank (1968). Rank believed that infants sense and fear potential abandonment even before they develop their capacity for speech. This fear of abandonment he labelled the "life fear." Rank stated that whenever the infant moves toward becoming separate from parental figures, this movement will result in a loss of connectedness. To be non-connected is to be alone, and such loneliness is terrifying. As a result, whenever an infant acts in an independent manner, her "life fear" is activated.

The infant simultaneously experiences an equally powerful fear which Rank labelled the "death fear." When the infant remains overly attached and dependent upon the parent, the excessive connectedness represents a psychological death. Being too connected represents a refusal to develop a sense of separateness and individuation. Consequently, each time the young child clings to parental figures rather than expressing separateness, her "death fear" is activated.

Rank believed that humans continually struggle to balance these two ongoing fears. Each time we move in one direction, the corresponding fear is activated. That is, the more fully I connect with another person, the stronger my death fear becomes as I am losing my separateness. The more independent I become, the more isolated I am; this is my life fear. According to Rank, only through the development of a personal will can individuals achieve a balance between these two fears. The initial signs of will are in a *counterwill*, such as the defiance of the two year old; later in life, the child can develop a will to move in positive directions

Rank wisely recognized that all humans need to make effective connections with others while at the same time retain a sense of their own unique separateness. Although it may be a struggle to find an even balance between these two poles of the life and death fears, a person has the greatest chance of achieving a successful resolution if she has been raised by healthy parents. Well-adjusted parents support their children and simultaneously encourage their movements toward individuation.

However, when parents have their own significant psychological problems, their difficulties extend into the relationship with their children. If the parent has many inappropriate needs which she expects the infant or child to satisfy, then she will find it intolerable for the child to become a fully separate and independent being. As a result, the parent strongly tries to maintain a symbiotic relationship with the child even as the child continues to mature. The mother's prepotent need to hold onto her child prevents the daughter from developing a healthy sense of a personal self. Any time her child behaves in ways which reflected being-for-herself, *i.e.*, individuating, it is highly threatening to the mother, and the mother withdraws from the child.

Parents can block the young child's movement toward individuation in other very destructive ways. The parents may try to decrease legitimate boundaries between themselves and the child, preventing the development of an autonomous self in the child. In still another variation of this destructive interaction, the parents may violate the child's natural boundaries and engulf the child in a symbiotic relationship.

Rank stated that all such movements toward individuation activate the life fear in children. Children are afraid of functioning independently in the world. However, when the parent also cannot tolerate such independent action because of her own psychopathology, then the child's fear of being separate and alone becomes exacerbated. This particular child's fear of isolation is very much based in reality, for her disturbed mother may punish, *i.e.*, psychologically abandon, the child whenever that child attempts to individuate. In such situations the young child is likely to remain firmly and symbiotically attached to the mother. Even though physical growth occurs, this maturation does not permit psychological movement away from such symbiotic connections.

Mahler (1972) made major contributions toward understanding the young child's conflict over separation-individuation. She described three subphases of the separation-individuation process: differentiation (beginning at four to five months); the beginning practicing period (seven to 10 months up to 15 to 16 months); and the subphase of rapprochement (16 to 25 months). Mahler considered the genesis of major forms of psychopathology, including psychosis, to lie in the massive difficulties experienced during these age periods.

Pathological Parent-Child Interactions

Individuals with personality disorders typically were raised in very destructive environments. They often were viciously beaten by either or both parents and frequently publicly humiliated and debased. They were regularly attacked for being stupid and incompetent. A number of these patients also may have been sexually abused by a family member. Many of their parents are addicts of either drugs or alcohol, and these parents may suffer from personality disorders as well.

While it is most common for personality disordered patients to have been victimized by blatantly malicious parents, some of these patients were traumatized through more subtle forms of destructive behavior. For example, they had parents who loudly professed deep love for their children, but these same parents behaved in ways which demonstrated a lack of caring. The simultaneous verbal expression of gushing, loving words while behaving in cold, rejecting manners exemplifies what Bateson, Jackson and Haley (1956) labelled "double bind" communication. It is extraordinarily difficult for children and adults to recognize that such discrepancies exist. Often children will deny their existence. At other times they rationalize and minimize the importance of those instances where they were hurt and rejected.

Personality disordered patients need to recognize that their parents actually did behave in intensely destructive ways. Many of these patients survived their horrendous home environments only by denying the hostility and destructiveness of their parents. When they enter therapy, many still retain strong bonds to these same destructive parents, even though the parents continue to exploit and abuse them. At times these patients acknowledge that they have been badly treated, but they find it difficult to regularly maintain this belief in their consciousness. As a result, they fluctuate between knowing and not knowing the truth about their parents' destructiveness.

Children who are badly treated and victimized by their parents have little control over their lives. Since they must remain in these psychologically destructive environments, they need to find reasons or explanations for their parents' frightening behaviors. When a parent becomes drunk, abusive, cold, hostile or rejecting, the child needs to understand why such behavior takes place. It is too threatening for the child to believe that such behaviors are random and outside the realm of potential control. To recognize this truth would require acknowledging fundamental helplessness. Rather, in order to feel empowered, the child in such an environment often creates the illusion that she could have, in some manner, prevented this destructive behavior. Whenever the parent behaves in a frightening way, the child then erroneously believes she is responsible for having upset her parent and instigating this hostile behavior. Children who are raised in unpredictable and destructive settings develop a distorted sense of responsibility. This kind of distortion is especially true for the children of alcoholic parents. Children can find some comfort in maintaining the illusion of potential power, especially since the alternative is a recognition that they are simply totally helpless victims.

Children raised in these destructive environments often come to believe they have been thoughtless, inadequate, ineffective, deficient and defective. Such deeply ingrained beliefs are the resultant, internalized representations of the words of the hostile parents as they displaced their violence upon their children. Because they were frequently, although inappropriately, blamed, these children consider themselves responsible for upsetting their parents. Sometimes they think they spoke too loudly, yet at other times they believe they were too quiet. They blame themselves for a host of events beyond their control. But, in order to feel empowered, they maintain the illusion of having potential control.

Other personality disordered children achieve a false sense of empowerment by extensively practicing denial. They define their homes as normal, and report "Yes, my father is always drinking, but it never affects his behavior." At other times they utilize reaction formation and mislabel their homes as loving rather than as destructive places.

In some extremely disturbed families the children may be labelled evil by the paranoid parents who believe this malevolence must be vanquished and driven out of their children's bodies. Current newspapers have described bizarre events such as parents who beat three year old children to death for soiling their pants. Stories like these are powerful reminders of the intensity of displaced rage which runs unchecked in some pathological parents.

Therapists need to acknowledge that the majority of their personality disordered patients are psychologically disturbed because of the parents' destructive behaviors. These patients did not acquire such deep-seated pathology through simple misinterpretations of parental behaviors. Rather, they were victimized by their parents' own serious pathology. Because the parents of personality disordered individuals were so hostile, rejecting and damaging to their children, they caused difficult if not immutable trauma. The inflicted pain is so extensive that it precludes the development of any positive relationship with the abusive parent. Even when the patient becomes healthier, her mother or father will, most likely, remain very hostile and intractable in their personal pathologies. For many personality disordered individuals, the best route to mental health will be achieved if they fully sever or at least severely limit future contact with their destructive parental figures.

In contrast, neurotic patients may only temporarily refuse contact with their parents during the course of their psychotherapy. The neurotic patients become angry with their parents and are likely to go through periods of acting-out, but ultimately they are usually able at some time to then establish a satisfactory relationship with parental figures. The parents of neurotic patients, even though they may have been too controlling or guilt inducing, still truly want their children to be successful. Unfortunately, they may have had incorrect definitions or goals for their children's success, and they may have tried to superimpose those ideas upon their children. However, once the neurotic patient is free of irrational guilt, she is then able to deal with her parents from a vantage point of strength and independence. Her underlying sense of self was not fundamentally damaged, and it is possible for her subsequently to achieve a positive resolution with her parents.

On the other hand, in most instances the parents of personality disordered patients are not child-centered at all. They are so narcissistic and/or hostile that they are incapable of being healthy, caring parents. They may profoundly reject their children, or they may clasp them so closely that these children cannot effectively individuate. Even when these children become adults with successfully completed therapy, they still cannot find a safe way to interact with their parents. In order to insure sustained mental health, they often decide to cease contact with such destructive people.

The Struggle Between Health and Pathology

Disturbed parents can block the child's early movements toward individuation and healthy development through two different pathological patterns. Some destructive parents will exacerbate the child's life fear to such an extent that she becomes terrified of acting in fundamentally separate ways. Her parents, by attending to their own overpowering need to retain their child as an integral part of themselves, render her powerless. The need to be symbiotically attached to their child is so strong that these parents can neither recognize nor support their child's natural need to become her own person.

In the other pathological pattern the parents express much overt hostility to their children. These parents regularly criticize, attack and abuse whenever they sense their children are about to function successfully on their own. Such parents want to retain power over their children and cannot tolerate being outperformed by their offspring. As a result, they undermine and berate their children's self-enhancing tendencies and thus prevent these children from developing positive self-esteem.

Both pathological patterns sow seeds for the development of a personality disorder, as the children who are subjected to these destructive behaviors frequently will, unfortunately, ultimately internalize those parental messages. These children adopt the voice of the parent as their own and soon begin to respond to their personal urges to individuate with the internalized self-criticism and hostility.

Children subjected to the first destructive form of parenting hear the subtle and destructive nonverbal message from their parent that says "If you move (psychologically) away from me, I will abandon you." Because the parent will not tolerate significant movements toward separateness, the child learns to block her own natural tendencies toward individuation. She accomplishes this by introjecting or internalizing the parental voice which does not tolerate independent action. In other words, she tells herself not "to be" for herself or not to act in ways that would be self-enhancing.

Children subjected to the second pathological pattern initially behave in ways that could ultimately prove self-enhancing; but they, too, have internalized a parental voice that does not allow them to succeed. Consequently, they will regularly and mercilessly berate themselves if they do attain interpersonal success as they have consistently been punished for demonstrating independent skills. As a result, these patients now possess a very powerful, sadistic, self-hating voice which parrots the hostile competitive parent's attack on their positive strivings when they were children.

The destructive power of these parents splits the personality structure of the child into opposing forces. One force contains all the natural healthy urges toward individuation, *i.e.*, becoming a separate, self-affirming being. The other force embodies the malevolent wishes of parents or their surrogates, which regularly negates most expressions of individuality, only allowing the individual to develop a self subservient to the wishes of the other.

Parents who cannot tolerate the psychological independence of their children will not permit the children's movements toward separateness even during the first year of life. Consequently, a very young child quickly feels overwhelmed whenever she moves away from such parental figures. These children learn a very powerful and primitive lesson under such conditions. They discover that "being-for-self" is wrought with danger and terror, and most attempts to individuate will fail. They learn that it is safest to stop moving toward such individuation and remain dependent upon and subservient to the controlling parental figures. This survival-based learning occurs even before the child has sufficient articulate speech to put the lesson into words. Because they experienced overwhelming terror whenever they tried to be separate beings, they cannot undo this primitive lesson through verbal dialogue alone, even in the safety of the therapist's office. Nonverbal lessons can only be extinguished and relearned at the nonverbal level.

Even when such a child matures and acquires the necessary skills to be able to function independently, she still blocks her tendencies toward individuation. Her psychological survival has been based upon retaining a symbiotic connection with her parental figure, and she will use all of the skills she has acquired throughout the developmental process to sustain this diminution of self. In other words, even as the child acquires verbal skills and the capacity to reason, these intellectual assets will be used to block all forms of "being-for-self," just as they would be used for purposes of self-enhancement in a healthy environment. The need to block individuation was acquired as a basic survival technique by these mistreated children; therefore, self-negation becomes the dominant factor in the child's personality structure.

This need to block the individuation process and natural tendencies toward "being-for-self" can be subsumed under the concept of "self-hatred" described earlier in this text. The personality disordered individual internalizes her parents' hatred of her own individuating and self-affirming tendencies. One part of her, therefore, undermines and hates the other part of her. Her natural tendencies to "be-for-herself" are the objects of her hatred, and she has a "voice" in her personality structure which attempts to block and to undermine all of her self-affirming actions. This self-hatred may represent the internalization of the parental figure who needed to make and keep the child as part of a symbiotic unit. On the other hand, this self-hatred may represent the internalized voice of the parent who needed to have this child function in an inferior and subservient role.

A powerful self-hating force is created through both forms of disturbed parent-child relationships; this opposes the natural tendencies toward individuation. The conflict between self-love and self-hate is the central dynamic in personality disordered individuals. An incessant internal battle wages between these two forces, and this struggle occurs both at the verbal and the nonverbal levels. When individuals suffering from personality disorders first enter therapy, they are usually unaware that such an internal struggle is present within them. However, all therapists can readily detect that their personality disordered patients are unable to act in healthy, self-affirming ways. It is only the pragmatic-existential therapist who identifies the inability to "be-for-self" as the struggle between self-hatred and self-affirmation.

In personality disordered patients, the need to individuate and to make self-affirming choices is regularly counteracted by the internalized parental voices which demand subjugation or selflessness. This struggle is unceasing. It is present throughout the child's developmental process, since simple maturation does not change or affect this fundamental conflict. In fact, the patient's maturation may make it more difficult for therapists to understand these underlying dynamics because the patient's basic struggle is often camouflaged by very high level verbiage.

The power of self-hatred is revealed through the patient's verbalizations in the following therapy session: Harry began the hour by documenting several ways in which his self-hating force had been operating during the past week. Soon he started to blame himself for not having been smart enough to anticipate and to circumvent this self-hating process. Then he blamed himself for not having solved his problems earlier in his therapy and earlier in his life. Despite his attempts to focus his energies upon detecting the presence of self-hatred, the internal attacks upon the self persisted and were able to circumvent his conscious awareness.

Most personality disordered patients have an intricately developed self-hating mechanism in their personality structures. In fact, this mechanism has the loudest internal voice, far more powerful than the voice which urges self-enhancement and self-affirmation. Such power is not surprising since self-hatred was developed very early as a basic survival mechanism. Whenever such an individual experiences the urge to move forward and be self-affirming, the urge activates the fear of severe pain and potential psychological death. Therefore, these patients desperately needed to acquire successful methods of blocking such tendencies to individuate very early in their development.

As a result of those early primitive defensive maneuvers, the patients now have an underdeveloped healthy self and rarely know how to counteract the self-hating forces in their personality structures. Because it was so dangerous to be an actively individuating process, these patients often used passivity as a cloak for all self-enhancing behaviors. These patients are unable to counteract the self-hatred with self-affirming messages. Frequently they are not even aware they are subjected to self-hatred.

One therapy patient described her basic problem as "disappearing." At different times in her life Joan psychologically withdrew to such an extent that her self-affirming voice became mute and she lost all sense of power and personal needs. At those times Joan essentially became a psychological non-being. During Joan's early years, her mother was so hostile that Joan learned to survive by what she described as "fading into the wallpaper." For example, the mother insisted that Joan accompany her on a shopping trip immediately after a dentist had extracted four impacted wisdom teeth from Joan's mouth. Her mother remained impervious to Joan's physical pain and proceeded to shop while Joan suffered in silence. Joan learned that if she did not announce her personal needs to her mother she would not be attacked. To assert herself would have incurred both wrath and psychological abandonment, so Joan learned to keep quiet about her needs and pain.

In such destructive environments, children learn that it is unsafe to affirm any self-enhancing, personal needs because such verbalizations will bring swift retaliation by the threatened parental figures. The nascent, separate self must remain hidden from the attacking parental figure and from the internalized representation of this figure. The young child will learn to "be-for-self" in some important ways; but more often than not, her self-affirming tendencies will be blocked by her self-hating mechanism.

The varying degrees to which personality disordered individuals can learn to "be-for-self" are largely a function of the degree to which the destructive parents allowed them to individuate. These parents wanted and permitted their children to develop certain skills, but they would not tolerate their children's basic movement toward psychological independence.

Destructive parental figures can negate healthy development in a myriad of ways. One patient recalled that his mother would repeatedly slap his face for minor infractions, such as going to school without wearing rubbers over his shoes. When he complained to his father about his mother's hostility, the boy was told to apologize for getting his mother upset: "I don't want to hear anything from you-- just apologize." Both parents collaborated in humiliating this child and in blocking his basic tendencies toward self-affirmation. Given such an upbringing, it is quite understandable that this patient had not learned how to effectively advocate for himself.

Children are unable to sustain angry feelings toward their parents until they have achieved significant psychological separation. Since the personality disordered patients were neither allowed to become fully individuated nor to be for themselves in healthy ways, they can not fully own angry feelings toward parental figures. Furthermore, they do not even realize the extent of the destructiveness wreaked by their parents.

It is essential to help such patients recognize that their parents behaved in fundamentally destructive ways, precipitating the patient's problems. These patients have been psychologically crippled by parents who blocked their natural tendencies toward healthy individuation. It is not the specific instances of parental rejection or abuse that are so important. Rather, the parents' primary needs to keep their children in either a symbiotic relationship or in the role of ancillary object stunted the child's healthy development.

These personality disordered patients first need to understand the malevolence directed toward them. Even in those situations where patients cannot recall overt physical hostility inflicted by parental figures, discussion of past interactions enables them to see the more subtle psychological forms of abuse they received. The patients need to recognize that they have been psychologically crippled by parents who blocked their tendencies toward individuation. The patients need to recognize that the horrible treatment they received was in no way justified; instead they must understand that they are the victims of their parents' destructive behavior. Patients need to correctly label those instances as destructive, hostile and bizarre parental behaviors in order to free themselves of the scars caused by such interactions.

Patients also need to recognize the widespread negative effects caused by parental interference with their individuation process. The patients have internalized the parental negation of individuation by creating a self-hating mechanism. They now have an inner voice which repeats parental hostility and often speaks in a tone that is even more cruel than that of their parents. This powerful mechanism is relentless as it continues to block healthy individuating tendencies. The introjection is so complete that it does not matter whether the patients remain in direct communication with their parents, for the self-destructive messages operate autonomously.

Self-awareness in personality disordered individuals is necessarily quite constricted as healthy introspection is an outgrowth of the natural need to individuate. Because much of the individuation process was blocked in personality disordered people, self-hatred is likely to remain a dominant, unchallenged voice in the personality structure. Even the knowledge from introspection can often be transformed into ammunition for further self-attacks.

Nonetheless, the patient must be told about the presence of self-hatred, the reason it exists and how one can diminish its power. This information cannot be simply and immediately imparted to all personality disordered patients. A pragmatic-existential therapist makes careful, timely interpretations at appropriate moments which will alert patients to the presence of such internal struggles. The therapist needs to make these interpretations in a rational, protective voice; this functions as an advocate for the patient's basic self-interest.

The self-hating mechanism in the personality structure produces insidiously clever strategies designed to block the individuation process. The self-hating mechanism is created through the internalization of the voices of all those individuals opposed to the healthy psychological development of the patient. Specifically, there can be a self-hating voice from the mother, another from the father; and there may also be additional internal voices representing siblings or significant others in the patient's life. Early in psychotherapy, the patient can use the term self-hatred to encompass all her tendencies to block individuation. Later in treatment, the patient will profit from identifying the source of the many different internal voices that are present within her.

Manifestations of the Underdeveloped Self

Sleep Patterns

The personality disordered patient can acquire important life affirming skills because she has within her a basic and intrinsic need to individuate. However, because self-hatred is such a dominant force in her personality structure, the skills that she does acquire will not be as solidly based as those developed by healthy people. An individual who has a firmly developed and well grounded sense of a personal self will acquire self-enhancing skills that can be brought to bear in many situations. On the other hand, an individual who has a powerful self-hating mechanism has a weak sense of self which is transient and becomes overrun or disappears under stress.

The instability of the underdeveloped self in personality disordered individuals is demonstrated in their erratic sleep/wake cycle. Infrequently, all people may awake at the wrong moment of a sleep cycle, terrified because they momentarily do not know who they are or where they are. This phenomenon, rare for most people, is a common occurrence among personality disordered individuals.

When asleep, people do not have the well-developed sense of self that is present during waking hours. In addition, the dream world does not operate with the same sense of logic as does the waking world, and the change from awake to asleep is a movement between radically different ways of experiencing. Upon awakening most humans will very quickly recapture their basic sense of self. Many of us may not feel particularly energized or ready to do battle with the world once our eyes are opened, but we usually know who we are and what we can do.

When the personality disordered individual sleeps, she is likely to experience terrifying dreams for she does not have a highly developed personal self present to protect her from the threats coming both from within and without. Furthermore, when she awakens, she does not immediately regain the sense of who she is or what her strengths are. She is more likely to awaken feeling very much like when she was a young child. As a result each new day holds terror for her; she must deal with the demands of the day as an adult, but when she awakens she does not own adult feelings.

Several of my personality disordered patients begin their days overwhelmed with such terror. They feel incapable of going to work even though they are highly successful professionals and have demonstrated their skills for decades. They recount frequent bouts of morning vomiting or an inability to get out of bed until they are substantially late for work. Once they force themselves to go to work, they begin to recapture the sense of being an adult self and they become quite productive. However, they lose that sense of "self" once they go to sleep and experience the same terrors again the next morning.

Relationships

Because of personality disordered individuals' underdeveloped sense of self, they gravitate to forming social relationships which are destructive rather than self-affirming. These patients are dominated by self-hatred and are likely to be attracted to people who will diminish them, thereby reenacting familiar patterns. They are most likely to be drawn into relationships consistent with their old ways of blocking individuation. It is rare for the personality disordered patients to be inclined toward relationships that could affirm their individuation tendencies; their self-hatred blocks them from choosing friends or lovers who might enhance them.

Correspondingly, people who desire healthy interpersonal relationships will not ordinarily be attracted to underdeveloped individuals who do not affirm themselves. Thus, healthy people rarely find personality disordered individuals to be appealing social partners. Even if they are initially viewed as attractive, their inherent deficiencies are likely to prevent them from being able to satisfy the needs of well-adjusted people. It is most common for personality disordered individuals to enter into and sustain relationships only with other seriously disturbed individuals.

Therefore, the personality disordered patient's fundamental problem in "being-for-self" causes her to have and to compound major problems in her interpersonal relationships. Personality disordered patients are most likely to become involved with destructive people who will continue to interfere with the patient's basic tendencies to individuate. As a result, these patients will experience profound interpersonal difficulties in addition to their extensive intrapsychic problems.

The Therapeutic Process

The exploration of the past is an important component in the therapy of personality disordered individuals as it enables them to become more open to their experiences at the moment. However, because each individual is an experiential process, the therapist must always place primary attention upon the immediacy of the patient as such a process rather than become preoccupied with a study of the patient's past. For example, if the patient is dominated by pain, it is necessary for the therapist to be soothing and supportive rather than inquisitive and demanding. When the therapist recognizes that the personality disordered patient has an underdeveloped sense of self and is easily threatened, it becomes imperative to tread lightly. Few positive changes can occur if the patient is threatened or feels too inadequate to be able to introspect. It makes no sense to try to outfit such a patient with expanded awareness if the patient is too insecure to put this awareness to good use. Hence, the therapist must try to make personality disordered patients feel comfortable and safe in the therapeutic setting, which in itself is a very difficult task.

The pragmatic-existential approach to therapy provides unique ways both of conceptualizing and treating this kind of patient. Once the patient is comfortable enough to begin the work of therapy, the initial task is to teach the patient how to become a phenomenologist. The patient must learn to describe herself as an experiential process;

careful questioning by the therapist will assist the patient in discovering how to look at and describe herself. The fundamental data for pragmatic-existential therapy will then be provided through such introspection by the therapy patient. By observing and reporting on herself as an experiential process, the patient becomes an active participant in her therapy and is able to detect and combat her problems.

As the personality disordered patient listens to and describes herself as an experiential process, she begins to see that self-hatred is prevalent in her experiential world. For many patients, their particular form of self-hatred is a loud voice which is quite easy to detect. As these patients carefully attend to their internal processes, they recognize that they are re-experiencing the internalized voice of a destructive parent.

In other patients, the self-hating mechanism, although primarily nonverbal, is still the force governing their behavior as they repeatedly act in self-destructive ways. The therapist's task is to help these patients recognize that such self-destructive actions are, indeed, purposive. These patients have a strong need to be in pain; and until they recognize the presence of such self-hatred, they will not be able to counteract it.

At the onset of therapy, the patient lacks both the self- awareness and strength to fight against self-hatred. The psychotherapist must then function as a wise and strong figure who can assist the patient in recognizing the presence of such self-negating tendencies. As the patient begins to see that self-hatred is extensive in her life, she will also begin to question the historical development of this powerful negative force.

The exploration of the patient's past leads to a discovery of the malevolence of particular parental figures. The patient begins to recognize that she has internalized the voice of the destructive parental figure, and that it regularly blocks her own individuating tendencies. The therapist must strongly support and encourage the patient's movement toward individuation.

For a therapist to effectively encourage individuation and for the patient to fully accept and internalize this message, a deep and nurturant relationship must develop between the therapist and patient. The therapist has to become the "good," nurturant parental figure who was always absent in the patient's life. This function can only occur if the patient finds the courage to reject the destructive parental figure, substituting the nurturant therapist. The transformation occurs primarily through the patient's leap of faith in the person who is the therapist. This kind of trust or connection cannot evolve if the therapist is immersed in the use of therapeutic techniques. Only when a therapist deeply cares for the patient in a professional manner that fosters the patient's individuation, can the patient become truly healthy.

Even when a therapist assumes such a role, some patients are still unable to internalize the power of the therapist and attach it to their underdeveloped life force. For such individuals, and in fact for many dependent and co-dependent people, the deficiency in the life force may be genetically or biochemically based. As a result, they may be unable to "be-for-self," not particularly because of destructive relationships with parental figures, but rather because they cannot marshall sufficient life forces to develop the "courage to be."

The psychotherapist may be able to sufficiently strengthen the life force so that major personality changes occur in some of these patients. However, progress is slow and limited in patients who do not have sufficient life energy to move forward and individuate. The field of mental health is not yet advanced enough to demonstrate the validity of this hypothesis regarding the life force. However, therapists do acknowledge that it is impossible for specific patients to progress beyond a limited point in treatment. In many of these cases, the limited progress is not due to deficiencies in the therapist, but may be due to biochemical deficiencies in the life force of the patient.

Other therapy patients will never be able to fully trust their therapists as they were so badly damaged as small children that they dare not risk re-experiencing such vulnerability. When a personality disordered patient can finally and fully trust her therapist, it only happens slowly and over time. This level of trust is a priceless gift that the patient bestows upon the therapist.

When such a deeply nurturant and reparative relationship is established, it provides the final necessary ingredient that enables the patient to move toward health and individuation. This healing therapeutic relationship not only allows the patient to experience herself differently but also to see the therapist in a fuller and more complete manner. The therapist had provided the missing supportive, nurturant relationship which then has enabled the patient to establish healthy and gratifying connections with others.

Seven:
Healthy Therapeutic
Parenting

The seeds of personality disorders are sown when children's natural needs to individuate are thwarted by their destructive parental figures. As these children mature, their need to individuate will be partially blocked by internalization of self-hatred. As a result, when as adults they arrive in a therapist's office, they will exhibit a diverse range of problems and strengths. In restricted areas of functioning they will operate as capable adults who are successful in particular endeavors. However, they will also be plagued by self-destructive tendencies which were instilled during their early childhood years. Since they were victims of very destructive parenting, they only can make major strides toward health when they replace that internalized destructive parental voice with a nurturant voice that advocates for their ongoing personal development and success. At that time, the pragmatic-existential psychotherapist becomes the healthy parental figure whom the patient internalizes in order to help bolster inherent tendencies toward individuation.

Many practitioners from diverse systems have asserted that therapists need to function as healthy parental figures for their patients. Adler (1964) considered the effective therapeutic stance to be the belated assumption of the maternal function. Jung (1971) engaged in parental type behaviors such as singing lullabies to his patients who suffered from insomnia. Sechehaye (1951), Fromm-Reichmann (1971) and Searles (1965) treated severely disturbed patients in basically the same ways that healthy parents nurture their young infants and children.

Even though many therapists function as effective parents to their patients, no school of therapy has yet encouraged therapists to systematically apply the full range of parental skills in their therapeutic work. Instead, most therapeutic systems view each form of psychopathology as having particular gestation periods. Correspondingly, effective parenting is then provided to those patients who were not given appropriate nurturance during the related developmental period. Of the therapists mentioned earlier, both Jung and Sechehaye offered the level of mothering usually provided to young infants, and Fromm-Reichmann, the kind usually given to the preschool child.

When patients are seen as evolving processes with unresolved problems dating from every crucial developmental period, a fuller range of therapeutic parental responses may be in order. A personality disordered patient needs the therapist to function as a good parent while he reenacts aspects of the entire developmental cycle. This means the therapist may have to nurture the patient through a repetition of infancy as well as be an effective parental figure while the patient faces the still unsolved problems of his psychological childhood, adolescence and adulthood.

Effective Parenting

The most complex task that any human tackles is learning how to function as a healthy and effective parent. Parenting is an extraordinarily difficult undertaking that calls for an incredible range of behavioral skills. Effective parents need to first be skilled at assessment as they must be able to detect the presence of the child's needs. During infancy the parent must decode nonverbal messages and determine when the child's biological and psychological needs require attention. Once the child acquires verbal skills, a different type of assessment is in order. The parent must attend to the child's overt messages and also recognize that underlying needs may be present, which are often at variance with the verbal messages the child communicates.

The parent has to be able to fully and wholeheartedly satisfy the needs of the infant. As the child matures, the parent must desist from functioning as the primary need satisfier to become the teacher who encourages the child to acquire skills leading toward self-sufficiency. The effective parent loves the child in healthy ways and uses a myriad of different responses to affirm this love. At times the parent will express love through physical contact with hugs and kisses; at other times love is communicated through verbal support and encouragement. Parental love is also expressed by setting limits and voicing anger when the child behaves inappropriately.

As the child matures, the effective parent has to express new and different behaviors that will assist the child's movement toward individuation. One treats a six month old differently from the way one deals with a six year old. Certainly, one must behave very differently toward a 16 year old than with a prepubescent child. Not only do effective parents radically change response styles as their infant progresses into adulthood, but they also respond in diverse ways to the child based upon his behavior at that particular moment. Because parents are fallible humans, their responses to their children will also reflect the prepotency of their own needs and emotions at specific times and situations.

The task of effective parenting becomes even more complicated with more than one child in the family, for an even greater repertoire of responses is usually required. Because children differ in their basic temperaments, parents have to adjust their responses to match the range of their children's emotional responses. Rivalries among children require parents to find dispassionate ways of responding to these competing needs. Parents also experience other pressing needs, such as the demands of their own jobs. External pressures often produce frustration and tension and may interfere with the parents' ability to fully attend to the needs of their children.

Even at those ideal times with little stress, the well-intentioned parent still may not be able to determine the best way of responding to his child's immediate situation. No matter how much the parent struggles to understand the child's needs, it is often very unclear what the needs are and whether the parent should even attempt to satisfy them. There is no complete manual which describes how to be an effective parent throughout the developmental cycle. If one were available, millions of parents would implement the desired strategies for most parents do want their children to become productive and be psychologically healthy.

Because it is so extraordinarily difficult to be an effective parent even when one has a great deal of internal resources, it is certainly understandable that people with many personal emotional difficulties will be particularly deficient as parents. These disturbed parents will not be able to suspend their own problems and attend to their children's needs in an effective manner. As a result, their children may be stunted in their psychological growth and are likely to develop serious psychopathology.

When such damaged children become adults and enter therapy to solve their emotional difficulties, they are attempting to undo the damage from their past. Personality disordered patients have had particularly destructive parenting which blocked them from developing in healthy ways. Although the therapist is treating a physically adult patient, that patient, in many ways, still utilizes child-like ways of seeing and responding to his world. Because the patient is an experiential process, he will at times experience his world as he did when he was six months old and must be treated accordingly, *i.e.*, given support and nurturance with no demands placed upon him. However, at other times the patient may behave like a defiant two year old who requires firm, even-handed treatment.

Effective therapists, just like effective parents, must alter their responses based upon their assessment of the needs in evidence at that particular moment. Therapists can, therefore, bring the skills of the capable parent into the consulting room to enhance their own effectiveness as they help their patients deal with their interpersonal worlds in more productive manners.

The variety of divergent theoretical models and treatment strategies in psychotherapy is as broad as the range of parenting styles. Patients are treated in therapy as individuals, as pairs, as couples, as family members, as group members and as co-workers. Depending upon the model of therapy provided, patients can be encouraged and supported, directed and taught, or confronted and challenged. Therapists may use combinations of these strategies at different times in treatment. Patients may be expected to work hard by introspecting or by complying with specific behavioral tasks. They may direct the course of their own therapy or follow the system or agenda suggested by their therapists. Patients may meet often or infrequently with their therapists, and these professional relationships will range from the very formal to the very casual.

It is startling that these different therapies can all legitimately lay claim to being successful treatment modalities. Every system of psychotherapy has proven beneficial for a significant number of patients. The reason that divergent approaches to therapy have all been effective at one time or another is that each therapeutic model satisfies the primary needs of specific patients at specific times. For example, certain people respond very well to encouragement and will show progress if they find a therapist who provides such continued support. Other patients need emotional distance and respond positively to therapists who utilize an intellectual and detached interactive style. If the consistently warm therapist were to treat both of these patients, only the first patient is likely to be a therapeutic success. However, if the reserved therapist were to see the same two patients, the second patient should have a successful therapeutic experience. Because patients have different needs, they respond best to intervention strategies based upon a holistic understanding of their own personality structures. The exclusive use of one style to conduct psychotherapy will necessarily limit a therapist's rate of success.

The ideal therapist would, therefore, function in a supportive way with the first patient and in a more reserved way with the second. Therapists raise their success rate when they can ascertain which response styles will be most effective with certain patients and when they correspondingly tailor their behaviors to complement these response styles. When a therapist exhibits such flexibility in behavior, he parallels the actions of the effective parent who changes styles and patterns of behavior in response to the needs of his child at the moment. The parent who cannot alter his patterns of responses across situations and with different children can be only a partially successful parent.

At times the effective parent functions as the firm authority figure and at other times encourages the child to make major decisions. The parent who refuses to set limits courts disaster, but so does the parent who cannot allow the child to become independent. Therapists as well must also set limits during instances when the patient needs external controls, even though the primary therapeutic stance is to respect the patient as a person, capable of making his own choices and assuming responsibility.

My first therapy patient taught me that limit setting is a necessary way to express love. This young unwed adult woman gave birth at age 19 and still lived at her parents' home along with her baby. She stated that she knew her parents did not love her because they had never imposed a curfew upon her. In this woman's mind, limit setting was a necessary expression of parental love. Her comments serve as a powerful reminder that unconditional love can be expressed through limit setting. Love can also be expressed through anger, as well as through warmth and support.

In establishing a therapeutic contract, therapists also set limits which are the necessary preconditions that allow treatment to work. I specifically tell prospective patients that I will not work with them if they use illegal drugs. They must choose either the therapeutic or the non-therapeutic way of coping with the world, and I will be the therapist only if they agree to choose the healthy alternative. Similarly, as a condition for entering into pragmatic-existential psychotherapy, the potentially suicidal patient must agree not to make suicidal gestures.

During the first meeting, I formulate an initial treatment strategy which establishes the basic parameters of the working relationship. Most patients can profit from frequent sessions, which means meeting more often than once a week. They should be told that increased frequency of sessions leads to quicker problem resolution; it does not mean they are very "sick." Statements like these demonstrate a willingness to affirm professional authority. Furthermore, such pronouncements typically reassure the patient as they set the basic conditions for successful therapy. Logistics, such as time and finances, may still restrict the frequency of therapeutic contact to weekly sessions.

Even though some patients have severe difficulties, they can only sustain weekly sessions: other patients even find weekly sessions too intense as they are enormously threatened by interpersonal relationships and afraid to face their problems. Consequently, they have to maintain significant space or distance from their therapists. These patients' needs must be respected, and the pragmatic-existential therapist must tailor the therapy to make the sessions the most tolerable for them. I worked with one patient over several years, where the frequency of therapy was bi-monthly. He needed infrequent sessions in order to consider himself healthier than the rest of his family, who had all participated in intensive therapy. He was able to make good progress at this pace because he saw himself as primarily in charge of his treatment.

At different points in psychotherapy, the effective therapist is authoritative, providing the patient with a clear representation of reality. Therapy patients sometimes state they feel their therapists do not care about them because they charge for their professional services. Most therapists initially become defensive when they hear such a comment. This criticism parallels the comments of the child who says his parent does not love him because the parent does not do what the child wants. Such a statement, of course, is the child's narcissistic distortion; it is often the patient's distortion as well.

I respond to this attempted manipulation by telling these patients they pay for my time and not for my affections. I state that my caring is my gift to them, and I do not "care" for people simply because they pay me. Furthermore, I point out that if I did not charge for my services, I would not be caring for myself or my own needs. These comments echo the responses the healthy parent makes to his complaining children. That parent tells his children he does not exist simply to gratify their needs. In speaking this way the parent teaches his children that love is an act of self-affirmation rather than of self-negation. The young child and the therapy patient both need to learn that in the healthiest form of caring, the "lover" never relinquishes his own individuality.

Prereflective and Reflective Consciousness

Most of the time, we all function in the mode called prereflective consciousness, which means we immediately apprehend our situations and behave in the moment without studied deliberation. The knowing that occurs in prereflective consciousness is the same immediate knowing described by Gestalt psychologists in their investigations of perception. Human action is immediate; and although we can usually explain "why" we behaved in a particular way, our explanations are *post hoc* analyses, *i.e.*, the consequence of reflective consciousness. For example, in the immediacy of the moment I find that I have opened the refrigerator door. I deduce (reflective consciousness) that I am hungry. However, I opened the refrigerator without having the conscious, deliberate thought that I am hungry. Yet I certainly did know that I was hungry, a knowing that was present without words or reflection. This form of knowing is the realm of prereflective consciousness.

Virtually all speech is spontaneously uttered and unrehearsed, which makes it a function of prereflective consciousness. We "know" what we are about to say, and we simply say the words. In the nineteenth century, James (1890) made this observation when he described the stream of consciousness. There are rare moments in human lives when people deliberately formulate the exact sentences they will utter; but almost all the time we understand, speak and behave immediately as prereflective consciousness. The initial draft of this book came largely from the province of prereflective consciousness. All of the studied rewriting was produced by the realm of my reflective consciousness.

Because almost all human actions emerge from the realm of prereflective consciousness, the healthy, effective parent immediately "knows" his child and his situation and acts accordingly. The effective parent functions primarily as prereflective rather than as reflective consciousness.

The personality disordered patient usually has a great deal of difficulty functioning as prereflective consciousness. Because this individual has internalized a self-hating mechanism, his immediacy of "knowing" is often an experience of self-hatred rather than an apprehension of the full meaning of himself and his situation. The therapist initially encourages such patients to function more regularly as reflective consciousness so they can distinguish between veridical "knowing" and instantaneous self-hatred. As therapy progresses, these patients will more readily come to behave as healthy prereflective consciousness.

The effective therapist himself usually speaks to the patient in the immediacy of the moment and thereby speaks prereflectively. Some of the therapist's verbalizations may be a consequence of his earlier formulated treatment plans or of his evaluations of prior sessions. Nonetheless, even when the therapist has used such reflective thinking when he actually speaks, his words are usually spontaneously stated and are, therefore, a product of his prereflective consciousness.

As patient and therapist speak with each other, they continue to move between the realms of prereflective and reflective consciousness throughout the entire course of therapy. When patients have sufficiently improved or no longer need therapeutic services, they have become individuals who can fully trust the "knowing" of their prereflective consciousness. By the conclusion of treatment, the self has sufficiently developed so that it is a valid, immediate process of knowing and can be implicitly trusted.

The best way for patients to learn ultimately to trust themselves as a process of prereflective consciousness is to be with a therapist who trusts his own prereflective consciousness. In other words, psychotherapists who function as models for their patients in many different ways can also be the model for trusting self as prereflective consciousness.

The fundamental distinction between existential and cognitive approaches to therapy can now be more clearly understood by using the distinctions between prereflective and reflective consciousness. Both systems advocate that by increasing the patient's knowledge, the patient will move toward greater mental health. However, the existentialist focuses upon the value of prereflective consciousness in mental health while the cognitive therapist stresses the importance of reflective consciousness. Even when existentialists attempt to enlarge the patient's understanding of his experiential world by expanding his meaning categories (Binswanger 1963), reflective thought is not viewed as the central, healthy dimension of functioning. Cognitive understanding and knowing are believed to be useful only if they are integrated into the intuitive knowing of prereflective consciousness. According to existentialists, to consider "thinking" as the best way of understanding the world is to restrict the manner and nature of "knowing."

Therapists Learn From Caring Parents

All existential therapies, and pragmatic-existentialism in particular, pay central attention to the experiential process that is the person. Existential therapists profit from understanding and emulating the experiences of the effective parent who encourages and assists his child in the individuation process. The existentialists learn from studying the experiences rather than the behaviors of the effective parent because change in experience is considered primary to change in behavior.

Healthy parents have strong, loving feelings toward their children, emotions which typically predate their child's birth and which are enhanced once the child arrives in the world. A loving parent has an immediate sense of awe upon seeing the infant. He recognizes how much this tiny helpless creature needs him, and he feels a deep sense of responsibility toward the baby. He wants to protect and nurture this helpless creature and assist this child in creating his own full and gratifying life. The reverence for life, the feeling of awe at seeing human potential, and the fundamental respect for the human are also essentials in the experience of the effective therapeutic parent. Boss (1963) uses the term "psychotherapeutic eros" to describe such a therapeutic interaction; and I, too, believe that such an emotionally-based caring is the central way effective therapists feel toward their patients. I also concur with Boss that when a therapist encounters a patient who does not elicit such caring feelings, the therapist needs to refer that patient elsewhere. A lack of psychotherapeutic eros blocks successful therapy.

Fundamental caring for the patient is the cornerstone for success. Caring enables therapists to behave as the healthy parent behaves with his child. This caring includes respecting the patient's separateness and allowing that separateness to be maintained. Like the healthy parent, the healthy therapist enjoys both watching and assisting his patient's movement in a direction which the patient has independently chosen. The effective therapist, just like the effective parent, is also willing to intervene and protect his "therapeutic child" from self-destructive behavior patterns that place the patient's life in jeopardy.

A deep healthy bonding should develop between therapist and the personality disordered patient; this connection will not reflect destructive countertransference. The term countertransference has been given too broad a definition by many professionals as it implies that any feelings that therapists have toward patients are inappropriate. A therapist will see a patient over many years, listen to his most intimate problems, and attempt to provide significant help. If therapists can participate in such meetings without some form of positive emotional connectedness, they would have to be cold, detached people, fundamentally unsuited for dispensing psychotherapy.

It is natural, healthy and growth-promoting when therapists have warm, caring feelings for their patients. While at rare times such caring could be problematic, the absence of any such feelings is necessarily very destructive. This kind of caring has a parallel in the effective parental role. While parental love may at times be excessive, the lack of any such love is far more destructive to the child.

Effective professional training instills high standards of ethics and responsibility which mitigate against excessive therapeutic involvement with patients. Patients are "therapeutic children" for one or two hours a week, but their lives are not the fundamental responsibility of the therapist. Existentialists state that every human is responsible for himself. Therapists assist patients only to the degree that patients allow, for each human always holds the basic responsibility for his own life. Even the most emotionally damaged patients are not healed by their therapists. Rather, therapists provide the climate in which the patients can begin to heal themselves. Even though therapists often are quite active and at times directive with their patients, therapeutic structure only provides patients with the basic tools which they lamentably lack. Patients always can choose whether to accept the survival tools which the therapists provide. As a healthy therapeutic parent, the therapist attempts to foster individuation rather than to encourage dependency. As a result, this therapist can monitor whether the patient is acquiring specific skills just to please the therapist. When such transference does occur, the therapist can point out that the patient need not please the therapist but rather has the right to behave in ways that will please himself.

Effective Responses to Child and Patient Needs

Effective parents complement the emotional states of their children. For example, healthy parents usually modulate their voice tone to be soothing and reassuring when their children are highly agitated. Their calm style of speaking parallels the verbal messages they give to their children. Attuned therapists also implement the same response strategy. They speak in reassuring tones when their patients feel overwhelmed with anxiety. Most of us can remember times in our own childhood when we were frightened and then comforted by both the verbal and nonverbal behaviors of a parent. At times, patients need comparable support, comfort and reassurance when they, too, are terrified. I recall holding an emergency session with a patient who had, very atypically, taken an illegal drug. I gave him a cup of tea which he later characterized as the best-tasting tea he had ever drunk. Of course, it was not the brand of tea that was so delicious but rather the parental warmth and reassurance that he so desperately needed.

Sometimes it is simply the physical presence or voice tone of the parent alone that is sufficient to reassure the child. At other times, a more active strategy is called for, and the parent must assist the child so that particular problems can be solved. In still other situations, the best parental strategy involves respecting the child's separateness and trusting his ability to independently solve his immediate difficulties.

Again, the parallel between child-rearing and therapy is quite relevant. There are times when a patient is sufficiently reassured simply by being in the presence of the therapist with no other interventions necessary. At other times the patient may need considerable therapeutic input to lessen his pain and depression. However, there are also occasions in treatment when the patient needs to hear that the therapist believes in him and in his ability to overcome the immediate difficulties by himself. In this last situation, any active intervention by the therapist would foster unnecessary dependency and heighten the patient's underlying feelings of inadequacy. The pragmatic-existential therapist is quite likely to select the appropriate strategy because he attends to the experiential process that is the patient.

Therapists are often most helpful just by carefully listening to their patients and by offering support rather than interpretations. Particularly at the beginning of therapy, many patients are in desperate need of a place of safety and a sympathetic ear. They cannot tolerate the heightened stress that would occur if the therapist immediately structured the treatment to focus upon behavior change. It is because they feel unable to do anything constructive about their current pain that these patients have entered therapy. By providing parental safety and comfort, the pragmatic-existential therapist supports the patient and reduces his stress. As a result, the patient can begin to evaluate and change his counterproductive behavior patterns later in treatment.

Some patients can only tolerate a therapeutic relationship that is formal and restrained. These patients have been deeply traumatized and are so frightened of people that, for them, safety lies in emotional distance. The sensitive therapist provides this safety through actions at both the verbal and nonverbal levels. For example, when I am with such patients I find myself sitting far back in the chair rather than at the edge. I do not shake hands with these patients; and whenever possible, I refrain from calling them by their first names. As therapy proceeds over time and these patients begin to feel much safer, I gradually express increased warmth at both nonverbal and verbal levels. However, when I see these patients again becoming uncomfortable, I resume a more distant pose. My own prereflective consciousness guides such behavioral choices, and I find myself sitting far away from a patient because it "feels right." I rely both upon my sense of the patient as an experiencing process and upon the trust in myself as a prereflective consciousness. These two factors are the main guideposts for effective therapeutic work.

Because therapists assume a parental function with their patients, their office serves as a shared "home" for both the psychological parent and child. How and where the office is situated and furnished is a statement of the nature of the role the therapist assumes. My decision to work in a home office expresses my conviction that the patient is to become a part of my "therapeutic" family. I have furnished the office to feel very much like a home. The antique furniture and book cases are complemented by pale yellow colors, while impressionistic paintings on the walls provide a sense of serenity. The two chairs are identical, conveying my belief in the fundamental equality of therapist and patient. A differential in size and comfort of the chairs would communicate a belief in a hierarchical therapist-patient relationship, comparable to the hierarchical parent-child relationship. Sitting in identical chairs gives the nonverbal expression of our underlying equality, which is then paralleled by verbal statements.

Parenting the
Personality Disordered Patient

When treating the personality disordered patient, a pragmatic-existential therapist usually draws upon the full scope of therapeutic parental behaviors. Because the patient's difficulties began in his earliest relationship with his parents, his therapy will have to undo and then replace this faulty connection with a healthier relationship. The therapist ultimately becomes his positive nurturing parent, a transformation which occurs through lengthy and painstaking work. Since the psychological problems first began before the patient had articulate speech, the therapist ultimately will have to function as his parent at nonverbal as well as verbal levels.

Specifically, the therapist recognizes that such patients have been deeply wounded and are enormously vulnerable to further pain. Because they are psychologically fragile, they would be quickly threatened by a task-oriented therapy. What they need, first and foremost, is a sense of safety and acceptance. Even though these patients may have many specific skills, they need a place of comfort, affiliation and protection. Basically they need to be protected from the internal self-hating voice, but first they must become aware that such a voice exists within them.

When patients initially enter therapy, they are meeting a stranger; and their reactions to strangers are expressions of the ways they feel about other people. Personality disordered patients are deficient in interpersonal trust, and for good reasons. Their own parents were deficient and at times acted very destructively toward them. When parents have been destructive, it is extraordinarily difficult for an individual to believe that other people are truly kind and capable of providing healthy nurturance. Usually, such mistreated individuals never allow others opportunities to prove that they may indeed be benevolent.

Personality disordered individuals will likely view a therapist as a very powerful figure. The therapist holds especial power with such patients because they are still childlike and, therefore, feel vulnerable in the presence of a capable adult. They see the strong therapist as a potential source of great good as well as great harm. This child-like perception of the other is common in many personality disordered patients but is rarely verbalized. Overt admission of such feelings indicates implicit trust of the other to be benevolent; such a level of trust takes a long time, if ever, to develop.

Most personality disordered patients also initially misperceive the person who is their therapist. Because of the pain of their upbringing, they have distorted perceptions of their parents, which have generalized into distorted perceptions of other people. One patient may seek a fantasied, omnipotent parental figure who will make everything right for him. Consequently, he feels very angry whenever he recognizes the human limitations of his therapist. Another patient may feel so intimidated by the excessive power he attributes to the therapist that he becomes very quiet and overtly submissive, but rages internally and undermines the therapeutic process. Still another patient may feel powerful only when he challenges the therapist, for he feels safety only through conflict. It takes much time and therapeutic patience for any of these distortions to diminish.

Nonetheless, the pragmatic-existential therapist exhibits behavior patterns reminiscent of the healthy caring parent. Initially, he provides safety and refuge followed by support, encouragement and, at times, direction. Because these patients were damaged at such early ages, they do not know how to proceed toward recovery and health. For this reason, the therapist needs to provide the personality disordered patient with a framework for studying his own pathology as well as for effective participation in therapy. One of the first functions the pragmatic-existential therapist has to assume is the role of teacher.

Attending to himself as an experiential process is an imperative first lesson for the patient. Psychotherapy is an interpersonal dialogue, and this dialogue begins with the patient's report of his own experiences. Hence, in the earliest stages of therapy the patient needs to acquire the skills of the phenomenologist. He must attend to his experiencing process and frame those experiences into words. The patient begins to learn how to function as a phenomenologist when he is asked to describe what he is feeling. Whenever the patient's descriptions of experience are unclear or vague, the therapist must ask for clarification which then allows the patient to improve upon his ability to observe and to communicate.

Personality disordered patients initially are poor at observing and describing their own experiences. They did not acquire such skills as children as it often was very dangerous for them to know and to own their own experiences of the world. In order to survive the destructive behavior of their parents, these patients learned to reject their own spontaneous, valid perceptions of the world and replace them with the distorted perceptions their parents "owned." Therapists usually are the first adult figures who show genuine interest and belief in the patients' own perceptions of the world.

When the therapist asks the patient to describe his experiences, he is giving major credence to the patient as a valid processor of reality. Such an expression of interest and concern is one basic way the therapist can show caring for the patient. By uncritically listening to the patient's report of his experience, the therapist validates the personality disordered patient as an experiential process. This experience is both novel and helpful for the patient.

Although these patients may have had some healthy interactions with parental figures, perhaps when they were in pain, they ordinarily did not receive healthy support or encouragement. When the child came home in tears, he was asked "What did you do wrong?" rather than "What happened?" If he had misunderstood the interpersonal behavior of other children, he was more likely to be criticized than helped. In some situations his parents might have encouraged him to share their paranoia by interpreting the actions of all other people as potentially hostile. The parents of the personality disordered patient rarely assisted him to acquire a full, complex cognitive interpretation of their world. Because their perceptions as children were rarely validated, these patients now as adults mistrust their own experiences and still do not have effective coping strategies. One cannot learn how to cope effectively if one cannot first trust what one sees.

Other parents of personality disordered patients may have been far from directly critical; instead, they were destructive by negating the child's participation in the world. Such a parent told his child that home was the only safe place and only the parent could be trusted. By negating the child's attempts to reach out in the world, such parents interfered with the individuation process.

The pragmatic-existential therapist will ask his patients to describe their experiences as a first step toward validation of themselves. In this interaction, the patients learn a new language—the language of phenomenological introspection. Simultaneously, the therapist attempts to learn the non-introspective language the patient typically uses within himself. The therapist must be especially sensitive to the patient's nonverbal communications, looking for cues which communicate the patient's underlying feelings. At such times, the therapist functions similarly to the parent of an infant or toddler. Both the parent and the therapist need to assess the internal working of the other because neither the toddler nor the patient can put his underlying feelings into words.

The pragmatic-existential therapist earns the patient's trust by demonstrating his sensitivity and understanding of the patient's needs. Because of that trust, the patient becomes increasingly willing to learn the language of therapy and engage in introspection. Trust is not an all-or-nothing event but rather a phenomenon which is likely to increase over time. Many patients may fundamentally trust their therapist. However, they also may need to maintain significant distance from them because full and complete trust would trigger massive fears of total annihilation. This dread of annihilation is the legacy from their malevolent parental figures. Because these patients have such pervasive underlying terror, their therapists must be gentle and proceed slowly with them. Sometimes such patients may never develop full trust in another which, unfortunately, restricts them from being able to completely overcome their destructive upbringing.

As the new therapy patient begins to describe his experiences, he carefully watches to see how his therapist reacts. Previously hurt by others, the personality disordered patient will be skilled at reading nonverbal signs of disapproval or disinterest. Occasionally a patient has asked me if it was time to leave the session, a question precipitated by my glance at my wristwatch. Such patients are wary of others and need to know how supportive or punitive a therapist will be. They do not believe an honest report of their experiences and feelings will bring about any help. Rather, these patients have learned the opposite—to verbalize experiences incurs the wrath and hostility of parents.

Therefore, the pragmatic-existential therapist must communicate appreciation of the patient's introspections. In that sense, once again, the therapist functions as the healthy parent who is pleased to see his child learn and develop. When the patient first learns to introspect, he is creating an observing ego. That is, he is able to develop a way of viewing reality that is veridical and untainted by destructive parental messages. Initially the perceptions of the observing ego are simply communicated to the parental figure, or here, to the psychotherapist. However, the observing ego eventually begins to observe itself and will ultimately become the central force moving the patient toward individuation. The observing ego within the patient provides the necessary information about the presence and the workings of the self-hating mechanism.

The patient's first descriptions of events and experiences typically are not the expressions of his observing ego but are rather are the manifestations of his self-hating force. Consequently, at times the therapist will challenge rather than simply accept the patient's descriptions of his experiences. When one of my personality disordered patients described having acted in ways which were clearly offensive to others, I asked him why. His answer was that he knew of no other way to behave. I contradicted him, for he did know how to be kind to others. The patient then agreed he had engaged in self-deception. Having recognized that he lied to himself, he then had to discover whether he also had lied to himself on other occasions.

In this interaction the patient was asked both to look at and question the validity of his experiencing process. All of one's experiences cannot be trusted, and healthy people do question the validity of what they think and feel at different times. Personality disordered patients need to question the validity of their experiences as well. Such questioning is central to an effective psychotherapeutic process as it acknowledges that individuals can profit from having a multidimensional frame of reference with which to view the world. Multiple explanations, meaning categories or frames of reference allow individuals to see their worlds most clearly. When children are not encouraged to develop different ways of interpreting their experiences, they retain only narrow, rigid viewpoints which will result in major distortions and inappropriate perceptions of self and others.

Pragmatic-existential therapy encourages a dialectic perspective as it recognizes the validity of many different ways of seeing the world. It encourages patients to entertain and then to choose among these different alternative viewpoints. The more possibilities the individual entertains, the more likely he is to discard the rigid world view propagated by destructive parental figures. By validating multidimensional explanations, the therapist increases the patient's ability to effectively process both internal and external events. The therapeutic question that allows the patient to expand his world view is posed as "Is that the only way this can be seen?"

By expanding patients' frameworks for understanding their worlds, therapists provide important cognitive tools which can be used to further the individuation process. In so doing, therapists assume the vital parental function of an advocate for the patient's healthy needs. The capacity of personality disordered patients to move in healthy personal directions was damaged quite early in their developmental histories. They cannot be-for-themselves in consistent ways without alienating others. When therapists help patients expand the ways they see themselves and other people, they provide basic tools which enable the patients to make self-affirming choices.

Because these personality disordered patients have much difficulty in being-for-themselves, they often are unable to detect the presence of destructive thoughts and behaviors which need to be eliminated. Therefore, it is necessary for the pragmatic-existential therapist to label these patterns as destructive whenever they are detected. Although the therapist should not interfere with the patient's right to make personal choices, he must verbally acknowledge to the personality disordered patient the presence of powerful, self-destructive tendencies. When such patients regularly become aware of the self-hating mechanism, they then can more judiciously reflect upon potential choices. The therapist may first ask the patient, "Is this the healthy part of you talking?" or "Will this particular choice make you happier or feel more fulfilled?" The patient must learn to ask these questions himself and detect whether his contemplated choices reflect self-hatred or the individuation process.

As the personality disordered patient focuses his attention upon specific problems, he may find himself changing in other spheres as well. When the patient moves toward individuation, he will spontaneously recognize and fix additional problems without ever discussing these issues with his therapist. This human capacity to independently heal oneself is a wonderful asset, especially since patients may never report the presence of specific difficulties. A patient can be crippled by psychopathology he does not even recognize and, therefore, he will not describe specific difficulties to his therapist. Consequently, if the patient is to move forward and make corrections in these areas, it will have to occur independently and without therapeutic input.

Such independent problem-solving was acutely described by one of my long-term patients. He began a therapy session by reporting he was pleased about the major progress he had just made in a social situation. He had begun to initiate sexual activity with a woman although she was sitting in a way that shut off the circulation in his hand. As his hand became numb, the patient removed his hand in order to regain feeling. He considered this behavior, removing his hand, to be a major accomplishment as previously he would have tolerated the pain of a numb hand rather than disturb the woman or make a demand of her. He had never previously used the therapy session to discuss any sexual intimidations. Consequently, the patient independently solved this problem without any direct therapeutic dialogue.

The patient progressed in this situation partially because he had internalized his therapist as a parent who wanted him to continue to individuate. When such a patient has been pervasively damaged, the therapist facilitates the patient's growth by functioning as the source of strength and support. The therapist is then the nurturing parent who draws upon a repertoire of interpersonal behavioral styles in order to satisfy the current needs of the patient.

A pragmatic-existential therapist may even teach the patient how to be assertive when the patient lacks these skills. However, patients frequently know how to be assertive but do not give themselves permission to utilize these dormant skills. Some patients can and will be highly assertive in business affairs but not in their personal lives. During therapy as they question why they do not allow themselves to be assertive, they usually discover that their reluctance is another manifestation of their self-hatred.

Despite the fact that personality disordered patients have been very emotionally damaged, many may possess high level skills. They may have certain talents which are even better developed than those of their peers. The pragmatic-existential therapist, functioning as the healthy therapeutic parent, is pleased to see these skills present, for he is neither competitive with nor threatened by his patients. Because this therapist is a positive nurturing figure, he encourages the patient to continue to develop any skill that will serve the patient's needs.

Each sign of burgeoning health in the patient is verbally encouraged because positive therapeutic comments facilitate emotional growth. The therapist functions like an athletic coach. The coach typically teaches and models specific skills, expressing his approval whenever he sees signs of progress. The athlete practices these skills until they become part of his repertoire. Therapists who function primarily in this manner are usually labelled behaviorists. However, a pragmatic-existential therapist can also function as a coach because such encouragement is encompassed within the functions of a healthy parental figure.

The pragmatic-existential therapist does not minimize the importance of behavioral changes; however, he recognizes that in most instances, behavior change does not occur simply as a result of coaching. Rather, the changes in experience make the individual receptive to the input of the coach. Comparably, a child learns to catch the ball because his "beloved" parent tries to teach him and also because he wants to develop this skill.

Owning the Role of
Healthy Therapeutic Parent

In pragmatic-existential therapy, the patient's internalized destructive parental figure is deposed and the therapist becomes the substitute or surrogate parental figure. It is an awesome responsibility to be so important in the life of another human. However, if the severely damaged personality disordered patient is to become healthy, he must be able to deeply trust his therapist, just as the very young child needs to be able to deeply trust his parent.

The essence of healthy parenting includes a deep caring for one's child and a willingness to assist that child to develop a personally fulfilling life. The pragmatic-existential therapist experiences the same feelings toward his patients. Because therapists, like parents, are fallible humans, they do not have all the answers and therefore cannot legitimately tell the patient how to lead his life. Therapists struggle to find the best ways of helping their patients just as parents struggle to find the best ways of being a parent. Both must come to terms with the fact that they act in the face of uncertainty and must cope with ongoing existential anxieties.

Being the therapeutic parent involves sharing in the patient's triumphs. The pragmatic-existential therapist is indeed very pleased for the patient and happy to share his elation. When a patient begins a session by describing recent successes, these discussions are important and productive. Because therapy contains the positive elements of a healthy parent-child relationship, the sharing of good feelings is a necessary part of effective therapy. Some therapists who unfortunately function as workaholics may always need to "get back to work." Productive therapeutic work is defined as problem solving; if there is no immediate problem that requires discussion, they search for one to solve. When treatment involves healthy therapeutic parenting, the therapist's expression of joy over the patient's successes clearly tells the patient that the therapist wants him to succeed and move forward in his individuation process.

The pragmatic-existential therapist demonstrates in simple ways that he cares for his patient. For example, one of my patients obtained his Ph.D. after many years of study. I felt it was very important to acknowledge he had reached a major milestone; consequently, I gave him a desk sign displaying his name and new title. This gift showed simple human caring and affirmation, not destructive countertransference.

In a similar instance, a new patient told me I was the second therapist she had consulted. Although she had been helped by her first therapist, she terminated the treatment because she felt the therapist did not care about her. After the patient had successfully completed long-dreaded, major surgery, she had heard nothing from her therapist. The patient had the courage to later confront the therapist on this issue; she was told the therapist was maintaining a necessary professional distance. When professionalism requires the exclusion of all overt signs of caring, the therapy cannot be fully reparative.

Certainly, it is of vital importance for therapists to maintain an appropriate professional distance from their patients. It is also true that there will be occasions when therapists have personal issues which can interfere with their effective professional functioning.

However, psychotherapy with personality disordered patients requires a healthy parental relationship, and such a relationship involves owning warm feelings. If a therapist believes that the elimination of all feelings from the relationship is desirable, that therapist would implicitly endorse the "schizoid" as the ideal parental figure.

When the therapist is emotionally healthy, he can detect and correct any signs of his own negative countertransference, as evidenced by the following example. A 40 year old man had been in an extremely destructive marriage; in the early phase of his therapy, we worked at helping him separate from and ultimately divorce his spouse. Shortly after leaving his wife, he became involved with a woman whom I perceived as very supportive and helpful to this patient. As their relationship continued to develop, the patient exhibited major personal growth, largely as a result of the intense introspective conversations he had with this woman. The closer they became, the healthier the patient became. I experienced momentary competitive jealousy as I felt this woman was "doing my job," perhaps even better than I was. However, I also realized that my work with this patient had prepared him to enter into such a positive relationship. Furthermore, this woman was making my job easy; all I basically had to do was listen to my patient and encourage his continued participation in the relationship.

Such momentary jealousy is again a common feeling for parents who experience rivalry with their adult child's lover. The healthy parent acknowledges this feeling, combats it and then feels happy to see the child in a healthy relationship. While the healthy parent may feel sadness in seeing their adult offspring mature and leave home, the healthy parent is also pleased for the child's successes and simultaneously relieved to relinquish the nurturing role.

Parenting a Large Family

Psychotherapy with personality disordered patients is quite intensive and demanding because the therapist must be willing to participate at a deep emotional level. When a therapist has to treat patients with significant depression, the work can be especially draining. The depressed patient is not proactive, and the therapist must initiate most of their discussions. It takes far less energy to react to a patient's comments than it does to spur a patient to action. Many therapists acknowledge that when treating only one patient with borderline pathology, they still feel as if they have done a full day's work. Consequently, it is important for therapists to question the number of patients they can effectively treat, both daily and weekly. The nature and intensity of the therapeutic hour varies greatly with the level of the patient's pathology; and if therapists must work with depressed or borderline patients, they need to have a lightened work load. Unfortunately, most mental health clinics do not give sufficient attention to this issue as they consider one therapeutic hour to be the same as another.

The healthy therapist works at a pace that does not interfere with a gratifying personal life style. The parent and the therapist once again share parallel issues. The parent needs to balance the gratification gained from being a parent with the gratification gained through other personal and work relationships. When individuals seek too much personal gratification from parenting, it can be destructive both to themselves and their children. Some therapists may seek too much gratification from their work, often manifested by scheduling excessive hours of therapy. If a therapist has countertransferential needs to be the dominant figure in his patient's life, he makes it extremely difficult for the patient to individuate and become fully separate and independent.

To function as a healthy therapeutic parent, the therapist must have many internal resources. He has to be able to make an emotional commitment to the patient, and he has to draw upon a wide range of professional skills which will enable him to balance the intellectual and the emotional dimensions of participation in the therapeutic process. Furthermore, the truly effective therapeutic parent is pragmatic, possesses a full understanding of psychopathology and can bring the truths of existentialism to bear in his therapeutic work.

Part Two:
The Practice of
Pragmatic-Existentialism

Eight:
Initial Contact
With Patients

Underlying Orienting Philosophy

The first half of the book proposes a theoretical model encompassing existentialism, pragmatism and healthy therapeutic parenting. These points of view need to be utilized in working with personality disordered individuals. Following such a model, the pragmatic-existentialist behaves quite differently as she utilizes each of the aforementioned theoretical components. When she follows the existential dimension of this system, she views the patient as a process of change and focuses her attention upon understanding the prepotent needs of the patient. In responding to these most pressing needs, this therapist is at one time especially pragmatic and at other times, functions as a healthy therapeutic parent. At other points in the treatment she uses the full range of traditional therapeutic strategies - reflecting, asking questions, posing tentative hypotheses and interpretations, and offering direction to her patients.

The key elements of pragmatic-existential therapy are to understand the patient as a changing process and correspondingly to change one's therapeutic responses to match the patient's pressing needs. Because the therapeutic responses are dictated by attending to the patient as a process, it is detrimental for a therapist to have a preset agenda for dealing with any particular case. Rather, the therapist will continually change her responses to the patient just as the patient continually changes her responses to the therapist.

Accordingly, the description of the actual conduct of psychotherapy fluctuates as it elucidates the different components of pragmatic-existentialism. This system is predicated upon the therapist's ability to change her responses to the personal process of the patient; while it is systematic, the practice of pragmatic-existential therapy is based upon ongoing changes of response. The reader should recognize that the changes in the level of the written dialogue reflect the changing nature of the therapeutic responses.

Any discussion of how to conduct the first therapy session must, of necessity, focus upon the behavior of the therapist. Because the therapist does not yet know the new patient, she must draw upon general principles of pragmatic-existentialism to guide her responses in the initial session. These general principles have proven helpful in early stages of therapy with patients who suffer from all forms of psychopathology.

However, the overwhelming majority of psychotherapy patients today are personality disordered, and the principles of pragmatic-existential therapy are designed primarily to assist this particular population. Personality disordered patients do not begin treatment with a strong commitment to the process. They usually enter a first therapy session with far less commitment to treatment than do neurotics. Personality disordered patients need to immediately discover that therapy will have significant value for them or else they will quickly discontinue the process. As a result, it is especially necessary for the therapist to make an important connection with the patient in the very first therapy session. Accordingly, this chapter describes different ways in which the pragmatic-existential therapist may conduct herself in an attempt to make significant first connections with her patients.

Preparing for the
Therapeutic Encounter

When an individual makes an initial appointment with a therapist, she is expressing an implicit commitment to become a regular psychotherapy patient. Her decision to explore the therapeutic process indicates a fundamentally healthy and self-affirming life choice. By contacting a psychotherapist, she expresses her wish to have a less painful and more personally fulfilling existence. By reaching out for professional assistance, the healthy side of the personality disordered patient has gained ascendence over the unhealthy self-destructive side. The voluntary psychotherapy patient has demonstrated her motivation for treatment through the act of making initial contact with a therapist. Correspondingly, the therapist's task is first to support and strengthen her motivation for treatment and second, to channel this motivation toward the establishment of an appropriate therapeutic contract. The therapist faces a quite different task when assigned an involuntary patient who may be court-ordered to participate in therapy. Here, the therapist must find a way to generate motivation for treatment in an individual who is likely to be resistant to most intervention strategies.

When a new patient voluntarily contacts a therapist, she is implicitly admitting an inability to exert sufficient control over herself and her life to feel either satisfied or fulfilled. Once she is willing to recognize and accept these personal shortcomings, she begins the process of seeking assistance from others. She may first turn to friends or to family members for either their direct assistance or even a psychotherapist's name. To ask family, friends or acquaintances for help is an overt acknowledgment of one's inability to solve personal problems independently. When a new patient first meets with a therapist, she must make a much fuller confession of personal weakness to an individual who, although possessing professional expertise, is a virtual stranger. Consequently, her anticipation of contact with a therapist is likely to evoke pain as it arouses feelings of inadequacy and shame. The very presence of a voluntary patient in the therapist's office represents the patient's implicit acknowledgment of her need for assistance. The patient does not need to directly say "help me" for the therapist to know that the patient is indeed asking for help.

Pragmatic-existential therapists recognize that many of a patient's wants, needs and intentions are implicit rather than explicit. It is necessary for practitioners to assess the presence of such intentions by drawing upon the multitude of ways that therapists can understand their patients (see chapter 2 and Potash, 1981). Not only do pragmatic-existential therapists utilize their professional knowledge to understand the intentions of their patients, but they also draw upon their own experiences as beings-in-the-world to enhance their understanding. Because therapists also live in the interpersonal world of shared meanings and symbols, they can draw upon this pool of common knowledge to better understand and communicate with their patients.

Pragmatic-existentialists also acknowledge that the process of personal experiencing cannot be fully conveyed through language. Individuals use words both to conceal and disclose intentions (Sullivan, 1953). Therefore, even as they attend to their patient's direct verbal communications, these therapists continue to attend to the nonverbal information provided by the patient's voice tone and body language. Therapists also draw upon a wide range of professional assessment skills in order to better understand the intentions of their patients.

In particular, pragmatic-existentialists use knowledge of interpersonal communication to further their understanding of the patient's experiencing even when it is not directly verbalized. For example, gestures convey meanings and intentions, and most humans are capable of effectively reading at least some of the other's intentions by attending to these nonverbal cues. An individual who is skilled at being interpersonally attentive can detect when people are anxious, angry or sexually provocative, and does not have to wait for them to verbally announce their intentions. If a therapist cannot draw upon such common interpersonal cues to understand her patient, this therapist will be deficient in delivering effective service. Because therapists acquire professional skills in assessment, they should trust their assessment ability to direct their therapeutic work in the most efficacious manner.

Consequently, the pragmatic-existential therapist who functions in the interpersonal world of shared meanings and symbols attends to both the nonverbal and verbal communications of people. She recognizes the intentions communicated through gesture and body movement, through silence and deceptive language, and does not restrict her understanding of the patient to the mirrored reflection of the patient's direct statements. The patient's experiential world is in constant change, and all of the involved nuances are not directly verbalized. Because only certain intentions and experiences of the patient are directly stated, the therapist must attempt to understand the person-process by drawing upon the full range of therapeutic expertise. Part of understanding the "other" involves knowing the common meanings of specific behaviors in our culture. One needs to attend to what is implicitly known and communicated as well as what is explicitly stated. If the therapist fails to address the implicit meanings of certain behaviors, the therapeutic process can be seriously compromised. Of course one must also draw upon knowledge of psychopathology and the therapeutic process in order to enhance the level of understanding of the patient. The more therapeutic meaning categories utilized, the more likely it is that the therapist will achieve full understanding of the patient.

The Necessity of Firm Therapeutic Limits

Like all other professionals, the pragmatic-existential therapist establishes firm limits and realistic conditions as part of the psychotherapeutic contract. For example, patients with alcohol or substance abuse histories must agree to desist from all substance use as a condition for entering psychotherapy. It is counterproductive to attempt psychotherapy with individuals who continue to use these means to escape from personal pain.

The therapist must confront substance-abusing patients with three possible choices: the patient can first enter a drug treatment center for assistance to end addiction and then later enter therapy; the patient can stop abusing drugs on her own and begin personal therapy; or the patient can continue to abuse substances and not participate in treatment. In any case, the patient must be free of substance abuse before therapy begins. One either chooses to self-medicate to reduce pain or to use therapeutic dialogue to reduce pain. These two are mutually contradictory strategies; if the therapist does not demand that the patient be drug free at the onset of treatment, the patient will continue to abuse substances even as therapy progresses.

Therapists need to establish other limits with certain patients in order to bring about meaningful participation in a therapeutic dialogue. This need for particular limits is clearly demonstrated in the following example with a novice therapist's case. In the initial session the patient stated that she came for counseling because her boyfriend had rejected her. She wished to discuss the poor judgment and "obvious, severe mental problems" of this male who had been foolish enough to reject her. The patient kept deflecting all the therapist's attempts to focus upon the patient and instead spent several therapeutic hours venting her hostility toward all the people who had treated her badly.

As long as this patient continued to deny that she shared the universal reason for entering therapy - to change herself - her sessions continued to serve a destructive purpose. By allowing the patient to voice a litany of complaints about other people, the therapist implicitly cooperated with the patient's denial of personal responsibility and her refusal to accept the basic terms of effective therapy. It is necessary for the therapist to establish a viable therapeutic contract; she must confront the patient with the fact that therapy can only work on solving the patient's problems and not those of other people. Only by setting such a firm limit can constructive therapy begin.

Even though an initial firm stance may be necessary with a small minority of patients, most new patients will respond best to therapists who adopt a supportive and understanding posture. It is extremely unlikely that a therapist will need to set limits with neurotic patients. However, a proportion of personality disordered patients require firm limits at the onset of treatment. The selection of initial response styles is based upon two general factors. First, therapists must draw upon their understanding of the necessary universal experiences of all therapy patients (see chapter 2 and Potash, 1981). Second, therapists must arrive at an understanding of the particular person-process sitting in the patient's chair.

All voluntary psychotherapy patients are implicitly communicating certain facts about themselves. The most immediately cogent experiences which describe new therapy patients are they (1) are experiencing psychological pain; (2) feel that their current pain is different from their previous level of pain; (3) feel powerless to eliminate their current pain; and (4) believe the professional will help them.

Individuals do not contact psychotherapists when they are satisfied with their lives. Even the most unsophisticated person knows that psychotherapy is both lengthy and costly and therefore will not undertake this process unless she has a very good reason to do so. Consequently, when an individual visits a psychotherapist, it is for the same reason that she sees other professionals; she is hurting, and she wants it to stop. Psychological pain is the primary impetus that propels an individual to contact a therapist. However, it is not the presence of the pain alone that prompts an individual to seek therapeutic intervention as all people experience psychological pain at times in their lives. It is when the level of pain has changed that an individual decides to contact a therapist. Perhaps the pain has increased so much that it is now perceived as intolerable where it was tolerable before. Or perhaps the individual now is beginning to view her longstanding psychological pain in a new light. She may believe that she does not have to tolerate such pain any longer, *i.e.*, change for her is now possible.

Certainly it is true that psychotherapy patients feel powerless to eliminate their pain by themselves. If they felt independently capable of fixing or curing their pain, they would have no need to seek outside assistance. They contact a therapist out of a sense of desperation. They feel powerless to stop or to mitigate the level of pain which they experience. By asking for therapeutic assistance, the prospective patient expresses an implicit belief in the power of the therapist to reduce her pain. If she fundamentally believed that psychotherapy was ineffective, she would not reach out for help. Therefore, prospective patients must possess at least the strong wish for, if not the implicit belief in, a therapist's ability to help.

This atypical state of pain and the belief in therapeutic assistance induce most new patients to be primarily receptive to the therapist's intervention strategies. If a new patient disputes and wards off a therapist's attempts to be of assistance, it is necessary to inform the patient that she has a strong need to undermine any therapeutic progress. This interpretation can then be used as a prelude to describing the battle between the healthy and unhealthy sides of the self (see chapter 6).

The Initial Meeting

Terms of Address

When the new patient enters the office, the general rules for social interaction are in order: the therapist needs to introduce herself and, usually, offer to shake hands. One encounters some patients who will use the therapist's first name during the initial session. This strategy typically signals the patient's need to remove the therapist from a position of expertise and treat her as an equal. Even though therapists do not possess any higher personal value than their patients, the patient's overriding need to immediately eliminate any reference to the therapist's professional credentials may signal the beginning of a power struggle between patient and therapist. Therapeutic interaction is not designed to be primarily social. Consequently, when a new patient immediately refers to her therapist by her first name, it represents a forced attempt at the social and a diminution of the essentially professional interaction.

In contrast, formality is a necessity when working in a clinic or hospital setting. At these facilities, one usually treats patients with severe psychopathology, some of whom have strong acting-out potential and others who manifest behaviors reflecting strong transference issues. Patients with severe pathology usually find it difficult to recognize and maintain personal boundaries. Consequently, professional contact with these and all patients needs to be carefully restricted to the office and not extended beyond the professional setting. In the initial meeting with these clinic or hospitalized patients, it is therefore necessary to create an atmosphere replete with professionalism. By restricting the initial introduction to the use of title and last name, the appropriate tone is set.

Novice psychotherapists often have strong needs to be liked by their patients and insist on being addressed by their first names. Doing so ignores the fact that many patients need to maintain interpersonal distance from the unknown therapist in order to feel safe. This need for safety is very common among individuals who suffer from personality disorders as most of these patients experience major difficulties in interpersonal relationships. Many of them feel invaded by other people; some are terribly frightened by others and need to maintain a distance, which they achieve by being basically aloof; still others overstep boundaries and need to be shown how to respect distance. When a therapist demands that her patients address her by her first name, the therapist is placing her prepotent need to be liked over the therapeutic needs of the patient.

Novice psychotherapists may erroneously assume that the use of a title or last name prevents a close relationship from developing between patient and therapist. The title "Doctor" can elicit a host of different reactions; it is as likely to conjure up the image of a warm practitioner as easily as it may elicit the image of a reserved, detached individual. Correspondingly, pragmatic-existential therapists are not engaged in hierarchical power relationships when they designate the population they service as "patients" rather than as "clients." The words "patient" and "client" do have somewhat different connotations, well documented by Rogers (1950). "Client" implies that the individual receiving therapeutic services is a person who experiences power and who evaluates the services that the therapist offers.

However, the use of the term "client" would distort both the regressed and significantly depressed patients who strongly resist making contact with a therapist. Indeed, the psychotherapeutic task in working with such individuals is to help them progress to where they can own the power associated with the word "client." Many outpatients as well lack feelings of entitlement, so to consider them "clients" is to misrepresent their own experiential processes. These individuals do not experience the freedom and control entailed by the word "client." As they progress in psychotherapy, these patients begin to own their personal power, can start to contradict and disagree with their therapists and then acquire the status of "clients."

The term "patient" is the better generic word to describe all individuals who receive therapeutic services. When the person receiving therapeutic services is designated as "patient," a certain hierarchical relationship between "doctor" and "patient" is implicitly acknowledged. At certain times therapists must assume the authoritative position and become directive, thereby protecting their patients from extreme self-destructive behavior, as outlined in chapter 7. There is both a hierarchy of knowledge and of power which may have to be used if a patient requires hospitalization. However, there is no hierarchy of personal worth between doctor and patient. The therapist has no higher personal value than does the patient; they are equals. Therefore, it is best to refer to the person receiving therapeutic services as a "patient." Rarely, if ever, do therapists need to directly use the word "patient" with the people they see in therapy.

It is best to characterize psychotherapy as an interaction between a doctor and a patient. The title "doctor" provides the patient with the necessary safe degree of personal distance; it also acknowledges the expertise of the professional whom she is consulting. As psychotherapy proceeds over time, the relationship between "doctor" and "patient" certainly begins to change. The patient feels a greater alliance with her therapist, recognizes that she is being encouraged and supported, and perceives the professional relationship as one of growing intimacy. At that juncture, many patients may prefer to call their therapists by their first names, which can be viewed as a sign of progress.

Sometimes the course of psychotherapy is clearly revealed by the changes in how the therapist is addressed. One of my patients demonstrated this phenomenon very clearly in the way he wrote out checks to pay for therapeutic services. At first, all checks were made out to Dr. Potash; after a few months the checks were written to Dr. H. Potash, then to Dr. Herbert Potash, then to Herb Potash and finally to Herb Potash, Ph.D. The patient changed his perceptions from initially viewing me as a distant professional devoid of personal identity, to later being a professional acquaintance, and then to functioning as his friend. In the last phase of therapy I finally was acknowledged as both his friend and a professional.

Preliminary Dialogue

Even during the social introductions the therapist has already begun to assess the level of distress the patient is experiencing. This assessment focuses both upon nonverbal cues, such as body language and voice tone, as well as upon the direct statements of the patient. If the patient appears to be under acute distress, some supportive comment is often the most useful place to begin. Statements such as "This must be very difficult for you" or "Take your time" often help the patient feel understood and able to begin the dialogue.

The first question for a therapist to raise is "How did you come to see me?" This is basically a two-fold question as it asks why the patient has chosen to enter therapy as well as how the patient came to choose this particular therapist. Often the patient will acknowledge a particular referral source who is the important link between this patient and the therapist. For moving on to substantial therapeutic dialogue, it is preferable to use a question like "What may I do for you?" This question immediately alerts the patient to the therapist's intention to be of assistance, focuses the patient's attention upon her need for help and enables her to begin to describe the nature of her current difficulties.

Beginning the Assessment Process

As the patient is describing what brought her into therapy, the therapist begins to collect preliminary information necessary for a fuller assessment. The patient's initial telephone comments may have led the therapist to generate certain diagnostic hypotheses, which may be either confirmed or rejected through the expanded dialogue. Certainly, the therapist generates additional hypotheses about the patient once the first meeting takes place. The therapist also attends to the patient's manner of dress, nature of eye contact and hand shake, as well as to the patient's general demeanor.

Noting the patient's style of dress provides important information. Since the date of the session was usually established a few days earlier, the patient has had opportunity to decide how to dress for the session. The patient's attire and appearance informs the therapist of the degree to which she is attempting to make a good impression on the therapist. The patient who tries to make a good impression by dressing well owns some sense of personal power. The well-dressed patient may still be personality disordered as the good external appearance can be an attempt to mask the internal self-hatred. Correspondingly, a patient who has taken few pains with her appearance is likely to be depressed, have low self-esteem, or be angry and resentful for needing help. This image, too, may be an early signal that this patient is personality disordered. These tentative hypotheses must be tempered with the realization that therapists often see patients immediately before or after their working day, where the patients have basically been in work clothes. When such is the case, the therapist still can see signs of how the patients view themselves and their possible attempts to influence others in their working world through their attire.

As the patient begins to describe her reason for making an appointment, the therapist attends to and assesses both her verbal and nonverbal communications. The patient's body posture and voice tone can indicate her emotional state. Depression is usually revealed through low voice tone and short verbalizations, while anxiety is often shown through rapid speech, fidgeting and a high-pitched voice. Effective therapists are particularly attentive to an assessment of the degree to which the patient attempts to make contact with them. It is important to discover the type of connection the patient wants: is she entreating, requesting answers, demanding sympathy, or is she withdrawn, depressed or evasive?

The most important determination to make during the first session is to what degree the patient feels out of control and helpless for excessive helpless feelings may warrant active intervention strategies. To some degree, all psychotherapy patients have experienced significant futility as their entry into psychotherapy affirms they feel unable to solve their own problems. Although the pain is present, it is not always directly visible or even verbalized. As a result, the pragmatic-existential therapist must look beyond the patient's words to assess the degree to which the patient feels overwhelmed and in need of very direct assistance.

In order to clearly acknowledge to another person that one feels desperate, a person must strongly believe that others can and will be of assistance to them. Some individuals may feel desperate and wish for assistance but do not have much faith that they will be helped. Correspondingly, they will not give any strong indications of being in intense pain. Other individuals, those who pride themselves on being in control of their lives, will be loathe to reveal a sense of desperation. For these latter patients, the therapist must attend to nonverbal cues such as voice tone, posture, and difficulty in sustaining eye contact in order to help ascertain the depth of the patients' pain.

Pragmatic-existential therapists assess both the degree of pain which the patient is experiencing as well as the degree to which the patient can continue to tolerate this pain. These practitioners evaluate whether their patients are in serious crisis, and they then adopt different types of intervention strategies that should prove most helpful in each particular case. The therapist directs the dialogue in the initial therapy so she can determine the patient's most immediate needs. The therapist first discovers whether the patient is in immediate crisis; and if such is not the case, the therapist focuses her attention on learning her patient's most urgent needs.

The new patient is experiencing at least one overriding concern that has prompted her entry into the therapist's office. The therapist must discover this primary need and then address it in some way that satisfies the patient. If the urgent need is not addressed in some fashion, the patient is not likely to return for subsequent sessions.

Personality disordered patients usually enter therapy because they are in a state of crisis, although it is quite difficult for them to articulate the extent and nature of their pain. Neurotic patients, too, may enter therapy because of a sense of crisis. However, for neurotics the pain is usually in the form of anxiety and the patient can directly specify the troubling symptomatology. The neurotic may be reassured simply by being heard. The personality disordered patient requires a much more active intervention, one that strengthens her hope.

Stated in the simplest terms, the therapist's first task is to insure that there will be a second psychotherapy session; an effective therapist will direct her energies to insure that the patient will return for this second meeting. The pragmatic-existential therapist seeks to discover the prepotent needs of the patient and then attempts to direct the initial interaction so the patient can see possible benefits in holding subsequent meetings.

Even though the voluntary therapy patient has a certain level of motivation for treatment, her interest in continuing therapy will be strongly affected during the initial session. If therapists are to deliver effective service, they must demonstrate to the patients that therapeutic dialogue will be helpful to them. It is therefore imperative that the therapist direct her energies to make patients feel the first therapeutic session is a positive experience.

As the therapist conducts an ongoing assessment of the patient during the first session, she may decide that a second session is not in order. When the therapist feels that the patient could be better served by a different professional, her dialogue needs to focus upon helping the patient accept such a referral. Also, a small number of new patients may not be suitable for any type of psychotherapy. They may prefer to receive medication or they need to be informed about the basic parameters of psychotherapy in order to make a determination as to whether these services fit their immediate needs. Some new patients may discover they are not prepared to make a commitment to psychotherapy. If such commitment is discussed during the first session, the patient will appreciate direct dialogue and may choose to reenter treatment at a later point in time.

It is unfortunate that most psychotherapy models and the written descriptions of "how to conduct initial interviews" concentrate upon the mildly disturbed or neurotic patients. Because neurotics are usually highly motivated people with good ego strength, these individuals are accustomed to delaying gratification and tolerating frustration. As patients they are likely to be very committed to participation in psychotherapy, even prior to contact with any therapist. Consequently, they are likely to tolerate an initial therapy session that is standardized and depersonalized. Such interviews, which often are devoid of significant feedback from therapists, rarely will impede a neurotic patient's successful psychotherapy.

On the other hand, patients with personality disorders have poor frustration tolerance, hold little hope for a successful psychotherapeutic experience, and are likely to be minimally involved at the onset of the therapeutic process. It is necessary for therapists to be very active in the first session and direct their energies toward making a good initial contact with these patients to insure that there will be a second session. A therapist needs to quickly prove her worth to a personality disordered patient.

To establish a meaningful connection with the personality disordered patient, the pragmatic-existential therapist conducts an especially focused assessment. Like most other therapists, she seeks to discover the nature and range of the patient's problems, which may then lead her to formulate a tentative DSM diagnosis. However, she specifically tries to discover the nature of the patient's participation in her world and how she succeeds and fails. Once the therapist tentatively understands the patient's destructive experiences and behaviors, she can formulate particular intervention strategies which will increase the patient's successes and reduce her failures.

During the first meeting with a patient the pragmatic-existential therapist tries to ascertain what style of interaction will be most helpful to each particular patient. The assessment here concerns the therapist's overt level of activity and method of communication. The therapist needs to know whether she can deliver the most effective service by being quite verbal or by being primarily silent. She also attempts to discover whether it would be best to attempt empathic communication or be more reserved in her style.

One of the first, and often the best, ways to effectively connect with a patient is through an empathic response. A comment such as "That must have been very difficult for you" represents an attempt to connect with the patient on a feeling level. It is very important to note how the patient responds to the warmth of the therapist. If the patient recoils or seems uncomfortable (*e.g.*, by moving back in her chair), these actions lead the therapist to change her style and provide the patient with more distance. As the therapy proceeds, the therapist can discover whether the patient's need for distance is characterological (and warm responses are contraindicated) or if the patient simply needed significant distance during the first therapeutic encounter.

Most patients, and indeed most humans, need to feel that other people can sense and share in their pain. Once it is apparent that the patient is appreciative of empathic comments, the therapist feels encouraged to continue communicating at that level of feeling. Consequently, supportive comments are crucial ways of making initial positive contact with the patient. Patients need to feel understood; empathic comments effectively convey this understanding.

When a patient exhibits a particularly high level of despair, it can be helpful to make a supportive comment such as "You have shown great courage by making contact with a therapist." It is useful to expand this message by stating that people who deny their problems and pretend that everything is fine are in worse condition than those who have the courage to ask for assistance. These comments affirm that the patient was wise to seek professional help.

The pragmatic-existential therapist also recognizes that empathic responses, while usually helpful, will be contraindicated when working with very depressed personality disordered patients. The patient does not need to hear that the therapist, too, would feel overwhelmed if she had to face the patient's difficulties. Rather, such patients need to become aware of the therapist as a powerful healing agent. Depressed patients feel so distraught by their difficulties that they need to draw upon the strength of the therapist in order to begin work on their problems.

It is counterproductive for therapists to adopt one interactive style and use it with all patients. The therapist needs to be flexible enough to change styles to meet the immediate needs of each particular patient. Even though expressions of therapeutic power are helpful when working with severely depressed patients, the pragmatic-existential therapist recognizes that other patients feel very threatened at entering treatment. Because personality disordered patients are so intimidated, the sensitive therapist presents herself as mild mannered and unassuming. This stance reduces the patient's anxiety level and makes it more possible to develop a healthy therapeutic alliance.

Through each of these interactive styles the therapist seeks to demonstrate her professional expertise. The sooner the therapist can find a way of connecting with the patient, the more likely it is that the patient will find the interaction rewarding. The new patient needs to believe that this first session is beneficial if she is going to return for a second meeting. Accordingly, when the patient senses an interpersonal connection or has the feeling that the therapist really understands her problems or leaves the session feeling reassured, she is likely to continue in treatment.

It may also be necessary to provide some patients with particular interpretations, such as a different perspective about problems or a preliminary insight as an anchor for future discussions. For example, some personality disordered patients may describe events in which they were victimized or abused but minimize the significance of the encounters. When a therapist labels such behavior as abusive, the patient may initially be startled, but she is also quite likely to believe that the therapist will be a protective and helpful person. When a therapist provides a different and more realistic view of her patient's difficulties, the patient begins to recognize the potential value of treatment.

In summary, the psychotherapist endeavors to make the following determinations during the first therapy session: (1) the degree of the patient's pain; (2) the most pressing needs of the patient; and (3) which intervention strategies have the most positive effect in meeting the patient's needs to move toward greater mental health.

Dealing With Patient's Expectations

When new patients have had no previous personal therapeutic experiences, it is very important to ask how they believe psychotherapy works. New patients often have many misconceptions about the therapeutic process and will feel confused, disappointed or angry if therapists fail to meet their assumed expectations. The pragmatic-existential therapist will simply explain how the therapeutic process unfolds and answer all of the questions patients raise about the process. Patients also should be encouraged to continue questioning throughout the course of therapy. Through these actions, the therapist implicitly affirms that the patient has the capacity to make rational judgments and effectively evaluate the information provided by the therapist.

If the therapist discovers that the patient has been in therapy before, she must inquire how the previous therapy helped or failed to meet her expectations. These questions make it possible to clarify both the nature of the patient's needs and the therapeutic behaviors which frustrated the patient in the past. When the patient provides a specific assessment of her previous therapy, one can evaluate those complaints and then ascertain whether it is possible to provide more effective therapeutic strategies and styles. When patients complain about certain behaviors of their previous therapists, it is vital to set a different tone at the onset of the new therapy experience.

One effective way of providing the patient with a different therapeutic experience is to make a specific contract with the patient whereby the patient is asked to immediately state any discomfort caused by the therapist's behavior. Such a contract expresses the therapist's respect for the patient, attempts to make the patient verbalize rather than hide her feelings of resentment, and fundamentally strengthens the therapeutic alliance. This particular agreement is a division of the more general contract for therapy that is negotiated at the end of the first therapeutic hour.

Special Needs of the Personality Disordered Patient

Therapists need to be the main advocates of positive mental health for their personality disordered patients. They cannot assume a neutral stance in their work. They are well aware of fundamentally destructive behaviors, and it is a legitimate part of their province to tell a patient to desist from abusing alcohol and drugs, to practice safe sex, or to stop provoking employers. The therapist also needs to clearly point out any destructive relationships which are injurious to the patient's positive mental health; the therapist must also inform the patient of available healthy alternatives.

When a pragmatic-existential therapist assumes this authoritative position, she is beginning to function as the healthy therapeutic parent. At times it is necessary to be directive as the therapist needs to counteract the self-hatred which is the core issue for personality disordered patients. At the beginning of treatment, the therapist cannot expect the patient to act independently out of self-love. The therapist must function as the clear voice of positive mental health and hope that her advocacy will ultimately become internalized by the patient.

Even though the pragmatic-existential therapist will be firm at times in setting limits upon destructive behaviors, she also recognizes that each patient alone must make the complex value decisions that set the course of a life. It is a violation of the therapist's role to tell a patient what career to choose or whom they should marry. Such interventions represent an invasion of the patient's boundaries and a refusal to accept the patient's fundamental responsibility to create her own life style.

A pragmatic-existential therapist is particularly concerned with establishing a clear boundary between functioning as the advocate for the patient's positive mental health yet not interfering with the patient's fundamental right to make personal choices. If a therapist fails to specify destructive behaviors, her patient will once again experience contact with a parental figure who does not provide necessary guidance and structure.

By functioning as the healthy therapeutic parent, the pragmatic-existential therapist is invested in actively helping her patient to further individuate. She will also be partial to her patient and, as a result, will advocate that her patient's needs be satisfied through the patient's interactions with others. Certainly the therapist will maintain a high sense of ethical responsibility and find ways to intervene if her patient acts in destructive ways toward other people. However, when working with a couple, a family or with a group, the therpaist cannot function as a particular advocate for one patient's needs. She must be fundamentally protective of all her patients in such interactions, for any sign of partiality when working with multiple patients spells disaster.

Some patients may enter therapy because a spouse has threatened divorce unless the patient makes significant behavioral changes. It is not possible to conduct viable therapy by establishing goals to please a third party. Rather, the pragmatic-existential therapist sets a different tone during the initial interview. She states a willingness to work in the patient's best interests, through helping the patient to make changes the *patient* considers desirable. The therapist can also inform the patient of possible changes that may further alienate her spouse. With this direct strategy, the therapist advocates for the patient and strengthens her independent motivation for treatment. Defining therapeutic goals in this manner makes it possible to strengthen the patient's need for personal growth.

A few personality disordered patients initially enter the therapist's office with a belligerent attitude. Because voluntary entry into therapy alone attests to a certain level of commitment on the part of the patient, it is counterproductive to force a verbal acknowledgement from a reluctant individual. The fundamental goal with all patients is to build a therapeutic alliance in order for treatment to continue; to demand that a patient respond in ways that chiefly satisfy the therapist's needs will necessarily undermine the potential alliance. Consequently, if a new patient voices skepticism about the therapeutic process, it is far more productive to support the skepticism rather than to directly challenge it. Statements like "I can understand why you do not believe this process will work, because you have no proof that it will" or "I do not expect you to believe in therapy now; what I hope is that you give it a try" are effective and reasonable responses to a patient's doubts. Healthy skepticism is actually a positive sign in a patient. There is no legitimate reason for patients to have blind faith in an unknown therapist or in the psychotherapeutic process, especially when the major figures in the patient's life have typically been destructive. When patients are encouraged to monitor and evaluate their own psychotherapy, the probability of ongoing resistance to treatment is significantly reduced.

The Therapeutic Contract

At the end of the first hour of psychotherapy, it is advisable to ask the new patient if she will accept a three or four session trial period before she makes a firm commitment to the process. A patient needs some time to decide whether she has found the right therapist. By asking the patient to reflect on and evaluate both the therapist and the process, the pragmatic-existential therapist again is affirming the patient's capacity to reason and make choices. It is premature to expect a patient to make a full commitment to work with a therapist on the basis of one hour's contact. The patient also should be informed that some therapists work best with certain kinds of people, and that effective therapy draws heavily upon the interpersonal relationship between therapist and patient. It is, therefore, imperative that a patient find a therapist with whom she is comfortable in order for her to receive maximum assistance.

Offering a three or four session assessment period serves three major functions. First, it increases the likelihood that the patient will return for another session, as she has not been forced to make a long term commitment to therapy. Second, the patient's power to make choices (a basic existential truth) is affirmed and her sense of powerlessness is implicitly challenged by suggesting that the patient evaluate the therapist. Third, asking the patient to conduct such an assessment admits the therapist's own human fallibility and demonstrates that respected, highly-functioning individuals can be willing to acknowledge their own imperfections.

By encouraging the patient to make such decisions, the therapist begins to diminish the hierarchical relationship that most patients have experienced when dealing with authority figures. Once again, the pragmatic-existential therapist thereby affirms that the hierarchical relationship exists only in terms of professional expertise. The patient is regarded as capable of independently making rational choices and evaluations.

In a few instances the therapist needs to state that the trial assessment period is for both the therapist and the patient. In other words, the therapist also must determine whether she is the right practitioner for a particular patient. Informing the patient that she, too, is being assessed is necessary only if the therapist senses a potential problem. It is important to alert patients to the possibility of referral elsewhere once the therapist sees a potential conflict. In some cases, the therapist may even need to specify where the source of potential difficulty lies, enabling both therapist and patient to address and to solve the problem that exists between them. However, at other times it may be more beneficial to give nonspecific reasons to the patient such as "This doctor works best with the kinds of problems that you have identified, and that is why I suggest you see this doctor."

Therapists refer patients to other practitioners when they sense negative countertransferential feelings. They also need to recognize that certain patients may work better in other modalities; therefore, they must be willing to make referrals to practitioners who are better suited to the particular needs of those patients.

Setting the terms and conditions for psychotherapy is one of the first ways therapists demonstrate their own sense of power and competence to the patient. Therapists know which basic conditions of therapy are acceptable (*i.e.*, regular attendance at scheduled meetings, advanced notice of cancellations) and which behaviors are unacceptable. These rules need to be communicated in ways that are authoritative yet neither hostile nor apologetic. Both the voice tone and overt speech of the pragmatic-existential therapist should demonstrate a belief in the efficacy of the therapeutic process. Such therapeutic actions bolster the personality disordered patient's faith in the process as well.

The first session should conclude with a restatement affirming the therapist's tentative understanding of the patient's problems. These comments need not be in the nature of in-depth analysis but can simply reveal either some empathic understanding or the therapist's positive feeling about working with the patient.

Logistics of Meetings

After the summary, the actual logistics of meeting times need to be discussed. Most personality disordered patients have been so extensively damaged that it is wise to suggest biweekly sessions. Therapy usually works three times as fast when biweekly rather than once a week. Almost all patients would profit from meeting at an accelerated pace, except for those who are terrified by intimate contact; however, limitations of both time and money prevent most people from affording twice-a-week therapy. If the patient can meet for biweekly sessions but is not immediately amenable to such an arrangement, it is better to allow the patient to begin with the reduced pace that she prefers. Again, it is crucial to demonstrate one's respect for the patient by deferring to her judgment.

In some instances the new patient is in a serious crisis and must be seen more often than once a week, at least at the onset of treatment. The therapist has to clearly tell the patient this heightened intensity of meetings is necessary. Even though financial considerations may make it impossible for the patient to maintain such commitment over a long period of time, the patient needs to accept this intensified pattern until she is more in control. The therapist cannot work at a reduced frequency of meetings when she believes it will result in ineffective treatment. One's professional responsibility mandates the establishment of a contract that does not violate the therapist's sense of correct treatment.

The final part of the contract necessitates a discussion of fees, insurance reimbursement and methods of payment. Because pragmatic-existential therapists encourage patients to accept responsibility for themselves and their actions, their responsibility can be directly encouraged through prompt payment of therapy bills. Not only does prompt payment affirm the patient's beliefs that she is receiving valued service, but it also minimizes friction between the patient and therapist. The financial dimension of therapy cannot be overlooked, but it should not become a central issue in treatment. Therefore, it is preferable for the therapist to turn that responsibility completely over to the patient. Following usual policies, therapists need to complete an initial insurance form for most patients; however, all subsequent bills and insurance forms can be taken care of by the patient. This kind of arrangement keeps the major financial responsibilities where they belong, upon the patient.

Finally, a therapist must explain her method of dealing with missed appointments. The simplest strategy is to request 24 hour notice for cancellation and state that payment is expected if the patient does not provide advance notification. After describing this policy, it is important to ask if the patient has any problems with the procedure. All too often therapists are so strongly invested in making sure of payment for each scheduled appointment that they alienate and ultimately lose some of their patients. There are emergencies which legitimately prevent patients from attending scheduled appointments, and patients should not be held financially liable for natural emergencies.

Effective therapy begins during the first session as it sets the tone for a working alliance between patient and therapist. Pragmatic-existential therapists develop such an alliance by first focusing upon understanding the nature of the patient's needs; this then enables them to encourage their patients to continue with the therapeutic process. The active stance which the therapist assumes with personality disordered patients is necessary to sustain the patient's motivation to continue with treatment. The aforementioned first session goals and procedures may not be accomplished in all occasions; however, as long as the therapist retains the primary goal of insuring a second therapy session, she is likely to be successful in her initial encounter with her patients.

Nine:
The Early Stages of Therapy
and Short-Term Work

In the beginning stages of therapy psychotherapists attempt to acquire a full understanding of their patients and their patients' problems. Pragmatic-existential therapists, however, seek a particular form of understanding—the knowledge of patients as experiential processes; this is used to guide their therapeutic work. Like all other therapists, pragmatic-existentialists convey their understanding of patients through both nonverbal cues and dialogue, including reflection, requests for clarification and formulation of tentative hypotheses. By expressing a tentative understanding of their patients' experiences, pragmatic-existential therapists enable their patients to see themselves and their problems in a different light. When patients accept such therapeutic feedback, they alter their perceptions of themselves and simultaneously recognize these changed perceptions as signs of progress. The therapeutic alliance between patient and therapist becomes strengthened each time that such positive changes occur.

The basic format and style of the therapeutic interaction is established in the early phases of psychotherapy. The pragmatic-existential therapist will adjust his methods of communication until he finds the most beneficial way of interacting with each patient. The shifts in methods of communication are again based upon the expanded understanding of the patient. The intentions of the pragmatic-existential therapist remain clear—to convey his understanding of the patient in ways that will encourage the patient to further expand his experiences and ultimately to change his behavior. The patient begins to move in positive directions during the early phase of therapy. In the middle and late stages of psychotherapy, these changes are intensified and reach to the core of the patient's personality structure.

All too frequently psychotherapy is conducted on a time limited basis, and further progress through long-term therapy is prevented. Extended psychotherapy is the best way to assist individuals whose psychological development has been seriously impaired. Individuals suffering from personality disorders cannot be provided with quick solutions for their long-standing difficulties. While it is possible to develop some successful therapeutic interventions with very damaged people, these strategies focus upon creating solutions for circumscribed problems. Profound assistance for such patients requires altering the underdeveloped and damaged core of their personality structures. These extensive changes cannot be accomplished in short-term work. Consequently, short-term therapy is not the treatment of choice for personality disordered individuals, even though it may become the treatment by necessity.

A number of factors currently restrict many patients' psychotherapy to short-term treatment. Numerous county, state and federally funded clinics provide only short-term treatment as a means of reducing extensive waiting lists. College counseling centers frequently offer only short-term treatment and refer designated long-term cases to private practitioners. In the private practice sphere, the duration of therapeutic treatment is increasingly dictated by insurance companies which will only provide reimbursement for limited maximum annual benefits. In particular, managed care companies frequently reimburse patients for short-term therapy only, and they demand that therapists provide focused treatment for specific problems.

Therefore, many factors totally distinct and separate from the nature and extent of a patient's psychopathology now dictate the duration of psychotherapy. Even though therapists may believe that their patients need long-term help, professional opinions do not determine the length of treatment. Rather, the nature of the patient's insurance contract or the policies of clinics often prescribe the duration of the treatment.

The pragmatic dimension in pragmatic-existentialism demands that therapists make a concession and offer time limited treatment to patients who actually would profit more from long-term therapy. At times it is necessary to conduct short-term psychotherapy with patients who suffer from serious psychopathology. The first phase of long-term treatment can be used as an effective model for short-term therapy by adding only a few modifications to the process. A model for short-term therapy is incorporated in the following description of the first phases of long-term therapy.

The Process of
Therapeutic Understanding

A pragmatic-existential therapist understands his patient first through the use of phenomenology; he attempts to know or apprehend the world as the patient sees it. The therapist adopts the patient's viewpoint, stands in his phenomenological field and uses the patient's language to share in his experiences (van den Berg, 1972). To experience the world as the patient does is to essentially become his alter ego. This form of phenomenological understanding is also the explicit stance taken in the client centered model (Rogers, 1951). Rogers considered this process of sharing the phenomenological world of the patient to be so taxing that it prevented him from maintaining his own separate perceptions of the world while in the presence of his clients.

In contrast to Rogers, the pragmatic-existential therapist moves beyond a simple sharing in the patient's experiencing of the world and seeks a separate and objective understanding of the patient as an experiential process. Specifically, he draws upon the insights of Binswanger and seeks to understand the patient's basic meaning categories. He also utilizes the universal and general elements of understanding as basic dimensions for making "sense" of the patient as an experiencing process (Potash, 1981 and chapter 2). In so doing, the therapist is then able to anticipate the patient's reactions to future events; he already knows the primary parameters the patient regularly uses to give meaning to his experiences.

Once the therapist detects the preferred ways in which a patient makes sense of his world, the nature of the patient's subsequent experiences appear to be logical consequences of these perceptions. For example, the seemingly bizarre experiences of the paranoid patient necessarily follow from the meaning categories he has utilized. If a patient believes there is a plot against him, it is logical that he would be suspicious, hostile and noncommunicative with others. His subsequent beliefs and behavior reflect his need to protect himself against the anticipated hostility of others.

Psychotherapy patients do not initially recognize that they use meaning categories or frames of reference inappropriate for a particular situation. They attempt to escape from the pain of being "thrown" (Binswanger, 1963) through using narrow and constricted ways to view the world. However, in sustaining this rigid and unidimensional way of viewing the world, patients will interpret diverse events with a meaning dimension that does not logically apply to all situations. For example, when a patient sees himself as deficient and inadequate and approaches all life situations with that point of view, he will interpret all events as further evidence of the validity of this belief. Whenever he experiences failure, his lack of success simply confirms his perceptions. If he is successful in some endeavors, these successes are attributed to luck rather than to skill. When another person responds favorably to him, he will either consider the other person ignorant of the real truth about his basic deficiencies (and believes the other will ultimately discover it), or he labels the other person also as inadequate and deficient. The classic Groucho Marx joke, "I'd never join a country club that would have me as a member," concisely expresses this latter point of view.

Psychotherapists who have rich personal lives, sufficient professional training and have successfully undergone personal psychotherapy possess a full range of meaning categories which they can bring to bear in understanding their patients as experiential processes. Effective pragmatic-existential therapists will thereby be able to understand their patients' experiences through empathic participation and by drawing upon their own personal and clinical sensitivities.

Some of the diagnostic skills used by pragmatic-existential therapists were present long before they began the process of professional training. These are the independent skills of people who function successfully in the interpersonal world. People with these skills learned which behavior patterns alienate people and which elicit positive responses by successfully coping with the interpersonal world. This knowledge is used not only to diagnose problems but also to select behavior strategies for initiating constructive personality changes.

This knowledge is also behaviorally expressed in seemingly simple acts such as the posture the therapist assumes in his chair. With some patients, a therapist sits forward, attempting to minimize the distance between therapist and patient; with other patients he remains far back in the chair and maintains distance to make his patient feel safer. At different points in the dialogue, the therapist will move forward to the edge of his seat; at other times he will move further back in his chair. Such shifts in postures are not a result of deliberate reflection but occur because the therapist as prereflective consciousness "knows" which patients will appreciate closeness and which patients will be threatened by a perceived violation of their space.

When psychotherapists are effective and well-individuated humans, they know how to succeed in the world; therefore they will understand how and why their patients do not succeed in vital life areas. Having personal experiences in successfully achieving goals and making good interpersonal connections are invaluable assets for guiding a therapist's interaction with his patients.

The pragmatic-existential therapist recognizes that the rigid and repeated use of inappropriate meaning categories is a major ideational process producing and perpetuating psychopathology. Once the therapist can detect the overuse of an inappropriate meaning category, he tries to understand why the individual restricts his sense of the world. While the general answer to this question remains the dread of being "thrown," a more specific answer is needed. The external world is particularly threatening to personality disordered patients because as children, they were deeply injured by destructive parental figures. They internalized such destructive messages thereby creating a self-hating force in their personality structures. These patients are threatened both from without and from within; they attempt to protect themselves against both types of threats through rigid perceptions of self and of others.

To better understand the ways in which rigid unidimensional meaning categories can constrict one's perceptions of the world, we can consider a particular example. A female college student who may primarily identify herself as a feminist would be sensitive to sexist views of the world. If she enrolls in one of my classes, she may hear and perceive my lectures as the verbalizations of a male. I am male and I lecture, which affirms that this student is not fundamentally distorting reality. At times it is true that my comments on a specific issue will reflect that fact that I have experienced life from a male perspective. However, my lectures will be better understood as the communications of a professor speaking to a class rather than as that of a male speaking to a female. If this student utilizes both of these meaning dimensions and listens to both the professor and to the male, she will obtain a fuller and deeper understanding of my communication pattern. Binswanger (1963) stated that people do not use two meaning categories simultaneously but rather alternate among several categories. If the student confines her attention to the use of only one meaning category, she will most likely perform best on her examinations if she classified me as the professor rather than as a male. Of course, if she increased her categories used for understanding (seeing me as older, or white or empathic), these could all further enrich her understanding of my lectures.

If we ask "Why does she restrict herself to the use of one meaning category?" we would again say that she feels highly threatened. Suppose that I were to begin communication with this student concerning her poor performance on an examination, having only the above limited information at my disposal. Because my primary hypothesis is that this woman is feeling threatened, my attempts at communication would first follow from this assumption; I would tread most carefully and be gentle in how I spoke with her.

It would be a mistake simply to tell her that she needs to listen to me in a different and fuller manner. Such a statement would, most likely, be interpreted as yet another message from a critical male; moreover, she may not know how to listen in a different manner. As I try to understand her further, I see that she has sexualized the classroom encounter. The therapist in me might wonder how often she sees nonsexual situations as sexualized. However, it would be inappropriate to raise such a question in the academic setting. If it were a therapeutic setting, it would still be an inappropriate question to raise at a time when the patient feels highly threatened as it would only make her more defensive. In addition, any empathic remark would be contraindicated because that would likely be interpreted as patronizing.

Taking the analysis a step further, this student must have a strong need to maintain distance from me, especially since she has reduced me to a one dimensional caricature (only a male and not a professor). This hypothesis leads me to determine that my best way of ultimately helping her to become a more successful student would be to first respect her need for distance.

If this student were to contact me because of her poor classroom performance, I would approach her from an existential perspective, both seeing and treating her as an equal participant in our dialogue. I would ask her to generate hypotheses concerning the reasons she performed below her expectations. This question is designed to help her recognize that she has the ultimate responsibility of understanding and facing her academic problems. Furthermore, such a question reflects my implicit acknowledgment that she already has the capability of gaining insight into herself through reflection.

If she is unable to raise any tentative hypotheses about her difficulties, I would ask a leading but indirect question that might help her to consider other possibilities—"Is there anything about my style and method of teaching that you find difficult?" Such a question allows her to maintain the initial negative feelings she might have toward me; but the question demonstrates that I am not just a critical male authority figure as I am trying to help. If she can directly state what she found disturbing about my teaching methods, I would ask her how I might change in order to make it easier for her to perform at a higher level. These intervention strategies all follow from my hypothesis that this woman is feeling highly threatened. The questions are designed to keep the discussions exclusively on an intellectual level so that they do not arouse any problematic emotions. Because the student is meeting to discuss academic issues, the interaction has to remain focused upon school performance; I would not venture into deeper personal issues.

This non-therapeutic example illustrates that the implicit understanding of "the other" leads one to use certain intervention strategies. The pragmatic-existential therapist does not have a pre-set agenda of ways to respond to patients. Rather, through his life, academic training and professional experiences, he has gained a better sense of ways to respond to particular situations, which can be used in both therapeutic and non-therapeutic dialogues. When conducting therapy, the pragmatic-existentialist typically responds immediately to his patients with comments from a prereflective consciousness. In a few instances he may use deliberate reflection and consciously decide exactly what he wants to say. His therapeutic responses are, therefore, usually intuitive and are based upon his apprehension of the patient. Only when therapists have the time and occasion to reflect and explain the reasons for their comments will they respond as reflective consciousness. At those points they can usually also furnish logical explanations for their immediate and intuitively-based remarks. When they use this reflective mode, they can acknowledge the connections between their intuitive responses and the underlying personal and professional knowledge which guided them.

Because an intuitive understanding of the patient's needs will guide the interactions of the pragmatic-existential therapist, he will use very contrasting response styles with different patients. These changes in therapeutic style are necessary as the therapist adjusts to complement each patient's individual needs. A therapeutic model which advocates behavioral constancy on the part of the therapist does not allow therapists to adjust their styles in order to make their patients most comfortable. When a therapist adopts a rigid means of treating all patients, he, too, is not allowing himself to be-in-the-world or to be the process of change that characterizes the fundamental human condition. As a result, he demands that the patient conform and adapt to the therapist's way of being. This demand is counterproductive as it reenacts the personality disordered patient's early experiences. Historically, this patient had to satisfy the needs of destructive parental figures who could or would not adapt themselves to satisfy the needs of their child.

As the therapist changes his style of response with different patients, there may be times when he occasionally peppers his speech with four-letter words. Therapists primarily need to maintain professional decorum and use well articulated speech to demonstrate that verbal skills are an invaluable way of being effective in the world. Nonetheless, with some patients it can be particularly helpful to minimally use vulgar language, especially in the early phases of therapy. Such strong language gives emotional expression to situations which the patient may have described in a bland and dissociated way. When working with adolescents, it also is helpful to use direct reflection in order to mirror the patient's verbal style.

These comments demonstrate that the therapist is willing to communicate at his patient's level. On the other hand, pragmatic-existential therapists never use vulgar language with those patients who maintain a rigid moral code and find such speech offensive.

When working with a patient who utilizes intellectualization as a defense, therapists may find it helpful to speak in a non-intellectualized manner. I recall working with one patient whose speech was replete with the most infrequently used multisyllabic words in the dictionary. Therefore, when I spoke to him, I was as direct and simple in my choice of words as possible, commenting at the level of feelings rather than at the level of high powered verbiage. Only after a year of work did the patient begin to communicate with a more casual level of dialogue. This change in his manner of speech was one factor that led him to acquire a larger and more diverse circle of friends.

Pragmatic-existential therapists also change their response manner when working with patients in varied age groups. For example, adolescent and young adult patients have a pressing developmental need to become independent adults. Even though these patients are satisfying their desires to participate in psychotherapy, this particular need for assistance is in basic conflict with their healthy need to function independently. As a result, the therapist must minimize instances in which he expresses himself as an authority figure. Such comments undermine the patient's basic needs to be a self-sufficient decision maker.

Because late adolescent patients have strong needs to be separate and independent, many of them will choose to terminate psychotherapy before all therapeutic goals are realized. If the therapist attempts to prolong treatment in order to achieve full problem resolution, he will undermine the patient's developmental needs. Long-term therapy should continue only for those adolescent patients who are so fixated at earlier developmental levels that they have not yet experienced powerful growing pains. When these patients progress to the point that they, too, need to be independent, it is advisable not to interfere with their desire to separate from their therapists.

As pragmatic-existential therapists respect the strong need for independence that is present in late adolescent patients, they correspondingly will minimize expressions of their own expertise. Because the existential perspective, that humans are necessarily creatures of choice, is quite consonant with the developmental needs of this group of patients, pragmatic-existential therapists can be particular adept in working with this population. In the practice of such therapy the patient is reminded that he always has options. As the therapist explains the choices and helps the patient see the relevant pros and cons, the patient becomes better able to select the healthier alternatives. The therapist encourages the patient's capacity to reason and thereby assists the patient in taking full responsibility for his life.

A number of young adult and adolescent patients may enter therapy because they are acting out against controlling parental figures. Even though their forms of rebellion are ultimately self-destructive, the rebellion still helps these individuals assert their own sense of self. As a result, therapists must establish a firm therapeutic contract with these patients that has well defined limits. When such limits are established at the onset of therapy (no drugs, only safe sex, 24 hour notice of cancellation), the therapist avoids power struggles over these issues.

If the contract does not cover necessary limits, these adolescent patients will often perpetuate self-destructive behavior patterns. The therapist will feel forced to become the controlling adult, and his attempts to stop destructive behaviors will most likely prove unsuccessful. If the therapist believes it necessary to attempt control with such patients, he will essentially be replicating the behavior of the patient's parents. This, in turn, will again trigger rebellion and self-destructive behavior on the part of the patient.

When the late adolescent patient agrees to a clearly defined therapeutic contract, the therapist is then able to refer to the terms of the contract whenever the patient attempts to act-out. It becomes possible to point out objectively that the patient is violating his agreement without allowing the discussion to evolve into a power issue. In fact, the therapist can interpret such behaviors as the actions of the self-hating part of the patient's personality structure.

Defiant adolescents expect adults to manipulate them and to lie to them; therefore, they believe adults cannot be trusted. Also, adolescents are continually bombarded by the eruptions of their own strong feelings. They are self-absorbed, which is another developmental phenomenon. Because it is so difficult for adolescents to see beyond themselves, they believe that other people react in the same ways that they themselves react. They think that other individuals, *i.e.*, adults, must also be overrun with the same strong emotions.

Staid therapists, those who attempt to maintain an unruffled professional role with masked personal feelings, will have major problems in developing good relationships with adolescent and young adult patients. These self-absorbed adolescents, riddled with pain, cannot believe there are people who exhibit no personal problems. These patients themselves lack control over their disruptive feeling states and hope to find someone with power who can take control. However, if such a patient senses that the therapist is not a fully emotive person, he will have major difficulties in trusting him. Instead, many adolescent patients will make it their goal to demonstrate that their therapists are not the understanding and unemotional people they seem to be. Such adolescents will frequently instigate, irritate and rebel until they elicit any genuine emotion from the therapist.

Access to one's emotions is the key to being a successful psychotherapist. Knowing what one feels and understanding how the patient's actions have aroused these feelings are basic sources of important diagnostic information about the patient. Psychotherapists are representative of all other humans in that the emotions aroused in the therapist are likely to be the same emotions aroused in others who interact with this patient. Knowing these feelings informs the therapist how the patient deals with his interpersonal world. Therapists can immediately apprehend how and why their patients lack success in some of their interpersonal transactions, based upon the emotions that the patient has activated.

By having access to the emotions aroused by the patient during psychotherapy, the therapist can help the patient see (1) what he did; (2) how it made the therapist feel; and (3) how such behaviors elicit similar emotions in other people. This knowledge can then lead the therapist (4) to ask the patient if he really wants to generate such feelings in others; and (5) to discover what feelings the patient would prefer to generate. Continuing this dialogue, the therapist (6) informs the patient what behavior patterns will generate these desired reactions in others; and (7) teaches or models the desired behavior patterns.

To follow the above paradigm the therapist has to be comfortable with self-disclosure and be willing to admit to the presence of negative emotions. In so doing, the therapist acknowledges that therapy is very much an interpersonal encounter and that his own emotions are important. His expressions of feelings are designed to penetrate the narcissistic preoccupation of the patient and to teach him about the emotional needs of other people.

The seven steps outlined above are best dealt with in a straightforward fashion. The therapist can directly point out the patient's actions and his own reactions and then ask if the patient wished to elicit these feelings. He will state that his own emotions are common reactions to such behaviors. By asking the patient if he wishes to elicit these feelings, he acknowledges the patient's potential power and control over his behavior.

The above communications often take place in pragmatic-existential psychotherapy. By adopting this strategy, the therapist functions as the "generalized other" and validates the interpersonal dimension of therapy. The dialogue is very rational and basically uses treatment strategies usually designated as behavioral. However, the crucial existential component of the model is expressed in step five where patients are asked to choose what sorts of power and effects they wish to have in the world. The therapist then becomes the agent of the patient and assists him in achieving his chosen goals. The therapist does not determine what is best for the patient; rather, the patient decides what is best for himself.

Directness, not evasiveness, characterizes the approach of pragmatic-existentialism. The initial contact with the patient requires a willingness to be forthright and honest. Too many schools of psychotherapy advocate that therapists should be quiet and passive in the first few sessions as a means of establishing rapport; then after rapport is established, the therapist may become more directive. However, no genuine rapport is established when the therapist role plays and is not forthright with the patient. When a therapist suddenly changes tactics and becomes directly expressive, he lacks credibility and the patient will accurately view him as deceptive. As already stated, the personality disordered patient particularly needs to have a clear and direct message from the therapist.

Directness must be present in the first session and persist throughout treatment, especially with the most problematic cases. For example, the therapist needs to become very active with the personality disordered patient who has suicidal tendencies. The therapeutic contract must be carefully negotiated, and the patient has to agree not to make any suicidal gestures while in psychotherapy. A negotiated contract decreases the occurrence of a patient's manipulations and suicidal threats.

Focusing Upon the Patient's Problems

Therapists and patients share the same immediate task at the onset of psychotherapy, which is to understand the nature and scope of the patients' problems. Although most patients have some idea of how and why they are in distress, their understanding is incomplete. As the therapist listens and acquires more information, he generates working hypotheses which provide a tentative understanding of the patient's difficulties. However, the most productive dialogue takes place when the patient can attend to and effectively describe his own experiences. These patient reports provide the necessary data for the therapeutic interaction. Therapists indirectly teach their patients the art of self-observation through both their own comments and questions.

Personality disordered patients who lack an effective self-observing process must learn to attend to their internal dialogue so they can gain awareness of the source of their difficulties. With a patient who has never previously focused or reported on his own behavior, the pragmatic-existential therapist must ask very detailed and concrete questions, designed to train the patient in self-observation. For example, the therapist will ask the patient to describe the events of the preceding day in minute detail, beginning with how he woke up (alarm clock or spontaneously) and proceeding to an account of each action undertaken. This strategy increases the patient's powers of observation and will lengthen his verbal reports.

After the personality disordered patient describes each of these events, the therapist then asks the patient to explain why he chose each particular behavior pattern. This question serves three major functions. First, it engages the patient in dialogue which is not essentially conflict related, making it easier for the patient to talk. Second, the question implicitly acknowledges that the patient always has choice in his actions. Finally, the question acquaints the patient with the fact that he has reasons for his actions; at this point he can begin to ask himself whether these reasons are, in fact, valid. Many patients will begin to see and understand themselves much better through the simple act of providing detailed self reports. Furthermore, the therapist will obtain a fuller sense of the patient's problems by hearing a description of the minutiae of the day's activities.

Another method of teaching observation and self report to personality disordered patients is to ask for descriptions of the internal processes or thoughts which occurred during specific interactions. Questions such as "What did you think about that?" or "Did that situation arouse any feelings in you?" help the patient describe the nature of his internal processes.

When a therapist asks a patient to describe the events of his day or his mental processes during different situations, he is making a significant intervention in the patient's life. Once the patient knows that he will subsequently report on his activities, he pays more careful attention to his behavior. When a patient is tempted to behave impulsively, he becomes aware that he will also have to explain this behavior to his therapist. He now has a new counteracting force in his personality structure, best described as the observing ego.

A similar phenomenon is used in certain behavioral interventions such as smoking cessation programs. Participants are first asked to record when they smoke cigarettes, and they smoke less frequently once they begin to carefully observe their own behavior. Increased self-awareness is again the first step toward increased self-control.

While it is certainly true that most patients begin therapy with some form of an observing ego already present, they have rarely had to report and describe their experiential world in any systematic manner. The necessity of transforming personal experiences into verbalizations changes the essentially private, or what Sullivan (1953) termed the parataxic experience, into a syntaxic experience where all humans share consensual meanings. In describing how they experience certain phenomena, the patients change those experiences by putting them into words. Patients may also spontaneously understand some of their distortions as they begin to listen to themselves speak.

A patient's description of experiences will be incomplete in many instances, prompting the therapist to ask for amplification. Most therapists routinely ask their patients to describe their emotional states while experiencing certain events. When a patient has no recollection of feelings in these situations, it becomes obvious that the patient is unconnected with his emotional life. Upon hearing this report, the pragmatic-existential therapist will once again draw upon his own experiences and function as the "generalized other" who knows the common emotional components of different situations.

When a personality disordered patient is unable to have access to his own emotions, the pragmatic-existential therapist may become so attuned to the natural emotions triggered by the described events that he himself will experience the feelings that were disowned by the patient. There have been moments in a therapy session when tears welled up in my eyes. I recognized that the pain I felt referred to the traumatic events in the patient's life which he had described in bland, unemotional ways. Telling the patient that I feel like crying often releases the underlying, unacknowledged pain in the patient, and he allows himself to cry.

It is usually quite instructive and helpful for the patient when the therapist functions as the generalized other and informs him of normal feelings in certain situations. It provides most patients with a completely different perspective on their problems. However, a personality disordered patient who is very unstable and must censor all emotional reactions to maintain self-control cannot tolerate the therapist's attempts to connect emotionally. It is necessary for the therapist to slowly and deliberately create an atmosphere of safety and trust before he tries to help the patient gain access to personal feelings. For example, at the onset of therapy, a patient may characterize his mother as "a wonderful person" but he may describe specific events that point to the contrary. Because the patient is strongly invested in maintaining a distorted perception of "mother," it would be counterproductive for the therapist to immediately challenge it. It is far wiser to defer the challenge of this distortion and instead proceed to a discussion of other topics where a consensus can be reached. When the therapist decides that the time is right to offer a different perspective on the patient's mother, he needs to do it gently and only after he has achieved a great deal of credibility in the patient's eyes.

It is far more important for the therapist to develop and sustain an alliance with the patient than it is for him to prove he is perceptive. The pragmatic-existential therapist continually attempts to understand the patient as process and therefore does not superimpose his own agenda upon the patient. Attention to process minimizes the phenomenon of premature interpretations. When a therapist makes an interpretation before the patient is ready to hear it, he is attempting to make the patient change in ways not immediately consonant with the process of the patient.

Patients enter psychotherapy because they feel they are not personally successful. They do not have sufficient control over their lives, and they wish assistance in reducing pain created by their failures. Throughout the treatment, the therapist must indicate that the patient can acquire the necessary skills to minimize future pain.

Depressed personality disordered patients initially need to believe that their therapist is powerful enough to provide them with the necessary skills to circumvent their pain. Because these patients feel so overwhelmed and powerless, it is best to allow them belief in the therapist's omnipotence, at least until they begin to acquire their own sense of power. These patients will need to lean heavily upon their therapists in order to acquire the necessary feelings of support and strength that makes change possible.

Supportive comments that affirm a patient's power to make the necessary and important changes in his life can have strong therapeutic effects upon those patients who feel less overwhelmed. Statements like "The hardest part of therapy is getting yourself to enter the door for the first time" and "Where there is a will there is a way" are important ways of building bridges to patients. Therapists themselves who struggled with entering personal psychotherapy should certainly be able to remember their own feelings of anguish. By recalling their own past emotions, the therapists can better appreciate the current struggle which their new patients face.

When therapy is effective, the patient takes charge of his own life. In order for such control to develop, the patient must first believe in himself. As the patient begins to feel empowered, he starts to acquire the necessary resources for coping with his problems. Supportive therapists who acquaint the patients with their own underlying strengths furnish a vital component of effective therapy. Teaching the patient specific skills also provides them with a greater sense of personal empowerment. However, when a therapist first offers support and then strengthens a patient's belief in himself, the patient will acquire the necessary skills more quickly than if no underlying support was provided.

For example, I have treated several individuals in psychotherapy who were experiencing great difficulty in completing their doctoral dissertations. It was important to tell them, quite early in the therapy, that their inability to complete the dissertation was an emotional problem and not an intellectual one. By repeatedly making this point, I informed these patients that their problems could be solved. As long as they argued that completing a dissertation was beyond their mental capacities, they were not able to obtain the degree. Correctly labelling their difficulties as an "emotional" problem enabled these patients to question themselves and then discover why they were reluctant to complete their degrees.

These particular personality disordered patients did not primarily need to learn new techniques in order to work efficiently. They had been successful up to the point of the dissertation, which demonstrated they did not lack the requisite academic skills. They now needed to understand and focus upon their basic emotional problems. Each of these patients had a strong need to fail, reflecting an underlying self-hating component in the personality structure. When these patients detected the complex manifestations of their self-destructive impulses, they became empowered to fight against the self-hatred. Once they were mobilized, they were able to utilize particular techniques and continue work on their dissertations. Until the patient understands the nature and pervasiveness of his self-hatred, he will be unable to counteract its power.

A Frame of Orientation for Personality Disordered Patients

A description of the nature of psychopathology will orient patients to the therapy process and assist them in understanding themselves. People typically enter psychotherapy with little or no understanding of what comprises psychological problems. A simple explanation of the battle within the self offers an important frame of reference for focusing upon the work to be done by both therapist and patient. Furthermore, once this information is provided, the therapist can refer back to the explanation at crucial times during therapy.

The patient needs to be reminded that an important part of himself wishes to be healthy—the side that brought him into treatment and wants therapeutic assistance. He needs to be told that another part of himself has actively produced all the problems; this is the unhealthy part of his personality. The process of therapy is described as initially an attempt to understand the nature and extent of the unhealthy part. Once both therapist and patient discover how this unhealthy side operates, they together will attempt to strengthen the healthy part of the patient's personality. The pragmatic-existential therapist can state that as treatment progresses, the healthy part of the patient's personality will become strong enough to fight and control the unhealthy tendencies.

This definition of psychopathology focuses upon the internal struggle that lies at the heart of the personality disordered individual. Although this kind of struggle exists in all forms of psychopathology, it especially needs to be clearly identified for the individual with a personality disorder. Even an experienced therapist can sometimes forget that the patient's struggle is fundamentally within the self, rather than between the patient and the therapist.

When the therapist frames psychopathology in the above manner, he can then redefine resistance as the unhealthy part of the patient's personality which at times may control his behavior during therapy. Simply put, the unhealthy part of the patient is fighting the healthy part; that drama is played out through the patient's attempts to undermine the therapeutic process. It is very important for the therapist to view the patient in this bifurcated manner so that he does not interpret resistance as reflecting the essence of the patient.

If the therapist does not have this understanding, he can easily be manipulated by the unhealthy part of the patient. The self-hating dimension of the patient's personality will then gain ascendence, and the therapist in turn will be forced to function as the healthy side of the patient's personality.

For example, if the patient begins a pattern of arriving late for therapy sessions, the therapist could view this as resistance, take an authoritative position and demand that the patient arrive on time. However, this reaction is counterproductive as it fails to ally the therapist with the healthy side of the patient's personality structure. If instead the therapist asks the patient "What part of you made you late?" the patient can quickly detect that "lateness" is a consequence of the actions of his unhealthy side. A further question like "What can you do about it?" will reaffirm the alliance between the therapist and the healthy side of the patient's personality. By operating in this manner, the therapist keeps the patient aware that he is participating in an ongoing internal struggle. The therapist must not allow the internal struggle to be transformed into an interpersonal battle between patient and therapist.

While it is best to provide the above description of psychopathology as early in treatment as possible, sometimes the explanation needs to be deferred because of even more pressing issues. In the early phases of therapy the therapist may see that the patient is in immediate crisis and therefore must direct his energies to help the crisis subside. On some occasions, the therapist may even have to demand immediate behavioral changes. Such interventions are the least desired therapeutic alternatives and are used only when the patient engages in extreme self-destructive behavior. In many instances the therapist can still proceed to describe the destructive behaviors as reflections of the unhealthy side of the patient's personality. Identifying the patient's problems as a struggle between the healthy and unhealthy sides of the personality orients the patient in a manner that will best energize his wish to become healthy.

Once the patient understands his psychopathology as a battle between the healthy and unhealthy sides of his personality, the therapeutic work has a clearly defined focus. Together, therapist and patient attempt to identify which are the healthy self-affirming urges and which are the self-destructive tendencies. Understanding is the first step toward change in both experience and behavior. It is premature to expect the patient to change his behavior until he understands the workings of the self-destructive part of his personality. Only after the patient has expanded his self-awareness can he acquire effective techniques to bolster the underdeveloped healthy self.

In its early phases, therapeutic work focuses upon an exploration of the self-hating or self-destructive tendencies within the personality structure. All thoughts that are self-injurious and all behavior patterns that instill pain in the subject are considered manifestations of the unhealthy self. The therapeutic dialogue is designed to enable patients to redefine themselves so they can become identified with the healthy core of their personality. Because a personality disordered patient lacked such a self-conception prior to beginning therapy, his self-image is replete with characterizations created by the self-hating force. As a result, the personality disordered patients are often full of self-loathing and have a very negative picture of themselves and their abilities.

Understanding self-hatred is a two-fold process. First, the patient needs to detect all manifestations of these self-destructive tendencies as they occur in his experiential world. He then needs to review his early childhood upbringing in order to better understand the roots of the self-destructive tendencies. As patients begin to describe the ways they were treated by their parents, it becomes obvious there was psychological abuse or injury by a major parental figure. In most instances, these patients entered therapy lacking any such insights. Instead, they regularly minimized, rationalized or denied that they were badly treated as children or young adults. As the patient reevaluates his past and sees how he was victimized, he begins to recognize the parallel between his current self-attacking behavior and the abuse he suffered at the hands of a malevolent parental figure.

Second, the therapist interprets that the patient has internalized and now perpetuates the attacks upon himself first initiated by one of his parents. All forms of self-derogation and all behaviors which produce failure and pain are considered outgrowths of this early, destructive parent-child relationship. His internal attacks and faulty behavior patterns are seen as the workings of the self-destructive side of his personality. In the early phases of therapy, the patient learns this paradigm and then uses it to explain his psychopathology. In the longer term working phase of therapy he will see all the manifestations of self-hatred and become successful at counteracting these self-destructive tendencies.

Personality disordered patients thus acquire a different and fuller understanding of themselves in the earliest phase of therapy. This new perspective provides them with insights into their problems, enabling them to begin a successful counteraction against their self-destructive tendencies. The first signs of increased health are likely to be in the form of self-questioning in which the patient starts to label certain experiences as manifestations of self-hatred. Later in treatment, the patient will begin to change his destructive behavior patterns as well.

The alliance between patient and therapist strengths over time. The patient senses that the therapist cares about assisting him in achieving pain reduction and a more fulfilling life style. He no longer feels alone in his attempt to combat his psychopathology as it is now a collaborative effort. This process of working together slowly begins to transform the patient's perception of the therapist. Instead of seeing the therapist simply as an authority figure and therefore reminiscent of the destructive parent, the patient begins to recognize that the therapist truly wants him to individuate. In this first phase of treatment the therapist is not yet endowed with the role of healthy therapeutic parent but is beginning to assume this important function (see chapter 7).

The first phase of therapy should produce changes in how the patient experiences and understands himself. This expanded cognitive understanding is an important step toward fundamental change. However, fuller psychological health will be best attained in the working-through stages of therapy, when the patient/therapist relationship provides the full impetus for the conquest of psychopathology.

Short-Term Treatment

When the pragmatic-existential therapist must use a short-term model of treatment, he conducts the work in the same way as during the first phase of long-term therapy. That is, he will help the personality disordered patient recognize the self-destructive forces within his personality structure. By enabling the patient to see himself as containing both healthy and unhealthy components, the therapist assists the patient in taking the first steps toward achieving fuller mental health.

When therapy is limited to 20 or fewer sessions, the best approach is to focus upon the one manifestation of the self-attacking force which the patient finds especially destructive. Directing attention to one problem area allows therapy to achieve a specific level of success. The patient should choose the particular experience or behavior that he wishes to change. When the patient makes this selection, once again, the therapeutic process endorses the existential principle that each individual is both capable of and responsible for his choices.

At times it may be possible to work on two specific problem areas, although it is preferable for the therapy to focus on only one issue. When two different problems are discussed, the self-hating part of the personality may lead the personality disordered patient to vacillate between both problems and ultimately avoid solving either one.

The time-limited nature of the work necessitates focused, task-oriented treatment. However, the pragmatic-existential therapist still provides the patient with an understanding of the inner battle to be waged against the self-hating mechanism in his personality structure. The therapist can teach the patient particular techniques to assist in his inner struggle as well as how to cope more successfully with his interpersonal world. Because the therapy process is time limited, the relationship between patient and therapist is unlikely to become very intense. The therapist cannot provide extensive healthy therapeutic parenting in short-term treatment.

The pragmatic-existential therapist believes that expanding the experiential world of the patient is the necessary precursor to behavior change, whereas most focused treatment models attempt to achieve behavior change without this attention to experience. While cognitive behaviorists do attend to aspects of the experiential process, they subsume all these activities under the concept of cognition. In contrast, the existential model has a broader notion of experience. For example, it helps some personality disordered patients recognize that their posture in the world reflects a preverbal and intuitive sense of the threat posed by others. Such a hypothesis would not be made by a cognitive behaviorist.

The model of psychopathology presented above, which describes the core conflict in the personality disordered patient as conflict between powerful self-hatred and underdeveloped self-love, has both experiential and behavioral manifestations. As a result, when it is used in short-term treatment, it can be defined as a therapy which attempts to strengthen self-love and minimize self-hate in both the experiential and behavioral realms.

The pragmatic dimension of pragmatic-existential therapy makes an important contribution to the success of short-term treatment. The therapist has the capacity to shift his manner of working to accomplish practical goals. It often is necessary to work with a patient in a time limited format, and the pragmatic-existentialist is flexible enough to adapt to these realities.

The pragmatic-existential therapist specifically recognizes that maintaining an unwavering focus in short-term psychotherapy is especially advantageous with particular patients. For example, when treating a patient who uses an avoidant defensive style, it is necessary for the therapist to maintain unwavering attention on a specific issue. Also, when treating a depressed patient, the therapist must be continually active in focusing upon the problem at hand. The therapist's high activity level counteracts the patient's passivity and offers a different model for behavior. Indeed, the therapist's focus upon a particular problem can activate and energize the depressed patient.

Focused dialogue creates a particular type of relationship between patient and therapist. It minimizes intimacy and warmth and concurrentlty elevates concrete problem solving strategies to the highest priority. Such an emphasis is of especial aid to schizoid and narcissistic patients. These individuals often respond better with focus on a given task than they do with confrontation on their fundamentally negative posture in the world.

When focusing upon solving a defined problem in a time limited basis, the therapist is very much a teacher, a role which heightens the hierarchical doctor-patient relationship. The therapist takes charge of the therapy by giving it a direction in the very first session; he maintains this focus throughout the limited time of the therapy.

Time-limited psychotherapy, which demands focused attention upon a particular problem in the patient's life, cannot deal with the patient as a totality. The structure of short-term therapy where diagnostic classifications and written goals take precedence, restricts the scope of treatment. Essentially, these constrictions built into time-limited therapy models move them closer to the approach of behaviorism.

Short-Term *vs* Long-Term Treatment

Short-term therapy therefore differs from long-term treatment by maintaining a focus upon solving a particular problem rather than in attempting to alter the patient's fundamental personality structure. The pragmatic-existential approach to short-term treatment still provides the basic framework for understanding and combating psychopathology, a framework which the patient can utilize himself after the short-term treatment has ended. Short-term therapy can assist the personality disordered patient with specific problems, but it cannot address his most fundamental difficulty. For the patient to show significant improvement, there must be a fundamental change in his basic personality structure.

Basic changes in the personality structure can only occur through long-term work. When treatment extends into long-term therapy, there necessarily will be a movement away from the more cognitive focus. Instead, therapy will provide fuller understanding and a reparative relationship with a healthy therapeutic parent. The long-term work succeeds because of the significance of the therapeutic relationship. It is not the specific interpretations and interventions of the therapist that are most curative but rather, the therapeutic caring.

When therapy moves beyond the initial phases of work and becomes long-term treatment, the process relies on different parameters for success. It no longer is crucial for the patient to gain insight into his psychopathology; instead, he must internalize the caring or the healthy therapeutic parenting which is being provided. As the alliance develops between the healthy side of the patient and the caring of the therapist, the patient moves toward fuller individuation and health.

Ten:
The Nature of
Long-Term Work

Introduction

No clear point demarcates the end of the initial phase of therapy and the beginning of long-term work. Therapy is a process with the basic elements of long-term work initiated during the early phase. The initial therapy phase and the long-term work can, however, be distinguished by outlining the central elements of both stages of treatment.

In the early phase of therapy, the therapist is usually quite active, providing the patient with both a general framework to understand herself and with a method of self-exploration to detect manifestations of self-hatred in her personality structure. The patient acquires a great deal of information during the initial phase of therapy. The therapist draws upon the wide range of her professional expertise and leads the patient toward increased self-understanding. At the end of the initial phase of therapy, the patient should have a fairly complete sense of why and how she is suffering from psychopathology.

In the long-term phase of treatment, the patient's primary need is not to acquire greater knowledge about herself but rather to transform that knowledge into action. She wants to change personal experience and behavior in ways that will produce greater individuation. The patient's ultimate movement toward health is not directed by the therapist. The most the therapist can accomplish in long-term work is to set the stage for the healthy side of the patient's personality to gain ascendence over her self-destructive tendencies.

During the long-term phase of therapy, the pragmatic-existential therapist primarily functions as the healthy therapeutic parent. She regularly expresses her interest and caring for the patient through her behavior in the ongoing therapy sessions. Therapeutic caring is the essential component of the therapist-patient relationship; the role of the therapist is fundamentally nurturing. The patient accepts the caring of the therapist and internalizes this caring by incorporating it into her underdeveloped healthy self.

The therapist's belief in the worth of the patient will become accepted by the patient over the course of therapeutic work. Concomitantly, the patient will believe and care for herself in much deeper ways than she has before. Belief in self and caring for self prompt the patient to fight her psychopathology and ultimately succeed in creating a healthy life style.

The pragmatic-existential therapist becomes the healthy therapeutic parent through the expression of her own unique ways of manifesting her interest and caring for patients. The behavior of the therapist is not based upon a series of carefully planned techniques, but instead represents genuine and spontaneous ways of being for the other that are nurturant and growth-inducing.

The best way to explain more specifically how this process unfolds is by drawing upon my own experiences in conducting long-term therapy. The use of personal examples expresses the existential position that each person is being-in-the-world and that each relationship is unique. The process that I-am is therapeutic just as is the process of other therapists. By carefully examining how one's own therapeutic process works, it is possible to better detect what one elicits in the patient. Personal experience is the guide to becoming a more capable therapist as it teaches the therapist both about the patient and about herself.

A Little of "Me"

I was raised in a very emotionally expressive family. We were vociferous and dramatic in making ourselves heard, and we utilized a wide range of verbal and nonverbal techniques to make our views known. I acquired the habit of accompanying my own speech with a series of idiosyncratic hand gestures, which are now quite familiar to all who spend any time in my company. I make these gestures when I speak to a class, during phone calls, in casual conversations, and also when I conduct psychotherapy. I may place my hands on my head or on my face or gesticulate excessively, usually without direct awareness.

On several occasions I have become startlingly aware of how regularly I use such hand gestures and posturing; I have noticed my patients, sitting across from me, making these same movements. When I initially noticed that these gestures had been adopted by my patients, I was embarrassed. I thought my patients had enough difficulties without adding nonproductive idiosyncracies to their behavioral repertoire. As I watched patients making these gestures, I became increasingly self-conscious, to the point of trying to keep my hands folded in my lap.

However, as I reflected upon what was happening with my patients, I recognized that imitation of nonverbal gestures is a phenomenon usually exhibited by young children. My patients were demonstrating that they had adopted me as a model to follow, and they were imitating my behavior in the same way that children copy some of their parents' actions. Moreover, I realized that the particular patients who copied my gestures were severely personality disordered. They had been extensively damaged during their very early upbringing by extremely destructive parents. A very positive phenomenon was actually occurring, even though I was uncomfortable with the particular form of imitative behavior that I noticed. As I was being adopted as a positive role model, the patients must also have been adopting the healthy and more objective view of themselves that I was trying to strengthen. These patients, though, were copying the total package, gestures and all. Much as I would have preferred for patients to acquire only my positive attributes, I accepted the fact that they were modelling my humanness which, too, contains its idiosyncracies.

This type of mirroring usually does not occur in neurotic patients. At times higher functioning patients, particularly adolescents, will deliberately copy the hair or dress style of their therapists. Therapists who engage in behavior rehearsal directly teach particular behaviors and encourage their patients to copy the therapist's actions. The types of modelling practiced in behavioral rehearsal are developmentally higher phenomena, specific adult skills designed to further the goal attainment.

The modelling of gestures is a behavior pattern which begins to appear before the child acquires speech. When this pattern reappears in adult patients, it affirms that a very deep connection has been made between the therapist and the patient, a process described by analysts as incorporation. Some of these patients may, nonetheless, state that they feel no attachment to their therapist. This split between the patient's verbalizations and behavior patterns classically demonstrates the vast gulf between what patients may consciously know and what is actually taking place.

Attending at the Nonverbal Level

Some patients do not let themselves know their emotional connection with their therapists because they sense that caring makes them vulnerable to potential destruction by the other. These patients were, most likely, deeply hurt when they previously demonstrated such caring to parental or other significant figures. By attending to the patient's imitative gestures, the therapist will detect the emergence of the patient's emotional connection and will not need verbal confirmation from her.

No matter how experienced the therapist is, there will be times when she attends only to the patient's immediate verbalizations and overlooks the fact that deeper and different feelings are occurring which the patient is not expressing. A therapist is not omniscient and cannot attend to all levels of communication at every moment. The lack of full and complete therapeutic knowledge of each communication is not a basic problem in therapy because the primary issues and emotions of the patient will be repeatedly expressed. If the therapist does not detect the hidden meaning of one particular communication, she will, nonetheless, hear other manifestations of the patient's primary issues.

Therapists have several reasons for the difficulty in regularly looking beneath the level of direct verbal communication where other phenomena are taking place. Therapists spend years in professional training, reading books and learning intervention strategies, which are all experiences that place great emphasis on the verbal sphere. Therapists feel an enormous pressure to view psychotherapy mainly as a verbal encounter and also to believe that verbal interventions are the major keys to patients' therapeutic growth. To believe otherwise would be to lose the sense of potential control in the therapeutic interaction.

On the other hand, it is certainly true that the analytic therapies minimize the importance of direct verbal communication and attempt to see the "real" hidden meanings beneath the words. However, all therapists recognize the multidimensional levels of communication. At times it is necessary to attend to the direct verbalizations, while at other times it is equally or more important to attend to the hidden or nonverbal messages the patient is indirectly communicating.

Another reason therapists rely on the verbal sphere is that the initial phase of therapy calls for direct expressions from the therapist. She sees the positive effects of her initial comments and recognizes that her interpretations of psychopathology are well accepted by the patient. It is very difficult to mistrust this way of being—verbal—that has proven successful in one's past.

Even a patient's acknowledgment that the therapist has said something of crucial importance can be a misinterpretation. For example, one of my patients entered therapy exhibiting classic obsessive-compulsive symptomatology. He felt trapped into performing many repetitive behaviors which interfered with his functioning. Therapy with this patient extended over a three year period, ending when the patient received a job transfer. At one point during the last year of therapy this patient explained "the most important thing" I ever said to him was the key which enabled him to gain control of his obsessive-compulsive behaviors. This "brilliant" utterance was actually a question: I had asked him "What is the worst thing that will happen if you do not engage in a compulsive ritual?"

However, that question was and is, indeed, useful. It indirectly implies that the patient has the capacity to evaluate his options and ultimately take control over his life. In that sense, my question epitomized an existential viewpoint as it affirms that the patient can choose to conquer his psychopathology. However, asking such a question, in and of itself, does not constitute brilliant intervention. This question or others like it are routinely asked by therapists in the very first assessment stages of therapy with most obsessive-compulsive patients. I said additional helpful things to this patient, by conveying to him several ways that he had the power to change—through my general stance, my words and my caring for him. However, this patient consciously processed my message as rational communication rather than emotional support and empowerment. If the patient's evaluation were the final word, he would have deduced that he participated in rational problem solving therapy.

If patients keep regular appointments despite their criticisms of the therapy or if they continually speak of their depressed symptomatology, their very commitment to therapy informs the therapist that positive events are nonetheless taking place. Some patients may immediately need a safe place in which to complain. The process of unburdening themselves enables them to feel love and acceptance. They also may need to devalue the therapist and the therapy as a way of protecting themselves from an intimate therapeutic relationship. Such patients are not fundamentally unhappy with the process; if that were the case, they would not remain in psychotherapy. Significant progress is revealed just by their regular attendance. The therapists must draw upon diagnostic skills to determine why a particular patient needs to devalue the process while simultaneously demonstrating her commitment to psychotherapy.

Some patients give conflicting verbal messages and then provide nonverbal cues which contradict their verbalizations, as demonstrated by the following example. A patient concluded his first therapy session by offering a warning. He said he had a terrible memory and would most likely miss sessions because he would forget the time of his appointments. However, this patient did not arrive even one minute late for any of his sessions. His promptness demonstrated that he had made a significant commitment to the therapeutic process. At the verbal level he was often critical of therapy and rarely would initiate conversation. Still, he did attempt to change the destructive behaviors discussed during his therapy sessions.

The dictum that "everything is data," borrowed from both projecive techniques and analytic practice, certainly applies to pragmatic-existential therapy. I discovered a useful measure of the patient's degree of safety and comfort in the therapeutic situation when I acquired a footstool for the office. I have one footstool, which is placed equidistant between two identical chairs. Sometimes I place my feet on the footstool, but I do not claim exclusive rights to this piece of furniture. I alternate between periods of using the footstool and resting my feet directly on the floor.

It is quite rare for a new patient to use or share the footstool with me. The patient who does so may be highly narcissistic and may be used to dominating interpersonal situations. What typically occurs is that some patients will, after a number of sessions, begin to tentatively place their own feet on the footstool. Occasionally they may even comment on the fact that we can both use it, or ask permission to rest their feet on the footstool. The size of the footstool makes sharing difficult, so it is typically used in some alternating fashion.

In addition, the small size of my office makes it too cumbersome to install two footstools, which would significantly widen the physical distance between therapist and patient. The presence of one footstool is not only a diagnostic indicator but also has become an important part of the therapeutic interaction. When patients begin to use the footstool, I know they feel very comfortable in their therapeutic home. When we share the footstool as equals, we are embodying the most fundamental existential message, that the therapist holds no higher value than the patient.

The footstool was a gift from family members, designed to enable me to rest my feet, so I can not lay claim to having the foresight of introducing this particular tool. However, like so much else that becomes important in psychotherapy, it was not a calculated therapeutic gambit. My footstool provides valuable data at the nonverbal level. Diverse information is presented through the patient's nonverbal cues, and the attentive therapist will process this information to gain insight into her connection with the patient.

Therapists, too, indirectly provide data to their patients through their posture and a host of other nonverbal cues. For example, if a therapist looks at her watch, some patients will immediately ask if it is time to leave. They interpret checking the time as rejection and do not want to be intrusive. Some therapists may circumvent this problem by having a clock positioned clearly in the vision of both therapist and patient. However, I believe that the patient does not need an omnipresent reminder of time. Furthermore, the patient could detect the therapist's glance at the clock as readily as she can see her looking at her wristwatch.

Caring in Long-Term Work

Long-term therapeutic work becomes effective when the patient incorporates the caring of her therapist and draws upon the therapeutic relationship for nurturance and support. The pragmatic-existential therapist does not abandon her attempts to increase the patient's cognitive understanding and insight; but such greater self-awareness becomes the secondary goal in long-term therapy. The primary goal is to provide a bonding relationship as a cornerstone upon which the patient can build better mental health. In the course of long-term pragmatic-existential therapy, patients will feel supported, valued and loved. They come to understand their therapists care for them and are invested in assisting them to develop a fulfilling life. Patients recognize the caring they receive is personal rather than simply part of a procedure that the therapist is required to perform. When they fully accept that the therapist is personally involved in their continued healthy development, they feel increased strength and can effectively conquer their psychopathology.

Pragmatic-existential therapists certainly do care deeply about their patients, but this caring is not manifested in the same way that Rogers (1951) expressed unconditional positive regard. Caring can and must be expressed in a variety of ways consistent with the personality of the therapist. Sometimes we show caring by being passive and accepting, but at other times we care by being confrontational and even angry. The love offered by the psychotherapist is, indeed, very much like the healthy parental love given to children. For example, the therapist expresses the fact that she, too, is pleased to share in the patient's successes.

The responses of the therapist must be adjusted to the psychological developmental level of the patient, just as is the case in healthy parenting. That is, pragmatic-existential therapists change their behavioral expressions of caring to match the needs and experiences of each patient. As the patient's experiences and developmental needs shift, so do the responses of the therapist. A patient who has been profoundly injured and traumatized needs a sanctuary, a place of safety that makes no demands upon her. Only after the patient feels very secure can the therapist encourage self-exploration and growth. Accordingly, the manner of expressed caring will change over time. These therapeutic responses are fundamentally synonymous with the actions of healthy parents who alter their behavior as their children move from infancy through childhood and adolescence, into full adulthood.

Pragmatic-existential psychotherapists express the type of love exhibited by the parent who is glad to see the child go to school, not the kind of love that wants to keep the child home. It is comparable to the love parents have for adult children; they enjoy each visit but are also pleased that their offspring have their own homes. Similarly, when the psychotherapy session ends, the healthy caring therapist stops thinking about that particular patient and shifts her attention to the next "therapeutic child" about to be seen. Even more importantly, she stops thinking about her patients at the end of the working day and devotes her attention to her own life. May (1969) described the type of therapeutic caring outlined above as "therapeutic eros."

In long-term work, therapeutic caring transforms the therapist into the good maternal or paternal figure which the patient never had. These parental ways of being for the patient are communicated in both the verbal and nonverbal realms. As the patient comes to view the therapist as a significant parental figure, she will look for cues that provide more information about the therapist and the therapist's regard for her. It is quite important for therapists to be aware of such scrutiny and to adjust their behaviors accordingly.

Even the way therapists decorate their offices can reflect their willingness to function as significant parental figures. When therapists are healthy therapeutic parents, their offices become the refuge, or the good home, that patients previously lacked. For this as well as for other reasons, I conduct my psychotherapy practice in my own home. It is important to create an atmosphere to maximize the patient's sense of belongingness, which is best provided by a warm environment.

Some patients comment on the garden they walk through on the way to the office door, or on the sounds of the house, or often on the smell of cooking. For some patients the office is such a special place that they become quite attached to the objects in the room, like the paintings as well as the placement of furniture. Patients have even expressed displeasure when they see any changes in the room, for that alters their "safe world." These patients' experiences are comparable to those of young adults who return home for holidays after their first semester at college. Students want their old homes to remain unchanged as they represent places of continuity, safety and security. They, too, respond unfavorably to change and new decorations. Many personality disordered patients feel so threatened by change that the consulting room should be kept as physically stable as possible.

Although patients become very attached to the therapy room and often feel that it is their own, such feelings are rarely directly expressed. Some patients may exhibit signs of resentment when appointments overlap and they meet the therapist's next patient. It is not only the room that some patients feel that they "own," but they make some attempts to "own" the therapist as well. The degree to which patients need to "own" the therapist is conveyed by their inability to acknowledge the occasional intrusive sounds which impinge upon the office.

A few patients I have worked with appeared to be totally oblivious to noises emanating from other parts of my home. The dogs may have barked incessantly, loud arguments may have occurred, the doorbell may have repeatedly rung, yet these patients were totally oblivious to all such sounds. (These intrusions are not everyday occurrences or I could not conduct therapy in the home.) Occasionally when I have had to leave the room to quiet a disturbance so that we could work without distraction, some patients were startled to discover that external noise had occurred. On the other hand, other patients have been hypervigilant to the slightest outside sound; they heard noises that I did not detect. Such keen watchfulness demonstrates that their anxiety keeps them living in a state of perpetual tension.

Because the pragmatic-existential therapist functions as the healthy therapeutic parent in long-term therapy, this work with adults is fundamentally very similar to effective psychotherapy conducted with children. Capable professionals can function as good therapeutic parents with both populations, and in so doing they validate the self-affirming tendencies of their patients. It is vital to provide both adults and children with the feeling they are loved and cared for. Therapists convey their acceptance and caring for adult patients through higher level verbal processes and sophisticated techniques that are inappropriate in therapy with children. Nonetheless, these therapeutic behaviors still convey the underlying message that the therapist cares for the patient and wants the patient to become healthy. Her caring is the most crucial message the therapist can ever provide, for it is the single communication that facilitates change in personality disordered patients.

Bettelheim (1968) stated that *Love is Not Enough*. The therapeutic "eros" or love is usually insufficient when it is passive and does not encourage the patient to take positive steps toward developing better mental health. Healthy therapeutic love is expressed in a multitude of ways, attuned to the patient's particular needs at that particular moment. As the therapist attends to the changing experiential process that is the patient, she may radically alter her form of interaction, from teaching to confrontation, from passivity to directness. To follow the dictates of existentialism, a therapist must continually be able to change her responses to match the needs and experiences of the patient.

Sometimes it is important to express caring for patients in very direct ways. In one therapy session a patient spoke of himself in sarcastic and self-deriding tones. I said, "Do not talk about yourself that way. I will not tolerate it. I do not accept that you are a monster or the worthless human that is described by the destructive part of you." In this situation it was imperative to identify the self-attacking mechanism of the patient and become the advocate for the healthy side of his personality. This intervention enabled the patient to identify his verbalizations as another unfair attack launched by the self-hating part of his personality.

Understanding Destructive Relationships

Through their ongoing participation in long-term pragmatic-existential therapy, personality disordered patients come to understand that their therapists care for them. The nature and content of therapeutic dialogue differs greatly from patient to patient as it must meet individual needs. Overtly, the therapist complies with the patient's desired topic of conversation, but a covert engagement and relationship is simultaneously developing. The fact that the therapist discusses the patient's chosen agenda is one small way she communicates her care for her patient. The overt therapeutic dialogue may range from problem solving and assertion training to the generation of insight; but the covert message, sometimes stated quite overtly, is that the therapist cares.

On rare occasions one direct statement or interpretation made by the therapist will prompt the patient to change her behavior. However, in most instances, any verbal statement a therapist makes is insufficient, in and of itself, to prompt behavior change. Rather, it is the covert message the therapist provides, that she cares for her patient, which enables the patient to move forward. Consider the group of patients who are involved in destructive relationships or marriages. Usually, but not always, the patients are well aware that they are in a destructive relationship when they first choose to enter psychotherapy. Indeed, many of them made that choice in order to receive help to end the relationship. A few of these patients simply want and need a therapist to give them permission to do so; once they obtain permission, they act upon it. These patients want to assign responsibility for their lives to other people and have chosen a therapist as their responsible authority figure.

However, for most patients it would be a significant therapeutic error simply to tell them to end the relationship, for the patients would be unable to do so. Rather, it is necessary to recount and to understand the history and nature of the destructive relationship; the patient must explore why she has needs to be in relationships which hurt her. Being able to answer the question of why she prolongs destructive relationships will not, in itself, enable the patient to behave in self-affirming ways. The ultimate therapeutic goal is for the patient to make the important and necessary changes in her life that she believes will satisfy her healthy needs. One way that the patient can be helped to face this choice point is by asking the existential question posed by Boss (1963), "Why not change?"

The question Boss raises can begin to empower the patient. By asking "Why not?" the therapist implicitly informs the patient that she has the capacity to make important changes in her life. Through the course of long-term treatment, pragmatic-existential therapists will communicate they care about their patients and want them to make the changes leading to more gratifying and fulfilling lives. These therapeutic communications provide the underlying support that enables the patients to move in positive directions. However, this change will not occur until such time as the patient gives herself both the power and the right to act in self-affirming ways.

Many patients suffering from personality disorders cannot end their destructive relationships because they feel unable to function as separate individuals. They sense a lack of the basic resources to cope with life independently, and they use relationships with others as a basic survival technique. To separate from the other means to risk a psychological death for they do not believe they can actually survive independently.

The above formulation parallels the analytic conception (Mahler, Pine & Bergman, 1975) of patients who could not effectively differentiate themselves from their mothering figures. In the earliest years when these individuals attempted such a separation, they were emotionally abandoned by their mothers and felt totally helpless. As a result, each maintained a symbiotic attachment to the mothering figure.

For still other personality disordered patients, allowing themselves to leave a destructive relationship means to act kindly to themselves, and they do not believe that they deserve such kindness. Rather, their lives continue to follow a masochistic pattern which usually was first exhibited in their relationship with a particular parent. These patients are dominated by the self-hating force in their personalities which originated in the destructive relationship with a parent.

For other personality disordered patients, leaving hurtful relationships requires first allowing themselves to believe that they can make choices. It is common in their developmental histories that they were restrained by at least one controlling parent from making separate and independent choices. This parent would not tolerate any signs of burgeoning independence in the child. When parents reject children for behaving in healthy independent ways, they block children from developing any firm sense of a personal self. This lack of a firm sense of self will interfere with an individual's ability to make independent choices later in life.

Destructive parents can threaten and control their children in a variety of different ways. Some personality disordered patients actually were allowed to have a limited independence when they were children. They could operate independently as long as the goal was to serve others, typically the parental figures. These personality disordered patients often now lead lives where they continue to serve others, but they cannot fundamentally "be" for themselves. They enter service professions and become effective helpers; however, they may be helping others at the cost of full affirmation of their own mental health.

Children of alcoholics frequently feel powerless because they cannot control a destructive parent. They often imagined that if they behaved perfectly, they could control the alcoholic parent. Such individuals may continue to live out this fantasy and attempt to control others who are self-destructive. These co-dependent people remain in destructive relationships with the hope of ultimately validating themselves. It becomes a cycle of self-defeating behavior, for the individual is never able to achieve sufficient interpersonal control.

Even when one of these explanations accurately expresses the patient's past history and is explored during therapy, this knowledge, by itself, does not necessarily lead to positive growth. Knowing the traumatic events which created emotional disturbances does not free the patient from the power of her traumas. The patient often still remains unable to make choices or to love herself. Gaining insight into these destructive forces is a necessary component for change, but it is insufficient by itself to produce change. The unfolding, caring therapeutic relationship provides the ultimate strength for the patient's growth.

Responding to Meet the Patient's Needs

Psychoanalytic theory (Fenichel, 1945) uses the concept of "working through" to explain the process of long-term therapy. When patients "work through" their problems, according to analysts, they ultimately comprehend the different manifestations of their historically based difficulties which, in turn, enables them to overcome the compulsion to reenact these problems in their lives. Increased self-understanding, at both a cognitive and an emotional level, is considered to be the central element of change in analysis.

In long-term pragmatic-existential psychotherapy, patients also come to understand the nature and manifestations of their own problems. They particularly recognize the presence of the self-attacking component in their personality structure, and they begin to counteract this force through the strengthening of the self-affirming force. The empowerment and development of a self-affirming force occurs through a patient's recognition that she is deeply cared for by her therapist. Healthy therapeutic parenting enables a patient to accept the fact that she deserves a healthier life; consequently, she begins to implement the different strategies, insights and problem solving techniques which she learned in therapy for her own enhancement.

Although therapeutic caring is the fundamental element which produces health and greater individuation, the patient still must cope with and counteract the powerful self-hating force in her personality structure. The therapist provides significant assistance in this endeavor, for she can readily detect the manifestations of self-hatred. As the therapist continues to interpret the presence of self-hatred in the therapeutic dialogue, the patient becomes more and more proficient at interpreting and then counteracting this destructive force herself.

The pragmatic-existential therapist will point out the presence of self-hatred when it is manifest; but at the more immediate level, she will address the issues that the patient wishes to discuss. The therapist's understanding of the nature of the patient's pain directs the intervention strategy. For some patients, unfortunately, high level strategies and words fall on deaf ears. These patients basically need healthy therapeutic parents; the therapist's words become the only mechanism which generates the sense of caring. In work with these patients, the therapist assumes a supportive stance and avoids trying to teach new behavioral strategies.

However, patients who lack basic coping skills require the expertise of the therapist, as they need to learn new behavioral techniques. This is the best way for the therapist to provide support. The therapist must be willing to assume a very active role, for these patients often feel helpless in problematic situations. The strategy for working with an overwhelmed patient is comparable to the style of intervention typically used with severely depressed patients. With both populations, the therapist becomes the powerful force who moves the patient. Since depression is self-generating, the therapist energizes the patient to break the destructive cycle.

Some patients need to be psychologically shaken, but other patients should never be shaken and instead need to be psychologically "held." For these latter patients, growth most likely occurs only after they feel safety in the office of the therapist. The pragmatic-existential therapist, by attending to the process of the patient, can determine which strategy is best for each patient.

There are also some patients who need to be "dazzled." These patients' defensive strategy of superiority can only be pierced when they recognize that the therapist is at least as smart or astute as they are. Even though therapists may occasionally need to demonstrate their prowess, it should be avoided, lest the therapist begin to participate in the same defensive maneuvers as the patient. This particular strategy, too, would prove disastrous for patients who painfully feel a sense of their own inadequacies. They do not need to be made to feel even more deficient.

Pragmatic-existential therapists avoid being directive with patients whenever possible and utilize such strategies only when it is vital to "save" the patient from a potentially harmful situation. When an authoritative intervention is utilized, it must be expressed in a protective voice. Ultimately the patient internalizes this caring message and learns to protect herself. When patients internalize the caring of the therapist, they learn to care for and protect themselves, thereby freeing the therapist from assuming the role of rescuer.

Direct authoritative intervention is used in the same way one throws a life preserver to a drowning person. It does not help the drowning person simply to tell her she has the capacity to swim. If she is to survive the immediate crisis, she must receive a life preserver. Any other strategy would prove fatal. Once the swimmer is no longer in danger, many possible strategies can be utilized to help avoid further jeopardy.

It is necessary to combine pragmatic elements with existential theory in order to be of maximal assistance to patients. When patients are in a profound crisis, they should not be told of their ultimate power; rather, they need to be given immediate assistance. At these times the patients' pressing needs must take precedence, and existential theory by itself does not provide a rationale for therapeutic directness and control.

When working with personality disordered patients who are not in crisis, the existential perspective of focusing upon the patient as process is the most important guide to successful therapy. Patients make significant changes only through enhanced self-understanding, therapeutic caring and the strengthening of their underdeveloped healthy self. When the patient is ready, she will move toward greater health, not necessarily when the therapist wants changes to occur. Consequently, when the patient says that the therapist must be tired of hearing her discuss the same issues again, the effective therapist states that such is not the case. The patient must have a need to keep discussing the same problems until she is ready to do otherwise. When she has found the ability to make necessary changes, she will do so.

Although some patients seem unable to change certain aspects of their lives despite continual discussion, they tend to exhibit spontaneous changes in areas that were not the subject of overt dialogue. One particular patient was trapped in a horrendous marriage and kept reiterating all the difficulties he had at home. Even though he was unable to be effectively self-assertive with his wife, he dramatically reversed his behavior in his business career. He used new skills in business that he could not practice at home. These changes occurred despite the fact that his business practices were not regularly addressed in therapy.

Similar changes occur in all patients. Some radically change their parenting style, becoming excellent parents. These same patients often are much slower to make progress dealing with the overt topics that are discussed. However, these changes do affirm that the therapist's attempts to enhance the patient's movement toward greater individuation are heard and incorporated by the patient. It seems to be far easier for a patient to improve her behavior in areas that have not been the source of major conflict than it is for her to change behavior patterns that epitomize her psychopathology. Pragmatic-existential therapists feel encouraged whenever they see any signs of positive growth, for it signals that therapeutic caring is working.

The Therapeutic Process in Long-Term Sessions

The pragmatic-existential therapist attempts to gain an understanding of the most immediate experiencing of all patients with whom she works. She focuses her attention on the process of her patient in order to gain as full an understanding as possible. Her overriding concern with obtaining immediate understanding is present in her work with patients who suffer from all forms of psychopathology, in all stages of treatment. She draws upon two major processes to obtain this knowledge. She attends to the patient's pitch (Boss, 1963) and tries to detect the ways in which her patient is immediately participating in the therapeutic interaction. In addition, she uses the phenomenological method to see the world through the patient's eyes.

When she utilizes the phenomenological method, the therapist is trying to understand the patient by sharing in the patient's experiential process; this understanding does not involve external judgment and evaluation. When she assesses the patient's pitch, she moves away from the shared experience and attempts to make an objective judgment about the patient's immediate condition.

As the pragmatic-existential therapist moves between phenomenological understanding and an assessment of pitch, she is alternating between the traditionally labelled subjective and objective poles of understanding. It is necessary for her to understand the patient both from within (phenomenologically) and from without (diagnosing pitch and making other evaluations as well) so that her apprehension of the patient can be as complete as possible. Furthermore, in the course of each therapy session she may draw upon many or all of the elements of therapeutic understanding, as described in chapter 2.

Because the therapist must understand the experiences of the patient at the immediate moment, she usually will wait for the patient to begin the therapeutic dialogue. If the therapist were to speak first, she would be superimposing a personal agenda upon the patient's experiential process and would not be attending to her patient as a phenomenological process. On other rare occasions it may be helpful for the therapist to comment on the patient's apparent emotional state before the patient actually begins to speak. If nonverbal cues suggest that the patient is significantly depressed or anxious, the therapist may choose to comment on her perception of the patient's emotional condition. Such a comment may well be in order, particularly if the patient has difficulty speaking. However, the best way to gain insight into the patient's process usually is to listen.

The long-term therapy patient typically begins her session by talking about significant events that occurred during the past week. A description of these events assists both therapist and patient in exploring the feelings precipitated by them. The patient will often attempt to identify which of her thoughts/feelings was produced by the self-attacking part of her personality structure. If the patient does not independently attempt such an analysis, a direct question is in order. The therapist may ask, "Is it the healthy or unhealthy part of yourself which thinks this way?" If this question does not give the patient enough information to make a determination, she can be asked to speculate upon the possible consequences of acting upon the particular thoughts she had. As patients begin to understand the consequences of carrying out thoughts or ideas, they can then better identify what is healthy and what is destructive. The therapeutic intention is for the patient to be able to distinguish between healthy and unhealthy ideation and response tendencies.

Often a patient may describe situations in which she has blatantly distorted the intentions and behaviors of other people. Although a therapist could point out the distortions, such immediate interpretations are rarely helpful. It is far more prudent and pragmatic to encourage the patient herself to participate in a reevaluation of the situation. As the therapist asks the patient to consider possible alternative explanations for the behavior of others, she is also asking the patient to question her own evaluative processes. With this approach, the therapist implicitly alerts the patient to the fact that her observing ego may be under the sway of her self-destructive force.

It is crucial for therapists to encourage patients to continually question their evaluations and interpretations of events. The patients' frequent misperceptions and distortions of others are the cause of many experienced difficulties. These distortions are, again, the function of the self-hating force in their personality structure. When patients learn to engage in such self-questioning during the therapeutic hour, they can then continue more effective self-evaluation outside of the therapeutic hour.

Asking patients for possible alternative explanations of events is another way to encourage expansion of their meaning categories. As they entertain different points of view, they will become more effective in making better sense of their immediate situations. Once a patient can understand other people more fully, she will be able to choose more effective behaviors in her interpersonal life.

Personality disordered patients have an underdeveloped healthy self. As they conduct themselves in the interpersonal world, their functioning is often invaded and dominated by the self-hating force. When the patient enters the therapy room and reviews the week's events, she becomes involved in a rational evaluation which calls for the presence of her observing ego as well as the participation of the healthy self.

Participation in therapeutic dialogue strengthens both the observing ego and the healthy side of the personality because each of these forces must be given voice during the therapeutic hour. Moreover, the content and the conclusions in the dialogue also serve to strengthen both the observing ego and the underdeveloped healthy self. The patient increases her understanding of the different ways in which self-attack occurs; and consequently, her understanding will alert her to possible repetitions of such self-destructive tendencies.

By reviewing destructive past events, both the therapist and the patient hope to prevent their reoccurrence. A primary method for providing better control of the present is an increased awareness of the past. The attention to recent events is designed to expand the patient's insight, but this increased insight in turn serves the pragmatic function of affecting the future.

While the overt dialogue focuses upon increasing the patient's self-understanding, a covert engagement takes place at the same time. The therapist demonstrates her caring for the patient through her active participation in the therapeutic process. The therapist is concerned with the patient's increased health, and this concern is eventually processed by the patient as an indication of her own personal worth.

The following sample therapy session reveals means by which awareness is increased and caring is demonstrated. Mary, a patient who resumed therapy after undergoing back surgery, reported that she felt angry after the surgery because she did not meet her dead mother when she was under anaesthetic. When prompted to describe her thinking more extensively, Mary said that she had hoped to see the light (that people see who have near death experiences) so she could meet with her mother and then return to living. During earlier therapy sessions with Mary, we had held only minor discussions of the self-hating mechanism of her personality.

I functioned as the "generalized other" and explained to Mary that anger and depression following successful surgery were not typical reactions; rather, most people would have felt joyous and relieved. Mary lacked a clear sense of natural and healthy emotional reactions to different situations, and therefore she needed to be provided with a framework of what is "normal." After absorbing this information, Mary's experiences of both anger and depression were interpreted as particular manifestations of the self-hating part in her personality structure.

When Mary wondered how it was possible for her to possess such self-destructive thoughts, she was informed of the ways in which parents can generate feelings of self-love or of self-hatred in their children. To assist her in understanding the distinction between the two, she was asked to identify how she treated her own children. Mary acknowledged that she showered them with much affection. She then recalled how her father had treated her; he had locked her in the apartment over entire weekends and had heaped verbal and physical abuse upon her throughout much of her childhood and adolescence. She was then offered the interpretation that she had learned to regard herself in the same ways that her father had treated her.

It was also important to begin to explore Mary's need to reconnect with her dead mother. Mary had been visiting her mother's grave site every two or three weeks during the three years subsequent to her mother's death. Her mother had been a withdrawn schizophrenic who was hospitalized for several years. Mary had tried to protect and nurture her mother, both before and after her illness. I pointed out that Mary's feelings of being a "good" person, as a child and as an adolescent, had been generated through her attempts to nurse her mother to psychological health. Mary commented that she was aware she was visiting the grave site too frequently and realized these visits should already have diminished.

It was important not to overload Mary with too much self-awareness, as she was psychologically quite fragile and had shown massive difficulties in speaking during therapy. So much of her life had been filled with stress that she needed intensive support rather than more self-understanding. In fact, Mary stated that she felt proud to have been able to tell me about her thoughts after surgery. I, too, concurred that this was a good prognostic sign for our continued work together.

Later in the session, Mary recounted a recent argument with her husband who had accused her of neither trusting nor leaning on him. When I asked her whom she had ever trusted in her life, she said "No one." In discussing her husband and his complaints, I pointed out that his behavior had been unreliable. Mary had stated that he forgot to pick up their children after school on the day she returned home from surgery; and after an hour and a half of waiting for him, the children called her to drive them home. She reported that she had wanted to call her husband at the very beginning of this session, which was held at two o'clock, to remind him again to pick up the children. When I replied I would have been glad to have her use the phone because I was there to help her, she acknowledged that apparently she did not fully trust me either. Although I concurred with her belief, I also felt it necessary to be supportive of her. I reminded her that it is enormously difficult to learn to trust as an adult when one has not been able to trust as a child. At the conclusion of the session I reiterated that we had been making very good progress in our work together.

As previously stated, the immediate and intuitive responses of the pragmatic-existential therapist are based upon the understanding of the patient as a process. These therapeutic responses are the result of a form of "knowing" that can later be explained through reflective consciousness. Accordingly, by reviewing the above session, I can now explain the reasons for my actions.

First of all, my responses in the session were spontaneous. I did not reflect upon what I wanted to say but simply trusted my immediate reactions to the patient. My spontaneity in conducting psychotherapy is used as a model to encourage spontaneity in the patient. Because I trust my own reactions, I implicitly teach patients to trust their own emotions as well. My presence in therapy is as a strong, vital, life force—a healthy self. This particular patient, like many others with whom I work, has an underdeveloped healthy self, or at least one that is often dominated by her self-attacking personality structure. Hence, as patients feel my own vitality, they can begin to share in it, draw strength from it, and use it to vitalize their own underdeveloped life forces.

I believed that Mary was bewildered and at a loss to explain the anger she had experienced at not reuniting with her mother. I began by counteracting her depression, which she described as steadily increasing. By providing her with a schema which might explain her feelings, I increased her capacity for self control. I was particularly active in this session because I believed that she did not have sufficient resources, at that moment, to find a way of coping with her powerful negative feelings.

Instead of acknowledging the need to reunite with her mother as a legitimate death wish, I preferred to activate and strengthen her life force. By labelling her experiences as manifestations of her self-destructive force, I was helping Mary recognize and separate the healthy side of her personality from her self-destructive tendencies. Mary may, in fact, possess strong death wishes. However, the therapeutic task is to move the patient toward health, and here it was best accomplished by strengthening the underdeveloped healthy self. To encourage her to discuss her wish for death would have energized her self-hatred, which was already threatening to overrun her personality.

At different points in the hour I tried to support and strengthen these healthy life forces. I affirmed her positive connection with her children; I praised her for being able to self-disclose, and I openly appreciated the fact that she recognized her difficulty with trust. Supporting an overwhelmed patient is a very powerful way of strengthening the patient's capacity to effectively engage in an internal struggle. Mary did not internalize or even remember all of my comments. Frequently she would acknowledge that she had no memory of the previous week's session. However, I sensed that she left that particular meeting with a renewed feeling of hope and a recognition that we had worked well together.

Mary is likely to remain in therapy for several years because she was pervasively damaged by a very destructive father and was poorly nurtured by a deficient mother. She never attempted college, and only after marriage did she receive occupational training. She is married to a man who has extensive physical and psychological problems, and she has children who are both learning impaired and emotionally disturbed. Because of all of these immediate problems, she truly needs extensive ongoing support. Only with such repeated support can she tentatively begin to face the historically based problems which regularly interfere with her functioning. However, she has to discuss so many immediate life crises during many of the therapy hours that it is often impossible to do more than attempt to help her cope with these massive everyday problems.

I very much admire Mary; she has dealt with so much adversity in her life, yet she continues trying to become healthy. There are times when I, too, feel overwhelmed by the unceasing problems that pervade her life. Still, we have a good working alliance which has strengthened her ability to cope and move forward.

Another Long-Term Session

Henry began a session complaining of flu-like symptoms. He was unsure whether he was experiencing another round of his long-standing chronic fatigue syndrome or if he was simply coming down with a bug. One of the repeated themes of Henry's therapy was his inability to take action in order to enhance his life style. Because of his present low level of energy, I opened the session by returning to the previous week's topic, the wisdom of purchasing his own home. Henry stated that he had acquired the names of a few realtors, one of whom specialized in selling town houses and condominiums, the properties in which he was most interested. Although he had not yet phoned any of these people, I chose not to comment on his lack of follow-through, but instead continued to support and bolster his feelings of self-esteem.

Even though Henry has virtually all the overt attributes that make a man attractive to most women, he has either become involved in destructive relationships or remained socially isolated for very long periods of time. In addition to a potential purchase of a house, he was currently in the last phases of a relationship which gave many indications of soon ending. When I asked him to describe how he thought most women saw him, he at first professed not to understand the question. I explained further, asking him what he believed most women saw when they met him. Henry's first reply was that he thought it would be a matter of taste. While I agreed, I also asked him to describe what about him might appear to be objectionable to women. He could come up with no such qualities. With further prompting, he said it seemed most single women would be interested in pursuing a relationship with him although this was not the view of himself that he carried. I connected his current negative view of himself with his persistent self-derogatory attitude, which had begun at least as early as his adolescent years.

Further discussion linked this negative self-image to his own self-attacking voice. While Henry acknowledged that the presence of such self-attack currently made him less of a desirable person, I pointed out that these self-attacks were not manifested in any of his overt behavior with women. In fact, his description of himself as intelligent, compassionate and successful was a very accurate portrayal of the ways in which most people see Henry.

Henry acknowledged that this was an unusual session as it made him feel especially good. He continued by stating our sessions were regularly helpful but this particular dialogue made him feel very optimistic. I pointed out to him that he needed to remind himself of who he really was, the adult who possessed all these desirable qualities, not the frightened adolescent, which was a central part of his self-image. The session concluded on this positive note.

During this meeting I was particularly active, responding to the lethargy and depressed feelings of the patient which might have been triggered by a combination of psychological and physical factors. I felt it was important to raise Henry's level of self-esteem, and I deliberately sought to do so by superimposing objective reality upon his negative feelings. As Henry rose to a more positive feeling state, he was then able to look at and analyze his behavior and then begin to counteract some of his self-destructive feelings.

Henry has been in therapy for a long time and is well aware of the power of his self-hating force. It was far more important to try to strengthen the therapeutic relationship and demonstrate my caring than it was to further describe the manifestations of self-hatred. Still, the presence of self-hatred was explained when it was present. Because I felt it was necessary to counteract his lethargy and depression, I had to find a different method of bolstering his underdeveloped healthy self by asking him to view himself through the eyes of others. It is necessary particularly when working with depressed patients for the therapists to draw upon their personal resources and continue to find new ways to elevate the patient's mood.

Productive Use of Negative Therapeutic Feelings

Caring and healthy therapeutic parenting are the central elements that make long-term therapy with personality disordered patients effective. However, there are occasions in which the therapist does not experience such caring feelings but instead has negative emotions directed toward her patients. At these times it is crucial for the therapist to engage in self-examination to discover why these negative feelings are present.

Three major factors likely to produce such negative feelings in the therapist are destructive countertransference, the experience of boredom, and angry feelings toward classic borderline patients. To resolve each of these issues, the therapist needs to utilize different strategies. However, the therapist must first be aware of the negative feelings before she can question why such feelings are occurring.

For a therapist to detect destructive countertransference, she needs to have a great deal of self-awareness. Heightened self-awareness is usually acquired through participation in one's own personal therapy. Yet, even when her personal therapy has been successful, remnants of unresolved personal issues may still be present which later can surface in therapeutic work with particular patients. When the therapist has basically come to terms with herself, she should be able to quickly recognize the presence of those remaining problematic issues as they become manifest in her therapeutic work. Because she is fundamentally psychologically healthy, she can resolve and undo the negative feelings that surfaced in her therapeutic work.

If a therapist has not had a successful personal therapy experience, she is much more apt to experience negative countertransference. She most likely will lack sufficient self-awareness to be able to recognize that her emotions are interfering with her work, and as a result she will be unable to counteract them. This lack of insight not only produces problematic emotions, but it also restricts her effectiveness. For example, she would not be able to use self-disclosure or draw upon her own emotions as reflective of the "generalized other" in order to demonstrate how the patient affects other people.

A therapist needs to be healthy and, ultimately, willing to share her own emotions in order to counteract feelings of boredom which are bound to surface in work with certain patients. When a therapist feels bored with a patient, she is likely to initially think there is something wrong with her, rather than recognize that her boredom is a genuine and valid reaction to the patient.

If the therapist feels bored and asks herself why, she should be able to recognize that the boredom is very atypical of her reactions to patients and therefore it must be a reaction to this particular patient's immediate behavior. Self-monitoring enables the therapist to ask the crucial question, "Would other people be bored when they listened to what this patient is saying?" If her answer is "No," then she is dealing with destructive countertransference. If her answer is "Yes," then she is functioning as the "generalized other" and is experiencing a common reaction to this patient's behavior.

Even when the therapist recognizes that her boredom is legitimate, she still must evaluate the risk of telling the patient that she is feeling bored. It is quite understandable that therapists do not want to alienate their patients by making a seemingly critical comment that might very well produce defensive anger. However, when the therapist trusts her feelings, she can risk the disclosure and help the patient move forward in therapy.

Although I am usually alert, attentive and participatory with almost all of my patients, I have found myself very fatigued and sleepy with a few specific patients almost as soon as the sessions began. With one patient I struggled to keep myself awake virtually throughout the entire session by such covert behavior as pinching myself to stay attentive.

Such feelings were unusual, especially as I noticed that I had been very alert in the immediately preceding session and was quite involved with the subsequent patient. However, fatigue still dominated my functioning with this particular person. When I decided my reaction did not reflect negative countertransference, I acknowledged my boredom to the patient. This admission elicited a confession from the patient. She said that she did not want to discuss difficult material and was, in fact, passing time by talking about irrelevant issues. I then recognized that fatigue was my own defense against her nonparticipation. By being honest about my reactions, I enabled the patient to own up to her own refusal to be honest.

When individual therapists are willing to share personal reactions with their patients, they enable the individual therapy process to provide some of the benefits that are usually only offered in group therapy. During group therapy, patients quickly learn how they affect others because their fellow group members feel no need to hide their reactions. When patients must face the reactions of others, they are forced to acknowledge the negative aspects of their own behavior. Thereby, the group develops more positive interpersonal skills. When a therapist in individual therapy shares some of her own personal reactions to her patient, she, too, provides valuable data which the patient can find very helpful. Of course, such self disclosure is prudent only if the therapist is sensitive and has had a successful personal therapy experience.

Most therapists feel a great deal of anger toward those personality disordered patients who have classic borderline symptomatology. Because borderline patients reverse the normal dimensions of relationships, they necessarily arouse negative feelings in their therapists when they regularly have had positive feelings toward their patients.

The therapeutic strategies must be radically altered when the therapists treat patients who have severe borderline symptomatology. To work comfortably with "borderlines," it is necessary to invert one's basic response tendencies. That is, one must be somewhat cold and reserved at those very times when one's natural tendency is to be warm. Classic borderline patients are frightened by closeness, yet they feel abandoned when they sense the therapist is distant. The therapists who work most effectively with this population are usually those individuals whose typical response style is somewhat aloof.

Therapists being themselves individuals with well-defined personalities will not always be able to radically modify their behavior patterns to work effectively with all the patients they encounter. When the therapist is healthy and highly functioning, she will be extremely flexible and should be able to work with a wide range of patients. However, she cannot be all things to all people. She needs to accept this truth, for it is part of accepting her own humanness.

Because healthy therapeutic parenting is the therapeutic gift which facilitates changes in patients, such caring cannot be faked or willed into existence. When a therapist must regularly block her natural response tendencies toward particular patients, the therapist and therapy will ultimately be ineffective. Even though I can behave in a strict, unyielding and distant manner, which is necessary in work with borderline patients, I cannot sustain these behaviors over a long time period and still personally feel comfortable. As a consequence, I typically refer classic borderline patients to other therapists who do not experience these difficulties.

The Limits of Therapy

Therapists wish that all their patients' problems could be fully resolved. The models of therapy designed to treat neurotic patients implied that such resolutions would, indeed, be possible. However, in the treatment of the personality disordered patient, a full resolution is often not within the realm of the possible. While it is true that some patients may be able to fully resolve many of their deep-seated issues, others will not be able to do so. Instead they may make partial progress and not ever be able to fully repair the pervasive damage done to them. Nonetheless, it is vital for therapists to still see such incomplete resolutions as successful forms of therapy.

I have seen one patient for over 20 years during which time he has married, become a father and has learned to be an effective parent. He has transformed himself from a person whom others immediately disliked into an individual who uses charm and caring as important ways of making his living. Still, this patient remains unable to discontinue his therapy, and the frequency has now stabilized to twice-a-month meetings. When we tried to reduce the meeting time further, he began to regress and experienced much disruptive anxiety. He still exhibits signs of some disordered thinking and describes his self-attacking mechanism, which he calls his "monsters," as being quite active. Yet, when he is in the therapy hour, we are able to quickly overcome distorted thinking patterns, and a few simple words from me enables him to be effectively redirected. The only reason to end contact with this patient would be one which is based on a belief in the dictum that therapy is supposed to end for all patients. Therapy continues to provide significant interpersonal support for this patient and therefore will continue.

One cannot forget that long-term therapy with personality disordered patients should provide the healthy parental figure lacking in the patient's early years. If so, it is unrealistic to believe that one should be able to end all contact with their surrogate parent forever and then label this total cessation of contact as "healthy" behavior. The most well-adjusted children visit with their parents upon occasion throughout their lives, and they draw upon parental support to bolster them in times of trouble. Certainly those individuals who were deeply damaged in their earliest years should have the same options as children raised in healthy families.

When therapy provides sufficient healthy parenting, patients internalize the message that they direct and control their own lives. As a result, they recognize they are able to end their therapy at any time they choose. Correspondingly, they should be told that if or when they choose to stop the meetings, they will always have the option of returning for additional sessions whenever they want to discuss something with the therapist. Patients need to retain the belief that they have a permanent connection with their therapists. Not only is the therapist a major internalized figure, but she is also the real person who has provided much assistance and support to them. Informing patients that she will be available in the future enables many patients to end therapy on a fully optimistic note. It is very reassuring to know that one can always receive further assistance.

Deep and meaningful connections should never be severed. Our caring for and being with significant others enables us all to face the painful realities of human existence. As Bugenthal stated, we are both apart from and yet a part of others. We can sustain being apart only if we sustain being together. Personality disordered patients need to retain their therapists as internalized parental figures and also to know that their therapists will remain available to them. At times, a patient may need to revisit the therapeutic parent after the therapy has formally concluded; this meeting may be a sign of healthy behavior. If a patient simply meets once more with her therapist to describe how well her life is proceeding, this is an important and productive activity. Therapists are necessarily involved with their patients, especially when they have functioned as their healthy therapeutic parents. If a therapist does not care about the patient's future once treatment ends, she would be a person with profound difficulties in her own interpersonal connections.

Therefore, when the formal therapy of a personality disordered patient ends, it does not always conclude with a full resolution and a termination of the relationship. Rather, it is best seen as the time when therapist and patient agree that they no longer need to meet regularly. The therapist can take some measure of pride in the patient's growth and development and should retain the option of meeting at future times. This policy keeps the relationship real and retains its therapeutic importance.

To promote the illusion that full resolution is possible is to negate the existential truth that all humans face which is, life is painful. Life involves difficult choices, and healthy people need to maintain important connections with others as ways of coping with the painful aspects of life. To say that we never need to reconnect with our parents is to maintain a neurotic or, better still, a narcissistic illusion. When two people have participated in a successful therapy, the connection between the two will be retained throughout the course of their lives.

Eleven:
The Case of John

I have described the theory and practice of pragmatic-existential psychotherapy in conceptual terms with a few limited examples. Another way to illustrate this treatment model more clearly is through the following case of John; the discussion gives a more detailed description of this therapeutic process with a personality disordered individual.

Initial Physical Impressions of John

John, a tall, fairly handsome man, arrived at my office dressed in blue jeans, flannel shirt and work boots. He sported a dark mustache which gave the impression that he was somewhat older than his actual 32 years. He appeared to be in excellent physical condition, and I later learned that he regularly participated in an exercise regimen. John's most striking physical feature were his blue eyes; they conveyed an animation and sparkling intelligence which was at variance with the rest of his demeanor. John was able to meet with me during his regular work day, and I later discovered that his high professional position in an office did not require him to dress in other than a blue collar fashion. In terms of his appearance, John was a mass of contradictions. He was very involved with maintaining a good physique and yet was seemingly totally uninvolved with his attire. His eyes showed extreme attentiveness to his surroundings, but his general physical stance was much more lethargic.

Important information about patients is regularly provided by nonverbal cues, as outlined in chapter 10. In John's case, the contradiction between his excellent physical condition and his lackadaisical interpersonal appearance signalled a possible split between an underdeveloped healthy self and the dominant unhealthy part of his personality. Another way to describe this distinction in more traditional existential terms is through the use of the three worlds - *umwelt*, *mitwelt* and *eigenwelt*. John was quite interested in his biological world - his *umwelt*. His interpersonal world, the *mitwelt*, was underdeveloped as he took little interest in appearing attractive. His individuality or *eigenwelt* was conveyed through the animation of his eyes, an attentiveness to the world around him.

Preliminary Background Information

As stated earlier, the primary concern of pragmatic-existential therapy is to understand the patient as an experiential process. Therefore, I do not obtain a detailed background history during the first session but instead attempt to make a significant connection with the patient during that time. I acquired a fuller sense of John's upbringing and important relationships over the course of many different sessions. To understand the workings of pragmatic-existential therapy, it is best to see how the therapeutic process unfolds over time.

I discovered during the first two sessions that (1) John was raised in an intact family whose members were all alive at the time he began therapy; (2) he was the youngest of three sons; (3) he was a divorced father of a seven year old girl who lived near him, spending every other weekend under his care; and (4) John's education stopped with an undergradate college degree, which was a hindrance to his career advancement.

Nature of the Referral

Like many therapy referrals, John came to my office through an unusual route. John belonged to a physical fitness facility; he had discussed his personal problems with one of the staff members who, in turn, recommended me to him. When I spoke to the referral source to thank him for the referral, I was given a further bit of information. John was described as perpetually trying to "hit on" all the women at the club.

Initial Psychotherapy Session

After only a few minutes in the first meeting I felt there was a major discrepancy between John's language and his underlying emotional tone. He seemed to be in great pain, but he was not describing overt problems that were likely to produce such distress. Here as well was another indication of two opposing forces. John's stated reason for entering psychotherapy was an inability to sleep alone in the dark. He said this problem had begun in grade school and had been a source of suffering ever since. In addition, the magnitude of this problem had increased because he had recently moved out of his girlfriend's apartment. John now slept alone much of the time, even though he still saw this woman on weekends.

I knew John's difficulties were more extensive than what he had described. After all, a night light would have resolved this problem without the intervention of a therapist. As I heard desperation in his voice tone, I hypothesized that John could not differentiate between major and minor problems. I continued to attend to the overt messages John communicated while I simultaneously attempted to understand his covert communications. My task at the onset of therapy was to obtain a sense of the range of John's problems, his level of awareness and the degree to which he would be amenable to different types of therapeutic interventions. Such a sustained focus of therapeutic attention is described in chapter 8.

In the initial session John rapidly fired questions at me which seemed to arise from a strong feeling of panic. He said "What does this mean?" "What should I do?" and "How can I stop that?" The questions were asked so quickly that it appeared he was not even interested in answers. After attempting to answer one or two of these questions, I sensed it would be an exercise in futility to continue to try. John did not appear capable of processing my answers as he was in too much distress.

My attempts to answer his questions reflected my belief that the therapist should try to satisfy the pressing needs of the patient. Once it became apparent that he needed something other than overt answers, as he could not attend to my responses, I had to change tactics in order to make a significant connection with him.

John told me that he had been a psychotherapy patient four to five years prior to this meeting. He had talked with three or four different therapists, but only one of them was seen for more than a few months. I asked for more details about these earlier therapies, following the strategy outlined in chapter 8; it is crucial to get a sense of the nature of the patient's previous therapy. One must learn from the patient how the therapy was of assistance and how it failed so one can design an intervention strategy that better fits the patient's needs.

The different therapists which John had consulted all appeared to be practicing on the fringe of the law. None of these people held licenses nor did they have degrees providing expertise in the treatment of psychopathology. John, nonetheless, stated that these therapists had been somewhat helpful. He had made a promise to one therapist that he would not commit suicide, neither at that time nor later in his life, and said he felt reasonably certain that he would be able to continue to fulfill this promise.

Assuming that John had seriously considered committing suicide only a few years earlier and sensing the enormous panic that seemed to pervade his immediate functioning, I believed that John must have serious characterological problems. Although I did not formulate this idea directly in words, I had a strong sense that I needed to find some unusual interventionist strategy to put into practice at that particular moment. I was not comfortable with a simple setting of basic parameters of therapy and a concluding comment of "I'll see you next week."

I thought it important to try to make a quick connection with John, and I decided to do so by raising questions about the nature of his previous therapies. I said I found it hard to believe that someone with his apparently high intelligence could not, at least, find a licensed and trained psychotherapist to assist him. It seemed very strange that he would only locate individuals performing therapy with no mental health degrees. His response was startling. He said that he did not believe psychotherapy would work anyway, and consequently had decided to obtain assistance as inexpensively as possible. When I mentioned insurance reimbursement, he was quite skeptical that he could be reimbursed for consulting me. I informed him that virtually all my patients were using their insurance policies to help pay for therapy. His pain was so intense that it led him to state that if I indeed could help him, he would willingly give me all of his money.

The above comments I made express some of the principles cited earlier concerning the process of pragmatic-existential therapy. I affirmed the patient's strength through my description of him as a person of high intelligence. At the same time, I implied that he had the capacity for effective problem solving but had not been able to draw upon these resources. Through such a comment, I acknowledged one manifestation of John's problems. My statements about insurance reimbursement reflected my teaching function as I was providing him with a method for safeguarding against unnecessary expenditures. Each of these comments was designed to relate to him by connecting at the rational, problem-solving level.

I also tried a different approach to make an emotional connection with John. I commented on my sense of his pain by telling him that I felt he was hurting a great deal. John appeared visibly shocked by my statement but then seemed to relax and appeared less tense. He not only acknowledged that I was, indeed, correct but also that he very much wanted to know how I could know he was hurting so much. His questioning had the quality of the incredulity one sees in young children who are amazed at the observational powers of adults.

By listening to the panic in his voice tone and in the rapid-fire questioning, I could hypothesize that much pain was present. By sharing this observation, I was not attempting to impress John but rather simply trying to convey that I did understand him. It is important for the patient to be able to feel understood at some point during the first session (as outlined in chapter 8) and my comment provided John with this sense of understanding. Although he apparently attributed an overly high level of power to me through his comments, I decided not to tamper with this perception. Sensing his panic, I recognized that he needed to draw strength from elsewhere. If he could temporarily see me as a powerful figure, this perception would serve to reduce his high level of anxiety.

His naivete, coupled with an immediate eagerness to learn, were two of many factors that made John a likable, appealing person. I could dimly sense, perhaps even then, what I would come to know later on: he was one of the brightest people I had ever met. His speed of comprehension and his ability to see several permutations of interpretation were wondrous. At later points in therapy I had to struggle to keep up with the rapidity of his self discovery; his understandings could be both brilliant and very complex. John was able to direct this intelligence toward furthering his mental health; in contrast, some patients use intelligence to defend against their problems.

Toward the end of the first session I offered John the four session exploratory contract mentioned earlier in chapter 8. I said I would attempt to help him primarily by increasing his understanding of himself and his problems. We would have to focus upon developing a fuller understanding of him which would prove far more helpful than if I tried to immediately answer all of his questions. I believed we would be able to discuss particular strategies of dealing with his problems later in our work together. I told John our most important task was to get to the source of his underlying pain, but we must first understand his pain before we could attempt to reduce it. John agreed to this exploratory contract.

My reference to "our most important task is to get to the source of your underlying pain" was designed to inform John of the collaborative nature of therapeutic work. Because he had already attributed to me a high level of power, I needed to let him know that the therapeutic work was a joint effort. The more he could engage in self-exploration, the greater was the likelihood of therapeutic success.

I did not include a "no-suicide" clause in our contract as John gave no indication during the first session that suicide was a current concern. I accepted his statement of promise to the previous therapist as a continuing binding contract. It would have served no useful purpose to enter into further discussion of suicide. Reintroducing the topic of suicide would have demonstrated that I did not believe in the validity of his promise and would also have indicated that I thought he was soon to lose self-control. Either interpretation would have been counterproductive to his new therapeutic contract.

Because John's level of distress was so high, I would have preferred to arrange twice-a-week therapy at the onset of treatment. However, as John had previously stated that money was his only source of security, I sensed that I would jeopardize his participation in therapy if I insisted on twice-weekly sessions. He was so desperate that he might have felt a twice-weekly schedule was exploitative. I believed we could move into twice-a-week sessions after he became more comfortable with me, so I mentioned that possibility but then quickly acceded to a once-a-week format.

My willingness to adapt to John's needs concerning the initial frequency of sessions reflects the discussion of therapeutic flexibility explained in chapter 8. It is crucial to build an alliance with a patient as early as possible, and the therapist must adapt to the patient's agenda as long as it does not undermine treatment. As the relationship develops, the patient may be more ready to accept the therapist's position concerning the frequency of therapy sessions.

Length of Treatment

Psychotherapy with John was conducted over a six year period. For the first six months of therapy, sessions were held weekly. Therapy sessions were held twice a week for the next 18 months. In the third year, the sessions reverted to a once-a-week format. In year four, therapy was conducted with twice-a-month sessions. However, weekly meetings were resumed in both the fifth and sixth year of therapy, until the time that our work together ended.

In the sixth month of treatment John's level of anxiety visibly increased. At that time he had just ended all contact with his girlfriend. I believed it was necessary to provide additional therapeutic support to reduce his stress and suggested that we increase the frequency of sessions. John then agreed to meet twice-weekly.

When we were well into the third year of therapy, it was apparent that John had a thorough intellectual understanding of his problems and had developed some effective mechanisms for fighting his pathology. I decided that once-a-week sessions would then be ample. During the fourth year, I became overly optimistic and tried to sustain the forward movements of therapy with twice-monthly sessions. This decrease was premature as it gradually became apparent that forward movement had ceased. We then returned to a weekly pattern of meetings until therapy was concluded.

Changing the frequency of meetings is necessary. When patients experience times of heightened crisis, they need additional therapeutic support. By attending to the immediate needs of the patient, the pragmatic-existential therapist adjusts the frequency of meetings to keep the therapy moving on the most optimal level. At times, the therapist may make errors in judgment concerning frequency of sessions. Because the therapist has established an effective working alliance with his patient, he can correct his mistakes and the patient is likely to concur with his decision. In so doing, the therapist affirms his own fallibility and demonstrates the existential truth that he is a human who makes attempts to correct his mistakes. Admission of therapeutic fallibility is an important form of modelling the therapist can provide to the patient (see chapter 9).

Complete Background History

I acquired a full sense of John's psychological development over the course of the therapy. These eventual discussions of his history led to reinterpretations of the crucial events of his life. John's parents were rather old when he was born; his mother was 43 and his father was several years older. When John was still of preschool age, his family lived outside of the continental United States as his father was a member of the armed services. John had fond memories of being cared for by a foreign nursemaid, but he had no clear recollection of his age at that time.

Both of his parents were non-practicing Catholics, and John received little formal religious training. John reported a recurrent childhood fear that his mother would be dead by the time he reached 30 years of age.

John described his family as very destructive and his childhood as being extremely painful. He was in constant fear of his father and would "walk on eggshells" whenever his father was at home. His father frequently and repeatedly "beat" him for minor infractions such as moving too slowly or handing his father the wrong tool in his workshop. One of his father's warnings prior to inflicting physical punishment was "I'll give you something to cry about." Indeed, when John was the recipient of his father's whippings, the father would not cease beating him until John was reduced to tears. The whippings were administered by belts with intact buckles, which were hung in the basement of the house. These belts were stored there in anticipation of future wrongdoings by any of the sons. John did not feel singled out for these beatings as his older brothers received their fair shares as well. John also stated he believed the beatings were not warranted; he thought his father expressed his work frustrations through beating the children. John said he hated his father as a child and had continued to do so as an adult.

In contrast, John reported feeling very close to his mother throughout his developing years. Through his earlier therapy John came to realize, however, that his mother had been destructive to him but in a way quite different from that of his father. As a result of this insight, he emotionally separated from his mother and now only met with her out of obligation. When he was a young boy, his mother frequently dressed him in girl's clothing, behavior which persisted, at least at home, well into his grade school years. His mother took photographs of John dressed up in this manner. John said his mother was never physically affectionate with him; he was never hugged or kissed by her. His mother never intervened on John's behalf when his father beat him. John could recall no occasions when his father struck his mother.

John's relationships with his siblings were quite poor. His two older brothers beat him up with regularity until his early teen years. His eldest brother, who was six years older than John, forced him to participate in homosexual activities when John was 11 years old. Not only did John feel isolated at home, but he also reported having few friendships or relationships outside of his home.

John described himself as a troublemaker throughout grade school and nearly all of his high school years. He was placed in the lower academic track classes for most of his education. When a teacher took special interest in John late in high school, he then began to excel academically. John was the only one of his siblings to enter college, where he received high grades. John acknowledged that he was full of rage and anger during college; he reported working with a classmate on building a bomb which they planned to detonate in an empty classroom. These plans did not come to fruition.

During his college years, John became sexually involved with a woman whom he characterized as "pursuing me relentlessly." John said he never loved her but still acquiesced to her wish to be married because he felt that he "would be unable to interest anyone else" in him. Very soon after the marriage John became involved in an affair. He said he loved the second woman, but she abruptly terminated their relationship.

John's marriage lasted for approximately five years, and one daughter was born early in their marriage. As the couple experienced heightened difficulties living together, they attempted marriage counseling, but they were ultimately divorced. John's wife remarried shortly afterward, but she remained in the same geographical area. John's description of his relationship with his daughter demonstrated that he was a very caring and available father, although he could not admit to loving his child.

Overview of John's Personality Dynamics

John had severe and extensive characterological difficulties. Not only had he been victimized by two destructive parents, but he had internalized their hostility to such a degree that he frequently would "beat himself" verbally for no rational reason, just as he had been beaten as a child. These beatings typically took the form of extensive verbal self-attacks. He often derogated his own abilities, beliefs and feelings and labelled himself as "wrong, evil and bad." The thought patterns which John engaged in during these attacks were quite irrational; and as his therapy progressed, John became aware that these thoughts significantly distorted the reality of who he was.

John's historical poor relationships with men were directly traceable to the terrible relationships he had with both his father and his brothers. He described himself as feeling awkward with other men and feared that if he made any friendly approach to males they would label him as homosexual. John said he had no desire to engage in homosexual activity. In the few friendships John had with men prior to beginning therapy, he felt powerless and exploited. He was typically isolated from other men and would usually eat lunch by himself at work.

Although John had several lengthy affairs, his heterosexual relationships were also quite troubled. John was unable to be psychologically intimate with a woman. His underlying emotional distance from women was certainly a consequence of his mother's emotional coldness. However, at the overt level John behaved as if he were desperate for female company. The type of woman he found attractive was invariably characterized as very cold and showing no interest in him. If one of these women became more attentive to him, John himself lost interest.

John was involved with a woman at the beginning of his psychotherapy. He described her as cold and inaccessible, yet she "surprisingly" agreed to a relationship with him. By the time John entered therapy, he had decided that the relationship was "going nowhere" because they "had little in common" despite seeing each other for over two years. John said he could completely leave a relationship only when the woman found another man. He reported that he felt very guilty and responsible for the woman's happiness and could not leave her alone and lonely. On the other hand, John could not tolerate abandonment by a woman. He had massive difficulties with the ending of all relationships.

More direct negative consequences of John's poor relationship with his mother were revealed by the presence of particular sexual aberrations. John had a history of cross-dressing, which was conducted in private and culminated in masturbation. At times he had worn female clothing when with female sexual partners. However, he said that he "hated" himself for engaging in this cross-dressing.

John also was experiencing significant difficulties in the areas of both self-assertion and hostility at the time he entered therapy. The only situation in which John expressed anger was when he was driving his automobile. Then he would "cut off" or "outdrag" other motorists. At work he neither asked for raises nor for promotions

John was also seemingly unable to engage in positive forms of self-indulgence. He did not spend money on himself, and some of the rooms in his home were devoid of furniture. He also suffered from bulimia, for there were times when he would eat compulsively to the point of nausea. He had poor control over eating habits and devoured large amounts of junk food. John said he wanted to be able to eat and live healthfully but he was unable to control his poor eating habits.

On the more positive side, John had extensive leisure interests and was very creative in carpentry and in many different arts. Unfortunatley, his involvement in these leisure activities would quickly become addictive behavior patterns as he was unable to take a moderate position in anything he did. The interests become more like obsessions than forms of gratification. Despite the extensiveness of his difficulties, John was quite easy to like. He had an engaging manner, and his varied pursuits made him an interesting conversationalist.

Early Stage of Psychotherapy

John's statement at the end of the first session, that he would give me all of his funds if he could be helped, was important diagnostic information. He lacked a clear sense of internal limits as most people would think "I still want some money for myself." John's willingness to abandon his primary source of security demonstrated that he could very easily be overrun by others. This lack of boundaries, coupled with John's panic, made me aware that I had to carefully define my position with him. I saw very quickly that John was an exceptionally bright person. His intelligence provided him with his only means of interpersonal protection, but it could also be turned to excellent advantage in the course of treatment. While John did not initially joust with me on an intellectual level, it was nonetheless important that I let him know that I was at least his intellectual peer.

John needed to see signs of my expertise so he could begin to respect and ultimately trust me. However, the demonstration of professional skill had to be carefully managed. John required a therapist who could appear very competent without making him feel intimidated at the same time. He needed to be able to draw strength from his therapist without being made to feel inadequate for needing professional help.

In the early meetings I primarily made empathic comments, acknowledging the depth of his pain and suffering. As he described his developmental history, I sensed it was important to validate that he had, indeed, been horribly treated by his father. I also focused on the fact that his mother failed to satisfy his normal needs either to be treated as a male or to be protected from his father's brutalization.

As therapy progressed, John made specific comments about his low self-esteem, and I countered these statements most directly with affirmations such as "You are a valuable human being" and "You are wise, perceptive, and intelligent." John was visibly shocked when I told him I thought he was extremely bright. He beamed at receiving this message and let me know how important these comments were by saying "I feel great when you say that." His honest and diligent participation in therapy was further revealed several months later when he said "I must watch myself so that I do not simply say things just to get you to say nice things to me."

Because John was feeling so overwhelmed at the onset of therapy, it was vital to be immediately supportive, empathic and non-demanding. Before he could attack his underlying problems, he needed to be comforted and to feel that I was his ally. I primarily deflected the discussion of his most immediate problems. For example, when he asked "How can I find the right woman?" I told him that he was not ready for the right woman. First we had to understand him better before we could attempt significant behavioral changes.

John's desperate need to have a relationship with a woman led to self-defeating behavior. He pursued women relentlessly and repeatedly asked them for dates. If a woman agreed on a Tuesday night that she would see him on Saturday, she would receive two to three phone calls before the date and John would also have a dozen roses delivered to her door. While it was apparent to me that John's desperation was destroying potential relationships, I also had to entertain the possibility that his behaviors were purposively self-destructive. Whenever a patient repeatedly engages in behavior with a particular negative effect, one must hypothesize that the effect is intended. In other words, because John was continually making women turn away from him, it was likely that, without direct awareness, he did not want to have a successful relationship with a woman.

Given John's panic and his sense of desperation, any attempt to immediately refine his behavior patterns would have been unsuccessful, especially since his fundamental intentions remained unclear. I felt we needed first to reduce the internal pressure and anxiety before any overt behavioral progress could be seen.

Following the basic strategy in pragmatic-existential therapy, we had to strengthen John's observing ego. He needed to look at and to report on the internal thoughts and perceptions which were the essence of his lived experiences. John began to describe a seemingly infinite number of ways in which irrational, self-attacking and self-deceptive thoughts dominated his consciousness. One such example was through the question "Should I give my daughter up for adoption?" When John described his relationship with his daughter, it was quite apparent that she doted on him; he saw her every other weekend, attempted very much to be a good parent, and would speak to the girl twice-a-week on the telephone. Even though John claimed to lack feelings for her, his behavior belied his verbalizations. Because there was no external demand that she be adopted by her mother's new husband, I interpreted the thought of adoption as a clear example of the self-attacking mechanism which was present within John.

Initially and frequently in the early phase of therapy, I labelled certain thoughts of John as reflecting self-hatred. I characterized these thoughts as the "destructive parental voice inside" him. John accepted this interpretation and devised his own label for these thoughts by describing them as "beatings." He recognized that these beatings were extensions of the beatings administered by his father. John could see that his pattern of behavior was intended to reenact the vicious and destructive actions of his father.

Even though we focused exclusively upon developing increased self-understanding during the first months of therapy, in the fourth month John informed me that he was now sleeping in the dark without difficulty. This marked the beginning of a pattern in which John would report significant behavioral changes without having specifically discussed these events during therapy. The therapeutic dialogue was having a major impact upon John, leading to behavioral changes far afield from the actual topics of conversation. This phenomenon is described earlier in chapter 10.

During the first six months of therapy John maintained minimal contact with the woman with whom he had previously been living. Because he viewed the relationship as nonproductive, he decided to stop all remaining contact and he moved his few remaining possessions out of her apartment.

The complete termination of this relationship proved to be very traumatic for John. He was besieged with internal self-attacks and then hated himself for leaving this "wonderful" woman. He had suicidal thoughts and was seemingly unable to stop the self-hatred. John was in excessive pain, and we consequently held several emergency sessions. We also began to meet twice a week, as I attempted to provide him with healthy therapeutic parenting to offset the destructive forces set in motion by his ending the relationship with this woman.

I became more active as John became increasingly overwhelmed. To counter his desperation, I was supportive and empathic. I was readily available during times of crisis, and I provided him with tools to fight against his pathology. Specifically, I helped him become aware of the self-attacks and the roots of this problem. I offered him concrete strategies such as imagining my presence when I was unavailable in order to lend him strength; I also taught him the technique of thought stoppage.

The use of all the above strategies epitomizes the work of the pragmatic-existential therapist during the early phase of therapy with a personality disordered patient. The patient is encouraged to develop an observing ego, he learns about the nature and presence of his self-hating mechanism, and he discovers how self-hatred developed through his early relationship with his parents. The therapist begins to assume the role of "healthy therapeutic parent" through listening, through empathy and by providing support. Also, the therapist assumes a parental role by teaching the patient techniques to cope with particular problems.

Extensiveness of John's Problems

As therapy proceeded, I became increasingly aware of the pervasiveness of John's difficulties and could find no areas in his life that appeared conflict-free. Several months into therapy, John said, "Now I see you as you are. I lose who you are when I am away from you, for I distort you into someone who will hurt me." John's statements appear to be a classic example of what analysts describe as problems in object constancy. Before a child develops object constancy, he knows a person only when that person is immediately present in his physical environment. Through the development of imagination, the child can subsequently conjure up the image of the parental figure when that person is not immediately present. The retention of a clear image of the parental figure when that figure is not physically present is designated as object constancy.

John's inability to remember who I was and what qualities I possessed indicated that he confused me with his parents. He needed my physical presence in order to view me as different from his parental figures. Because John could not clearly retain his perception of his therapist, it was very likely that his perceptions of all other people he encountered were distorted as well. These misperceptions helped initially to explain why John was unable to sustain healthy relationships. He could not retain a clear image of the other person but distorted people into the images of his parents.

Although the overt therapeutic dialogue was helping John to recognize the nature and extent of his problems, a large gap remained between the intellectual recognition and the emotional resolution. It is only possible to transform this intellectual recognition into an emotional reality through long-term therapeutic work, as discussed in chapter 10.

When John first described his compulsion to cross-dress, I simply responded empathically with "That must be very difficult for you." Although I recognized that cross-dressing was a major concern, I felt there were more immediate issues requiring attention. When I later introduced the concept of the "destructive internal parental voice," I was able to use this concept as a tentative explanation for his cross-dressing. I told him that engaging in cross-dressing was not the behavior of the "wise internal you" but was directed by the destructive parent (in this case, his mother's voice). I interpreted cross-dressing in this manner because John claimed that he did not want to do it and felt ashamed for engaging in this behavior.

Somewhat later, John reported he had returned some women's shoes that he had ordered by mail as he recognized his compulsion to cross-dress was the manifestation of his mother's destructive voice. Only once or twice in the remaining five years of the therapeutic work was cross-dressing ever mentioned again; it appeared to be another problem area which was successfully resolved with minimal therapeutic dialogue.

The recognition of the extensiveness of the "internal beatings" led John to see the malevolence of both of his parents. Approximately nine months into therapy, John wrote to his parents to tell them they would not be hearing from him for a long time. His hatred for his father was long standing, in contrast to his developing hatred of his mother. However, as he became aware of many diverse ways in which his mother currently undermined him and did not satisfy his basic needs, John made no further attempts to communicate with his parents.

Approximately one year after formal therapy ended, John came to see me because his mother had died and he did not want to attend her funeral. He wanted my permission not to attend, and I gave it to him. I believe it is important for therapists to recognize there can be no healthy resolution for patients who have very malevolent parents. For these patients, contact with their parents opens themselves to continual pain. Rarely, if ever, would I encourage patients to sever such contact, but certainly I do not challenge this decision once they make it.

John's inability to treat himself kindly was apparent in the lack of material possessions, in his inability to buy nice clothes or even sufficient equipment to pursue his various interests. Over the course of therapy John's regard for himself dramatically changed, to the point where he developed a passion for art and bought expensive paintings. Again, over time, and with no prompting, John was able to initiate changes without direct therapeutic dialogue.

The Long-Term Work

As stated in chapter 10, there is no clear point of demarcation where the early phase of therapy ends and long-term work begins. In

John's case, I consider the transition to have occurred during the sixth month of therapy when he completely terminated the relationship with his girlfriend. Even though the end of the relationship precipitated a major crisis in John's life, it marked a significant change in our therapeutic relationship as well.

Once John recognized his need for therapy more often than once a week and began to rely on our relationship for renewed strength and support, I became the significant healthy therapeutic parent. At this time, his therapy assumed the qualities of long-term work.

In the first six months of therapy the nature and extent of John's problems had become apparent to both of us. Self-hatred was diagnosed as the core of John's difficulties. John was repeatedly seeking to establish a symbiotic tie with a woman, but in these relationships John needed to be ultimately rejected. In this manner he was reenacting his relationship with his mother. While such a pattern is reminiscent of the strategy used by classic borderline patients, John was, nonetheless, developing a very positive relationship with me, even though he could not directly admit to feeling an important tie with his therapist.

It also became very apparent that John was unable to be-for-himself in the most basic ways. Since his attempts at healthy individuation had been thwarted by his parents, all aspects of his functioning had been significantly impaired. His pattern of pervasive impairment is quite common among individuals who suffer from personality disorders. The therapeutic task was to repair and to strengthen his fundamental need for individuation.

Following the model of pragmatic-existentialism, it was necessary for me to become his significant new parental figure, one who would nurture and encourage his personal growth. When the psychological damage done to an individual is as extensive as it was with John and particularly when the roots of the difficulties can be traced to preverbal development, therapeutic progress necessarily is quite slow.

Once John increased the frequency of meetings to twice-a-week, he was able to agree to defer his attempts to find a special woman in his life. Rather, he accepted the strategy of focusing his attention upon understanding the extensiveness of the self-attacks which pervaded his consciousness. He became proficient at separating the thoughts that could be attributed to the wise, healthy side of his personality from the conceptions which were generated by his self-attacking mechanism. However, when we discussed his relationships with women, it was particularly difficult to decipher whether his stated dissatisfactions were the consequences of healthy or self-destructive thought patterns.

In the second year of therapy John resumed dating patterns, but he often wanted to end these relationship quite abruptly. He offered legitimate reasons for feeling dissatisfied, and we were both very much aware he was attracted to cold women similar in personality to his mother. He knew he liked women who were fundamentally wrong for him; and when he met a kind, pleasant woman, he would usually feel no attraction toward her.

Also in the second year of the therapy I recognized the depth of our therapeutic connection as John began to imitate my gestures (a process described in chapter 10). My basic approach with John remained to support his study of internal self-attacks and to encourage him to act in his own best interests. I told him his refusal to take vacations, his inability to change physicians when he was dissatisfied, and his tolerance of hostile behavior by other people were all indicators of continual self-attacks.

John began to exhibit gradual behavior changes in many aspects of his life as therapy progressed. Instead of passively regarding lunch plans, John began to invite other people to eat with him. Very soon he became a regular part of the lunch crowd. In fact, he became the coordinator for the noontime meal and often made the decisions as to where the group would eat. Instead of being socially isolated, John became popular.

John also developed a mutually supportive relationship with a woman who was his office mate. After she received a job transfer, he became quite friendly with his new male office mate, a friendship that quickly blossomed outside of work and endured after this individual also left the company. This new social relationship expanded as John also befriended the co-worker's wife. I continued to affirm and support John in these relationships and in his new and satisfying interpersonal life. By the third year of therapy, the nature of therapeutic discussions had undergone significant change. John was doing the bulk of the interpretive work, and I was functioning as the supportive parental figure who continued to affirm the positive aspects of John's behavior.

John started to verbally express his anger toward people who were treating him badly. He demanded pay raises and was quite effective in substantially increasing his salary. At one point, later in therapy, he acknowledged that entering psychotherapy was a very sound economic strategy; he had increased his earning power far more than he had spent for his psychotherapy sessions.

At the end of the third year of therapy, John entered into a serious relationship with a woman. Joan was described as exhibiting some of the same personality dynamics John had possessed, and she briefly entered into her own psychotherapy to deal with these issues. She, too, responded best to John when he was withdrawn and cold. She became detached and distant when he displayed signs of affection.

John fluctuated in his feelings about Joan and their relationship. He would vow to leave her but then changed his mind and remained in the relationship. Whenever he expressed serious dissatisfactions with how he was treated, Joan would become more compliant and would adapt to his needs. It was enormously difficult for me to ascertain whether this could be a deeply satisfying relationship since it contained many positive and negative elements. As the healthy therapeutic parent, it was important for me to help John detect all aspects of self-hatred. However, John's ambivalence about the relationship seemed to be a mixture of both self-hatred and rational evaluation.

Following the existential principle that we all are responsible for our choices, John and Joan ultimately had to make the final decision about their relationship. They decided that they should first live together so they could more fully determine whether they could have a satisfying life together. Once Joan moved into his home, John felt quite resentful and thought that he had made a mistake. However, his anger began to diminish, and he then decided he had in fact done the right thing by becoming closer to her. Confirming the positive nature of the relationship, Joan was able to establish a good relationship with John's daughter. Relying upon John's descriptions, I concluded that Joan was an intelligent, successful woman who did not need sustained closeness. These dynamics fit well with John's fundamental needs.

Periodically in therapy, when I felt the timing was appropriate, I asked John to discuss his feelings toward me. John continued to have difficulty in accepting the fact that I cared about him, even though I told him this most directly. On the other hand, he kept denying that he had any feelings about me. According to John, I was a therapist and could not be seen as a person. I did not challenge John's explanation because it would have been counterproductive for him to admit that he had positive feelings toward me. The deep connection between us was nonetheless apparent, and I knew how threatening it was for him to acknowledge this connection and neediness. John often denied caring for his daughter and yet he would regularly bask in her accomplishments. He did not admit that his pride conveyed his caring. Loving and caring had such negative connotations in John's personal history that he continued to avoid acknowledging the presence of these feelings in himself.

It was John's suggestion that we terminate our sessions. As he described it, his life had become very fulfilling. He was respected and well paid for his work, he had friends with whom to socialize, he was in a satisfying sexual relationship and he had full control over the internal "beatings." Self-attacks had become a rare event; and whenever they began, he could counteract their power very quickly. I concurred with his decision and acknowledged that we both could feel very satisfied with the work we had accomplished.

The basic elements of pragmatic-existentialism were used to guide the long-term work. I assumed the function of the healthy therapeutic parent, expressing my interest and caring over the course of treatment. The depth of our emotional connection was displayed in one way through the imitation of gestures that John exhibited in long-term therapy. I expressed caring through my availability for emergency sessions and directly in my verbal statements.

As a caring therapist, I was involved with John's movement toward greater health and individuation. I repeatedly acknowledged each sign of progress that he displayed. I was pleased to see him take a more active role in the therapy as my own role diminished. John would speak of his progress, and I would nod my assent; the work became increasingly easier over time. By functioning as the good parent that John had lacked, I was able to experience the satisfaction that all healthy parents feel when they see their children mature into healthy and happy adults. I was able to participate in the undoing of his psychopathology and in his creation of a healthy person. These are the benefits of working within the framework of pragmatic-existentialism.

The more John developed the healthy side of his personality, the more he moved toward healthy adult functioning. When he reached the point where he believed he could continue to control his life without my regular participation, he decided to terminate therapy. It was a decision that I could readily and gladly endorse even though I recognized that there was still some unfinished business for him. To discourage him at this point would be to react in a manner which was similar to his parents' attempts to discourage him and prevent positive growth.

John had a successful therapy experience, and I am pleased to have been a significant participant in that process. However, the success represents John's endeavor far more than it reflects my own work. It is ultimately the patient who must do all of the important work in therapy. The patient must fight against his own psychopathology. The therapist can provide the support and some of the tools to outfit the patient for the struggle; but successful therapy is based upon the resolve of the patient, not upon the expertise of the therapist.

Final Comments

Pragmatic-existential therapy offers therapists a valuable framework which can be used to assist personality disordered patients in learning how to combat their psychopathology. By focusing upon the patient as process, this particular model of therapy necessarily draws upon the therapist as process as well. The effective pragmatic-existential therapist must be a healthy, highly-functioning individual. He must be able to trust the process he is in order to guide his work with patients. The model of therapy provided by pragmatic-existentialism will prove disastrous if the therapist is not well aware of himself or if he has significant unresolved issues that interfere with his functioning as a healthy therapeutic parent.

Pragmatic-existential therapy is not a system of techniques; rather, it is a way of being with patients that has proven to be quite helpful and therapeutic. It is an approach that respects the humanness of the patient as it draws upon the essential humanness of the therapist. Still, the essence of the acceptance of our own humanness demands that we acknowledge the limited power of the therapist to produce changes in the patient. The most that therapists can provide are knowledge and caring, which patients can then use to move forward in their lives.

It is ultimately the patient's own resolve that moves therapy forward. Sometimes patients are unable to change sufficiently to meet their own expectations because they have been so extensively damaged that they are unable to repair this destruction. Even when patients improve and overcome significant manifestations of their psychopathology, they rarely implement changes at a pace which meets their expectations.

Therapy with personality disordered patients is painstaking and extensive and will prove successful only through long-term work. The inevitable frustrations the patient feels during treatment are part of the incessant human struggles we all face. To accept this ongoing struggle with one's self as an inevitable part of the human condition is as necessary for the personality disordered patient as it is for the rest of us. When the patient accepts this truth, he can end therapy as a successful, although fallible, human.

References

Adler, A. (1964). *Problems of neurosis*. New York: Harper & Row.

Adler, A. (1968). *The practice and theory of individual psychology*. Totowa, NJ: Littlefield, Adams, & Co.

Agnew, S. (1971). *Collected speeches of Spiro Agnew*. Speech at a Republican fund raising dinner, New Orleans, October 19, 1969. New York: Audubon Books.

Allport, G.W. (1960). *Becoming: Basic considerations for a psychology of personality*. New Haven, CT: Yale University Press.

Allport, G.W., & Cantril, H. (1934). Judging personality from voice. *Journal of Social Psychology, 5*, 37-55.

Arieti, S. (1955). *Interpretation of schizophrenia*. New York: Robert Brunner.

Barnes, H.E. (1983). Sartre's concept of the self. *Review of Existential Psychology and Psychiatry, 17*, 41-65.

Bateson, G., Jackson, D.D., Haley, J., & Weakland, J. (1956). Toward a theory of schizophrenia. *Behavioral Science, 1*, 241-264.

Bettelheim, B. (1950). *Love is not enough*. Glencoe, IL: Free Press.

Binswanger, L. (1963). *Being-in-the-world* (translated and with a critical introduction by J. Needleman). New York: Basic Books, Inc.

Boring, E.G. (1963). (Eds. Watson, R.I & Campbell, D.T.) *History, psychology and science: Selected papers.* New York: John Wiley and Sons, Inc.

Burton, A. (1974). *Operational theories of personality.* New York: Brunner/Mazel Publishers.

Boss, M. (1963). *Psychoanalysis and daseinanalysis.* New York: Basic Books, Inc.

Braginsky, B.M., & Braginsky, D. (1969). *Methods of madness: The mental hospital as the last resort.* New York: Holt, Rinehart and Winston.

Brentano, F. (1874). *Psychology from an empirical standpoint.* Volume 1. Leipzig: Duncker & Humblot.

Buber, M. (1958). *I and thou* (2nd ed.). (R.G. Smith, Trans.) New York: New York Philosophical Library.

Bugenthal, J.F.T. (1965). *The search for authenticity.* New York: Holt, Rinehart and Winston.

Conkling, M. (1986-7). Sartre's refutation of the Freudian unconscious. *Review of Existential Psychology and Psychiatry, 20,* 251-265.

Dewey, J. (1899). *Psychology and philosophic method.* Berkeley, CA: University of California Press.

Dewey, J. (1910). *The influence of Darwin on philosophy and other essays.* New York: Holt.

Ellis, A. (Sagarin, E. Ed). (1973). *Humanistic psychotherapy: The rational emotive approach.* New York: McGraw Hill.

Fairbairn, W.R.D. (1986). The repression and the return of bad objects (with special reference to the "war neuroses"). In P. Buckley (Ed.) *Essential papers on object relations.* New York: New York University Press.

Fechner, G. (1960). *Elements of psychophysics.* New York: Holt, Rinehart and Winston, Inc.

Fenichel, O. (1945). *The psychoanalytic theory of neurosis.* New York: W.W. Norton & Co.

Frank, J.D. (1961). *Persuasion and healing: A comparative study of psychotherapy*. New York: Schocken Books.

Frankl, V. (1960). *The doctor and the soul*. New York: Alfred A. Knopf, Inc.

Frankl, V. (1963). *Man's search for meaning: An introduction to logotherapy* . New York: Pocket Books.

Frankl, V. (1967). *Psychotherapy and existentialism*. New York: Simon and Schuster.

Freud, S. (J. Strachey, Trans.) (1950). *Beyond the pleasure principle*. New York: Liveright.

Freud, S. (J. Strachey, Trans. & Ed.) (1966). *The complete introductory lectures on psychoanalysis*. New York: W.W. Norton & Co., Inc.

Fromm, E. (1941). *Escape from freedom*. New York: Farrar and Rinehart.

Fromm, E. (1973). *The anatomy of human destructiveness*. New York: Holt, Rinehart and Winston.

Fromm, E. (1981). *On disobedience and other essays*. New York: The Seabury Press.

Fromm-Reichmann, F. (1971). *Principles of intensive psychotherapy*. Chicago: The University of Chicago Press.

Guntrip, H. (1968). *Schizoid phenomena, object-relations and the self*. London: Hogarth Press.

Hall, M.H. (1968, December) A conversation with M. Boss or the evolution of psychoanalysis. *Psychology Today*. 58-65.

Heidegger, M. (1962). *Being and time*. New York: Harper & Row.

Husserl, E. (1965). *Phenomenology and the crisis for philosophy*. (Q. Lauer, Trans.) New York: Harper & Row Torchbooks.

James, W. (1890). *The principles of psychology*. New York: Dover Publications, Inc.

Jaspers, K. (1955). *Reason and existenz: Five lectures*. (W. Earle, Trans.) New York: Noonday.

Jaspers, K. (1963). *General psychopathology*. (J. Hoenig & M.W. Hamilton, Trans.) Chicago: The University of Chicago Press.

Jung, C.G. (1946). *Psychological types*. London: Kegan Paul, Trench, Trubner & Co. Ltd., and New York: Harcourt, Brace & Co. (This work appears in the Bollingen Series as Vol. 6.)

Jung, C.G. (1971). *Psychological reflections: An anthology of his writings*. London: Ark Paperbacks.

Kaufmann, W.A. (Ed.). (1975). *Existentialism from Dostoevsky to Sartre*. New York: Meridian.

Kierkegaard, S. (1957). *The concept of dread* (2nd ed.). (W. Lowrie, Trans.) Princeton, NJ: Princeton University Press.

Koffka, K. (1935). *Principles of gestalt psychology*. New York: Harcourt, Brace & Co.

Kohler, W. (1947). *Gestalt psychology*. New York: Leverlight Publishing Co.

Laing, R.D. (1965). *The divided self*. Baltimore: Penguin Books.

Mahler, M.S. (1986). On the first three phases of the separation-individuation process. In P. Buckley (Ed.) *Essential papers on object relations*. New York: New York University Press.

Mahler, M.S., Pine, F., & Bergman, A. (1975). *The psychological birth of the human infant: Symbiosis and individuation*. New York: Basic Books, Inc.

Maslow, A. (1954). *Motivation and personality*. New York: Harper.

Maslow, A. (1968). *Toward a psychology of being*. Princeton, NJ: D. Van Nostrand Co., Inc.

Masterson, J.F. (1972). *Treatment of the borderline adolescent: A developmental approach*. New York: John Wiley & Sons, Inc.

May, R. (1969). *Love and will*. New York: W.W. Norton & Co., Inc.

May, R. (1977). *The meaning of anxiety* (rev. ed.). New York: W.W. Norton & Co., Inc.

May, R. (1979). *Psychology and the human dilemma*. New York: W.W. Norton & Co. Inc.

May, R., Angel, E., & Ellenberger, F. (1958). *Existence: A new dimension in psychiatry and psychology*. New York: Basic Books.

Mezzich, A. C. & Mezzich, J.E. (1979). Diagnostic reliability of childhood and adolescent behavior disorders. Paper presented at American Psychological Association, 87th Annual Convention, New York.

Nietzsche, F.W. (1968). *The will to power*. (W. Kaufmann and R.J. Hollingdale, Trans.) New York: Vintage Books.

Potash, H.M. (1981). *Inside clinical psychology*. Madison, NJ: Gordon Handwerk Publishers.

Perls, F.S. (1969). *Gestalt therapy verbatim*. Lafayette, CA: Real People Press.

Rank, O. (1968). *Will therapy and truth and reality*. New York: Alfred A. Knopf, Inc.

Ramsland, K. (1984-5). Engaging the immediate: Kierkegaard and psychotherapy. *Review of Existential Psychology and Psychiatry, 19*, 189-204.

Reik, T. (1949). *Listening with the third ear: The inner experience of a psychoanalyst*. New York: Farrar, Straus and Co.

Rogers, C.R. (1951). *Client-centered therapy*. Boston: Houghton Mifflin Co.

Rogers, C.R. (1961). *On becoming a person: A therapist's view of psychotherapy*. Boston: Houghton Mifflin Co.

Rogers, C.R. (1980). *A way of being*. Boston: Houghton Mifflin Co.

Rogers, C.R. (1984). Client-centered therapy. In I.L. Kutash & A. Wolf (Eds.) *Psychotherapist's casebook: therapy and technique in practice*. San Francisco: Jossey-Bass.

Rychlak, J.F. (1981). *Introduction to personality and psychotherapy*. Boston: Houghton Mifflin Co.

Sartre, J.P. (1956). *Being and nothingness*. (H.E. Barnes, Trans.) New York: The Philosophical Library.

Sartre, J.P. (1962). *Nausea*. (L. Alexander, Trans.) London: H. Hamilton.

Scheftner, W. A. (1980). DSM-III and the schizophrenias. Presented at the symposium, The ABC's of DSM-III, Illinois Hospital

Association, Illinois Psychiatric Society and Illinois Medical Records Association.

Schroder, M.L. & Livesley, W.J. (1991). An evaluation of DSM-III-R personality disorders. *Acta-Psychiatrica-Scandinavica, 84,* 512-519.

Searles, H.F. (1965). *Collected papers on schizophrenia and related subjects.* (with a preface by Robert P. Knight) New York: International Universities Press Inc.

Sechehaye, M. (1951). *Symbolic realization.* New York: International Universities Press Inc.

Skinner, B.F. (1971). *Beyond freedom and dignity.* New York: Alfred A. Knopf, Inc.

Sullivan, H.S. (1953). *The interpersonal theory of psychiatry* New York: W.W. Norton & Co., Inc.

Sullivan, H.S. (1964). *The fusion of psychiatry and social science.* New York: W.W Norton & Co., Inc.

Tillich, P. (1952). *The courage to be.* New Haven, CT: Yale University Press.

Titchener, E.B. (1901-1905). *Experimental psychology.* New York: The Macmillan Co.

Titchener, E.B. (1915). *A textbook of psychology.* New York: The Macmillan Co.

Tolstoy, L. (1960). *The death of Ivan Ilyich, and other stories.* New York: New American Library.

van den Berg, J.H. (1972). *A different existence.* Pittsburg: Duquesne University Press.

van Kaam, A. (1969). *Existential foundations of psychology.* New York: Image Books.

Wallraff, C.F. (1970). *Karl Jaspers: An introduction to his philosophy.* Princeton, NJ: Princeton University Press.

Watson, J.B. (1924). *Behaviorism.* New York: W.W. Norton & Co., Inc.

Wertheimer, M. (1945). *Productive thinking.* New York: Harper & Bros.

Winnicott, D.W. (1986). The theory of the parent-infant relationship. In P. Buckley (Ed.) *Essential papers on object relations*. New York: New York University Press.

Yalom, I. (1981). *Existential Psychotherapy*. New York: Basic Books Inc.

Author Index

Subject Index

M

Meaning categories   28, 29, 31, 43, 114, 115, 149, 157, 171, 234

Meaninglessness   43, 44, 51

Mitwelt   98

Modelling of gestures   218

N

Neurotic anxiety   40

Nonverbal communication 32, 33, 191

Now   111, 112, 116

O

Observing ego   157, 204, 234, 260, 261, 260, 261

Obsessive-compulsive personality disorder   88

Ontological "givens" 28, 37, 38, 49

P

Personality pattern disturbances   88

Personality trait disturbances   88

Phenomenology   18, 19, 21, 30, 32, 193

Pitch   30, 66, 73

Prereflective consciousness   147, 148, 149, 152

Proprium   20

Psychology, definitions of 11, 12

Psychopathic personality   87

Psychophysics   13

Purkinje Phenomenon   14

R

Reflective Consciousness   147, 148, 149